To Eileen & Rhodri

With all our

mum & Dad.

Supertips

Supertips
To make life easy

MOYRA BREMNER

Illustrated by
Marie-Hélène Jeeves

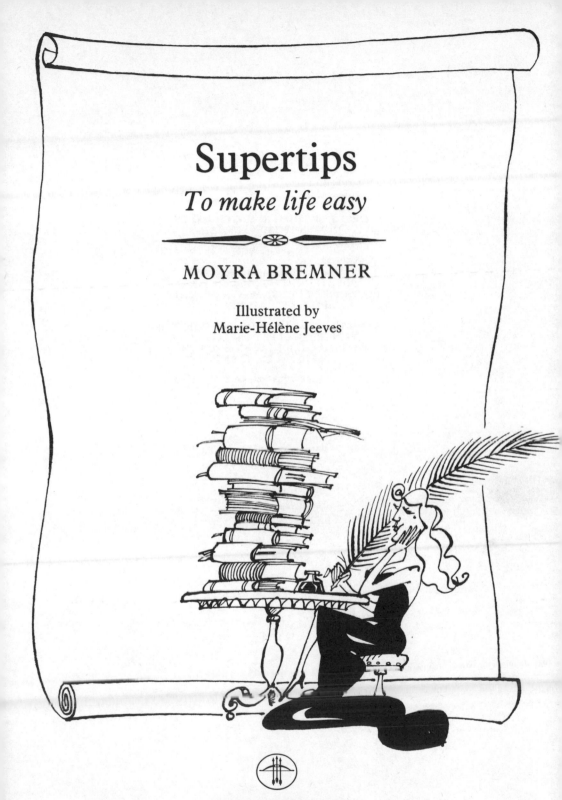

ANDRE DEUTSCH

FIRST PUBLISHED IN MARCH 1983 BY
ANDRE DEUTSCH LIMITED
105 GREAT RUSSELL STREET
LONDON WC1
SECOND IMPRESSION APRIL 1983
THIRD IMPRESSION MAY 1983
FOURTH IMPRESSION JUNE 1983
COPYRIGHT © 1983 BY MOYRA BREMNER
ALL RIGHTS RESERVED

TYPESET BY INFORUM LTD, PORTSMOUTH
PRINTED IN GREAT BRITAIN BY
WILLIAM COLLINS SONS & CO LTD,
GLASGOW, SCOTLAND

SBN 233 97466 0

*To my mother
who taught me so much more than I realised
and above all
to my children, Siobhan, Fergus and Rory
who make everything possible.*

CONTENTS

INTRODUCTION

Supertips is a collection of know-how shamelessly dedicated to making life easier. For though some of the ideas have been included just for pleasure, most are designed to save time, money and energy.

Most of us have become so conditioned to the idea that modern methods are labour-saving that, at first sight, a book which includes so many old methods may seem like nostalgia for its own sake. Far from it. Though I haven't been able to resist including some nuggets of curious information, this is not a collection of old wives' tales of doubtful value and practicality. It's a collection of best ways — both old and new. The surprising thing is how often old ways, which were in danger of being lost, turn out to be faster, easier and cheaper while modern methods are a waste of time and energy.

I have to confess that the collection started because I am a lazy perfectionist. A difficult combination which from a very early age compelled me to pick the brains of everyone I met to find the quickest and best methods. Of course not everyone is willing to part with their secrets. My nursery school teacher, for instance, refused to give me the secret of the wonderful peppermint lumps she used to make — on the grounds that I couldn't read at the time — and so far as I know she took the secret with her to the grave.

At four it is difficult to get adults to take you seriously, but I became more persuasive with the years, wandering into workshops and restaurant kitchens wherever I went, gathering trade secrets. Slowly I formed a collection of some of the basic knowledge which was once handed on from father to son, mother to daughter, and craftsman to apprentice.

Most of us know some of these hints — how to remove a red wine stain, or take out a rusty screw, perhaps — but few people know more than a handful. So as my collection grew I became used to phone calls from friends which began 'Moyra, you'll know. How does one . . .' Even so, this book would never have been written if I hadn't come across the recipe book my grandmother compiled when she was first married. In it recipes for flea powder, cough mixture and shoe polish were hugger-mugger with those for Hunter's Beef or Queen's Pudding. Reading it made me compare my own skills with those of my comparatively uneducated grandmother and brought home to me just how much my generation had lost.

For the first time I was struck by the irony of the fact that universal education, with all its benefits, had also created a situation in which most people can tell you what a square root is but few can detect a fresh egg on sight — even when they use eggs daily and square roots not at all. It seems that although we haven't exactly sold our birthright for a mess of potage, we have allowed the skills which make people competent and independent to be steadily downgraded over the years. With the obvious result that we have been left vulnerable to the blandishments of any manufacturer with a slick advertising campaign claiming his product is the ultimate answer, or to any rule-making bureaucrat who comes along saying that apples should be judged by size not flavour. So perhaps in gaining all the freedoms of the twentieth century we have lost other quite basic ones.

It was time, I decided, to stop being haphazard, make a systematic study of traditional know-how, add my own collection and compile a book combining the best of the old with the best of the new. That was seven years ago. Since then I have sifted through ancient household manuals and magazines, gathered family hints and tips from all over the world, and systematically searched out people with special skills — such as silver polishers, cabinet makers, butlers and engineers — who had preserved old skills and could tell me the best and cheapest methods to use. Most of the methods I checked and tested myself, for others I went to those who had the expertise to tell the safe and effective from the dangerous and useless.

The result is this book. It isn't an encyclopaedia, nor is it designed to persuade anyone to abandon detergents or weave their own hair shirt. It is just a lazy perfectionist's personal collection of know-how designed to turn mountains into molehills by giving the way to do almost anything in or around the home with the best possible results and the least possible expense or effort. Though naturally the good sense of the user plays a part in their effectiveness. The collection isn't exhaustive but I have tried to include both the information one needs most often and that which is hardest to find elsewhere, whether it's how to clean a drain, cherish the family jewels, or stop a cock crowing. Some tips are designed to be useful constantly, some are just there to fall back on, and others are included because they charmed or amused me. All of them made me wish I had known them sooner — which is why this is as much a book for browsing through as for using.

Introduction

Browsers will find the information collected into groups and sub-
divided into chapters covering special topics. Those who need a
particular piece of information may find it quicker to refer to the detailed
index at the back. (Incidentally if your favourite isn't in here, let me
know. Like the Windmill Theatre my collection never closes.)

Making this collection would never have been possible without the
help of all those who have advised me and shared their knowledge with
me. I am deeply indebted to

Asprey and Co Ltd   Moyses Stevens
Berry Bros and Rudd Ltd   Gwen Shirley
Cyril A. Castle   David Butcher
Englefields (London) Ltd   Thompson and Morgan
Harrods p.l.c.   The Tortoise-shell and Ivory House Ltd
Jeeves of Belgravia

and to all those in other companies, organisations, museums, and areas of
public service who have given me their time and shared their expertise. I
also want to thank Elizabeth David who, through her books, nursed me
through my first steps in the kitchen and provided the foundation to any
culinary skill I possess. And in particular I owe a special debt to the
hundreds of people all over the world who have trusted me with old and
treasured books and passed on their know-how, and to my friends and
acquaintances who have so patiently allowed me to pick their brains over
the years. The credit for this book belongs to all of them. Any errors or
omissions are mine.

Your Home

SPIT AND POLISH

Such is the pressure of marketing and advertising that over the last half century most of us have been persuaded to believe that all the smartly presented proprietory cleaners are superior to the dowdy bottles used in the past. This is far from the truth. For me, one of the great surprises has been to discover just how good some of the old methods are. Those I have included here either work better than branded products or provide an excellent fall-back when more modern products are unobtainable. Using them also carries an unexpected bonus. After a little experience it becomes easy to see why certain combinations produce the results they do and suddenly all those odd, seemingly useless, bits of simple chemistry one learnt at school fall into place. After that it becomes possible to work out one's own combinations — which is extraordinarily satisfying and puts one, at long last, out of the thrall of the manufacturers.

BAKELITE

Strangely, the impregnated wadding metal polish is excellent for cleaning bakelite and celluloid. This is especially useful on electric switches and plugs as it avoids the danger of using water. Rub the residue of polish off with a soft cloth.

BAKING TINS

Tins for baking and roasting which have become black and encrusted with food burnt onto them will come clean when boiled with a good handful of washing soda. Very bad tins may need a long boil, and a scour to get the softened debris off afterwards, but the very worst will come clean if you give the soda time.

BATHS

Cleaning
Only a glutton for punishment will use any sort of abrasive, whether

3

powder or paste, on a new bath. Keeping the glassy surface scratch-free is half the secret of an easily cleaned bath. The other half of the secret is to install a bath brush and washing-up liquid in the bathroom and instil into everyone that as the water is running out they squeeze washing-up liquid on the brush, brush the bath out, and rinse it. The washing-up liquid must be the slightly thick sort and it *must* be a brush not a cloth. Even in the home you get consumer resistance. Having just become clean and fresh in the bath people don't want to handle messy-looking cloths, so without a brush they opt out.

Once the system is running the bath keeps immaculately clean without the houseperson lifting a finger.

If a bath is already dirty the substance which cleans it best is paraffin, which is equally good at getting off soapy scum and limescale, and brings the surface up to a fine shine. The only drawback is the smell which must be thoroughly rinsed away. Paraffin is equally good on basins and makes short work of taps.

If a bath has become very dirty and greasy, fill it with very hot water and add several cups of washing soda. A soak in this and a good brush with a bath brush should clean all but the foulest bath.

If that fails the answer is hydrochloric acid. Mix 1 part of the acid to 9 parts of water. *Wearing rubber gloves*, wipe this on the dirt and rinse each patch as soon as it is clean. Great care has to be taken not to spill or splash the acid — especially near the face — and it should be in contact with the bath for as short a time as possible, as acid left on will eat into the bath's surface. However, this method would restore even a former doss-house bath to reasonable whiteness and cleanliness.

Stains

The commonest stain is the brownish deposit which forms in hard-water areas, where the last of the water lies or a tap drips. A rub with salt and vinegar removes this quite easily.

Rust marks on baths will usually bleach out if a mixture of salt and lemon juice is applied to the stain and left on. It works very slowly, so give it a day or so, and keep adding more juice as it dries. If that fails (and the bath is a white one) try rubbing the mark with hydrogen peroxide.

BEESWAX POLISH

A beautiful beeswax polish can be made very easily, using real beeswax and turpentine. Ironmongers still stock cakes of yellow beeswax looking like cakes of soap. Grate one of these on a coarse grater and put it in a jam jar. Cover the grated wax with turpentine, or turpentine substitute, and leave it for 2 days. Shake it well and it's ready for use.

If a beeswax-polished surface becomes spotted with water or other liquids rub the spots with turpentine or white spirit until they disappear and polish again while the area is still moist from this treatment.

BLINDS

The simplest way to clean venetian blinds is to take an 'L' of crust from a new loaf and run it along each slat, holding it firmly on either side of it. Take a fresh crust as each becomes dirty. Roller blinds can be cleaned, if they have a hard surface, by rubbing them with a slice of fresh bread or rolling across them a very firm flour and water dough. This is assuming they are not the washable type.

BOARDS

Chopping-boards, and pastry boards, should be scrubbed clean in running water as soon as they have been used. They are much easier to clean at this stage and the risk of food going bad on a porous surface is avoided. They must not be left soaking in water. It warps them and expands the wood at the joints so they become loose when dry. Floury boards, and rolling pins, clean up fastest with cold water. Hot water cooks the flour and makes it cling.

The way to get stained boards clean is to scrub them with salt water, cover the stains with salt and lemon juice and put the board in the sunlight to whiten.

BRUSHES

Bristle Brushes
In Edwardian days, when nannies applied a hundred strokes of the brush to each head of hair, the bristles had to be kept in perfect condition. The way they did this was to wash them in warm water with a walnut of washing soda and a few drops of ammonia. The bristles were gently tapped up and down in this without letting the roots get wet. Rinsing was done in the same way and the brushes were put, bristle down, to dry away from direct heat. This is still the best way to wash pure bristle brushes.

Shoe Brushes
When shoe brushes become clogged with polish, washing them in hot soapy water to which a dash of ammonia has been added, will clean them, although soapy water alone will fail.

CANE AND FRIENDS

Soap can discolour cane, rush, coconut matting and bamboo. So all these should be cleaned with strong salt water instead. If the material is greasy, adding a very little ammonia to the water will clean it. Any marks which remain can be treated with methylated spirits.

If a chair seat is being cleaned both sides should be washed to make it shrink evenly and remove the sag.

CARPETS

Burns
On a wool carpet rubbing the burn immediately with a slice of potato takes the singe out of the surface. The brown tips which are left to the ends of the threads will sometimes wash out. If they don't, they could be discreetly trimmed with nail scissors, if the burn is small enough.

Dents
If a carpet has become dented with heavy furniture, put an ice cube on the dent and leave it to melt. Or leave a large tablespoon of water on the place. On wool carpets this makes the pile spring up like new, on acrylics it isn't always so successful.

Dirty Carpets
No old method of cleaning carpets can touch the modern foam shampoos. When using them remember acrylic carpets become over-wet far more easily than wool ones. The danger of over-wetting is that it damages the backing to the carpet and can make it shrink and buckle.

Good though these shampoos are, carpet dyes are among those most likely to run, so a test patch should always be washed where it won't show.

However dry a carpet may feel, put a piece of plastic bag under the legs of furniture as you put it back, and leave it there for several days. Then a hidden nail won't leave a rust stain because of below-the-surface damp.

In old books a dash of vinegar in warm water is always acclaimed as being the sure way to bring the colours in carpets up 'like new'. I may have tried it on the wrong types of carpet, but I don't find it does that. It is, however, an excellent spot remover. A few drops of ammonia in water are equally good.

If you can count on having snow each year you can always clean your carpets the Austrian way. A routine part of their spring cleaning is to take carpets out and beat them face down on the snow. I'm told snow cleans the carpets quite beautifully. Presumably one has to keep them out of the way of skiers lest they turn into a modern version of magic carpets.

Man-made Fibre Carpets

Man-made fibres tend to build up static and attract fluff. The way to reduce this problem is to mix about 4–6 tablespoons of water with 1 tablespoon of fabric softener, and spray this over the carpet with a plant sprayer and allow it to dry. The exact proportions of softener to water depend on the softener you use.

A cloth dampened with this mixture and kept in a jar should be used to dust acrylic and perspex fittings. It will keep them free of static and make them stay clean much longer.

New Carpets

A new carpet should not be vacuum cleaned for 4–6 weeks to give the pile time to bed down. Leave it longer than this if the carpet is little walked on.

Soot

If soot falls on a carpet it should immediately be sprinkled heavily with salt and left for half an hour before being carefully brushed up.

Stains see Stain Removal, pages 151–161.

Sweeping

If the hoover gives out and a carpet has to be swept by hand the way to stop all the dust rising and making the furniture filthy is to first sprinkle the carpet with slightly damp salt or tea leaves. On no account use *wet* tea leaves or you will have tea stains on the carpet.

CHROME

A little household ammonia in water is the best chrome cleaner. Rinse and dry the chrome well afterwards, to polish it up. The great advantage of ammonia is that it is equally good at removing the grease which gets onto the chrome on cars, and the fly-marks which dirty chrome fires and lights. On stubborn marks use a little neat ammonia on the damp cloth.

If you have no ammonia, paraffin or toothpaste on a damp cloth are quite good substitutes.

If chrome taps are marked with water deposits rub the marks with salt and vinegar or vinegar and whiting. If there are no deposits, whiting and water gives a good polish to chrome. Just rub it on, rinse it off and rub up with a dry cloth or, best of all, a chamois leather.

DRAINS

If drains have plenty of hot soapy water going through them, and grease and refuse aren't put down to clog them up, they should stay smelling sweet. If they do start to smell — or you know they aren't getting enough soap and water through to keep them clean — put half a cup or so of washing soda in the sink, and pour on boiling water. As soon as it has dissolved pull the plug out. Outside drains may need caustic soda and water poured down them. (*See* Paint Stripping, page 45, for hazards.)

If the water from a sink or basin starts to be slow in running out there is a blockage somewhere. Dealing with it before it becomes a total block will save a lot of trouble. The first place to look is in the trap or U-bend under the sink itself. Removing it and cleaning it out is a mucky job but easy enough if you have a long-handled monkey-wrench to undo the rings which hold it in place. Work with a bowl or pail underneath, to catch spills. If cleaning this out has no effect, try shoving a piece of stout wire bent into a hook at the end into the outside gulley. Only when this fails do you need a plumber.

When water refuses to run out at all, repeatedly pushing a sink plunger up and down over the open plug hole should get it going. If you have no plunger use a large softish rubber ball.

Drain Covers
The least unpleasant way to clean a cast iron drain cover is to put it on a bonfire for just long enough to burn off the slime and debris.

ELECTRIC BULBS

Both damp and vibration shorten the life of electric bulbs. If you need to clean them hold them steady and dust with a dry duster. Fly-marks can be removed with a drop of vinegar or methylated spirits.

FLOWER VASES

I have always wished I could perform miracles. The nearest I have ever got to it is the effect of bleach on really filthy flower vases. You can take the dirtiest glass vase, fill it with water and add a good dash of bleach, and in a few minutes the dirt will have totally disappeared leaving both the glass and the water completely clear.

It is a good plan to clean all glass vases and metal plant holders like this each time they are used. Then the bacteria which shorten the life of flowers are destroyed. But check if other vases can take bleach.

FREEZERS AND REFRIGERATORS

If glycerine is brushed on the inside of a freezer after it is defrosted the ice will fall off in sheets next time it is cleaned out, which speeds up the defrosting.

Switched-off refrigerators should be left with the door open. The dust which may get in is a far smaller problem than the mould which will grow if the door is closed. (*See also* Smells.)

FUNGUS

When fungus is a problem on damp walls, or on windows which receive a lot of condensation, a short-term solution is to scrub it off and paint the area with neat bleach. This usually has no ill effect on the paint, but do a test patch first, where it won't show. From then on put a dash of bleach in the water whenever the windows are washed. Wear rubber gloves as bleach is bad for the skin.

As mould spores are in the air the only long-term solution is to get rid of the damp conditions in which mould likes to live.

GLUE

The adhesives from transparent tape and sticky labels should come off paint with methylated spirits. (*See also* Adhesives and Stains.)

KETTLES

A kettle which becomes encrusted with deposits from the water takes longer to boil and uses up more fuel, so it's not a bad idea to keep it clean. The traditional way to prevent it furring up is to keep a rough shell in the bottom of it. This attracts the scale and keeps it off the inside of the kettle.

If a deposit has already formed it can be cleaned off with equal amounts of vinegar and water. Half fill the kettle with this mixture — the vinegar rises dramatically as it heats — and boil it up. Leave it to get cold before emptying and rinsing. This will cope with a light deposit. On a heavy one you will need to keep bringing it to the boil and rubbing at the inside, as it cools, to break off the part which the vinegar has softened.

9

Borax and water used in the same way is another possible cleaner, much recommended in old books. But it is less effective than vinegar and has the disadvantage of being poisonous.

KNIFE WASHING

In old sculleries there was often a stone jar of water beside the sink. Knives were stood in this to prevent food hardening on them while the other items were washed. The point of this was that, until about 1970, the fixative for knife handles was a resin which expanded when hot or wet. So if knives were dropped in the washing-up water the blade was gradually pushed from its socket. No knife made before 1970 should ever have the junction between the blade and the handle put in water, unless the handle is clearly pinned on. Ordinary steel knives should only stand in water for a very brief period or they will mark and rust, and even stainless steel knives are more vulnerable than you might think. The acids in some foods can mark them and the part of the blade near the handle can be extra vulnerable.

A curious fact is that steel knives are soldered to metal handles at such a high temperature that an arc of blade nearest the handle changes its character and ceases to be 'stainless'. Left to soak overnight this part alone may be stained by food acids. Even the rest of the blade is vulnerable to some chemicals. Silver dip, for example, can leave permanent marks. So it should not be used to clean silver handles on knives.

It is now very hard to get emery powder, which is the best thing for stains on a plain steel knife. Scouring powder on the end of a damp cork is next best. Failing that steel wool, or wood ash on a piece of potato.

If a steel knife acquires an unpleasant smell it normally washes off. If it doesn't, plunging it into the earth several times will cure it.

LACQUERED METAL

When lacquer on copper or brass starts to peel off in patches the lacquer must be stripped before it can be thoroughly cleaned and re-lacquered. Either methylated spirits or acetone will strip it, depending on the lacquer. Both will damage polish on furniture, so knobs and handles should be taken off before they are treated. One of the acrylic lacquers gives the best finish when re-lacquering.

LAVATORIES

Plain bleach is very much the most powerful cleaner for lavatories. Pour it into the lavatory over the lavatory brush so you are applying neat bleach onto the upper edges when you brush round them. The more time you give the chemicals to work before flushing the better.

If you have the common problem of moving into a house with a neglected loo then repeated overnight soaking is the answer. If the upper edges are encrusted, carefully make a paste of bleach and flour and apply this with an old paint brush – a foul job, but the flour will hold the bleach on the area where it needs to work. Once clean, a lavatory should be cleaned out at least every two days. This prevents urine stains, but scale from hard water is a different matter.

Lime Scale

When drips from taps or the trickle at the back of a loo create hard deposits it's wise to remove them sooner rather than later. The thicker they get the harder they are to remove. In the early stages brushing hard with hot vinegar will remove them. Thick deposits should be brushed with 1 teaspoonful of oxalic acid dissolved in $\frac{1}{2}$ a cup of hot water. Let it work on the scale for a little, then scrape at it with a hard plastic edge, such as the end of a toothbrush handle. Keep applying and scraping till it has gone. Wear rubber gloves for this job and keep the acid mixture off the skin and clothes.

LIGHT OAK

When it gets very dirty light oak can be cleaned by scrubbing with a moderately stiff brush. Work with the grain using a teaspoonful of ammonia in 2 pints (1 litre) of warm water. Wipe the oak dry and when completely dry powder lightly with French chalk and rub off any excess.

MARKS ON FRENCH POLISH

Every good butler keeps a little jar of cigarette or cigar ash tucked away. This is against the day when some careless guest will place a cup or glass on a French–polished surface, leaving a large white ring. A mixture of that ash and a good vegetable oil rubbed on the mark will remove it completely — though some marks take more rubbing than others. This mixture is for dark woods only, the oil could stain pale woods. On light woods rubbing with an oily Brazil nut is safer.

Some people recommend oil with salt instead of ash. Even if this works there is a risk that the salt will scratch the French polish.

OILING FURNITURE

Teak, afrormosia, and other tropical hardwoods have a very high resin content — natural protection, perhaps, against the creatures which would otherwise have eaten them. It is because this resin must never be sealed in that these woods must be oiled not polished. Boiled (*not* raw) linseed oil is excellent for all these woods and a great deal cheaper than so called 'teak oil', which mysteriously smells exactly the same.

To apply the linseed oil put it on a ball of cotton wool and wrap the cotton wool in a piece of rag. This gives a far more even spread of oil than applying oil to the cloth itself.

OIL LAMPS

I never like to be without an old fashioned oil lamp. The light is beautiful to eat by and it's a boon when the power fails. They need far less maintenance than you might suppose. The vital thing is to keep the wick trimmed perfectly straight. If it isn't it will smoke. But even a perfectly trimmed wick gives off some smoke. When the chimney becomes blackened it should not be washed — washing weakens it and makes it liable to crack, don't ask me why. Instead, push a soft twist of dry newspaper into it and work it against the glass. Every trace of soot will come off easily. Wicks smoke less if soaked in vinegar and allowed to dry before being put in.

OVEN CLEANING

Sometimes when bent double and hanging bat-like upside down — the only position in which one can clean the roof of an oven with a drop-down door — I think how I would like to condemn the manufacturers to daily oven cleaning. I would not, of course, make it easy for them by applying bicarbonate of soda. For, if a strong solution of bicarbonate of soda is wiped over a newly cleaned oven, future dirt will come off remarkably easily. The bicarbonate needs to be reapplied after each cleaning. Use about 1 tablespoon of bicarbonate to $\frac{1}{2}$ pint (250 ml) of water.

If an oven is really dirty caustic soda will take the dirt off with the least effort. In fact I find it rather better than the proprietory oven-cleaning pads, as well as considerably cheaper.

Put 1 tablespoon of caustic soda into a pint (500 ml) of hot water — *don't reverse this and put the water on the soda, it's dangerous.* (*See* Paint Stripping for explanation.) *Wearing thick rubber gloves*, swab the inside of the oven with this, being careful not to splash it on your skin. Leave it to work for at least half an hour, but preferably overnight. Then just wipe the dirt off. Time is the most important factor with this cleaner. So if the dirt doesn't come off very easily the caustic needs longer to work on it. Only an excessively dirty oven will need a stronger solution than this to get it clean. *Keep this mixture off vinyl floors and surfaces.*

PANS

Aluminium

If you are one of those who must have every pan bright and shiny, you can save a lot of elbow grease by using Cream of Tartar on blackened pans. Fill the pan with a solution of 1 teaspoon of Cream of Tartar to each pint (½ litre) of water and boil it for 10 minutes. This won't bring it to a shine but it will take the black tone out of the metal, so it only needs a quick wipe with a scouring pad to bring it up. The leaves and trimmings of rhubarb do an even better job, especially if left to stand in the pan after being boiled, but they aren't always to hand. As they are poisonous the pan must be rinsed well afterwards.

Burnt Pans

Salt is the certain cure for burnt pans of every sort. I must have thrown away days of my life scouring burnt pans before I discovered this.

How you use the salt, and how much you use, depends on how badly burnt the pan is. If it is only slightly burnt an hour's soak in strong salt water will do the trick. But if it is really caked it may need as long as twelve hours, with a boil-up before and after. The deposits should virtually wipe off. So if they don't, boil it, leave it longer, or add more salt.

There are those who swear by boiling a beetroot in a burnt pan — but this seems a waste of a beetroot. Others say cold tea does the job, but salt is so good I prefer to stick to it.

Enamel Pans

Enamel will craze if subjected to sudden changes of temperature. This will make it look dirty for good. It will also scratch if harsh abrasives are used on it. If it becomes stained or yellow washing soda will clean it without harming the surface. Rub a little powdered washing soda on the stain or fill the pan with water and add soda, boil, then brush thoroughly clean.

Frying Pans

A new iron frying pan or griddle is less likely to burn food if it is seasoned first. Cover the bottom well with salt and heat it thoroughly. Rub the salt in with some paper. Repeat the process twice more, then wipe out the salt without washing the pan.

As they get older iron and heavy aluminium pans will gradually become non-stick if they are simply brushed out after use under very hot water, without soap or scouring. Trying to keep them shiny is a waste of time.

Milk Pans and Friends

Milk is less likely to stick to a pan if the pan is rinsed in cold water first. It also cleans off more easily if the pan is filled with water the moment the milk is emptied out. Pans which have had egg in, especially scrambled egg, should also be filled with water immediately. In fact the essence of cleaning any pan easily is to fill it with water and leave it to soak. Use hot water because cold water could warp or craze hot pans. The trouble is that it's possible to forget all about a soaking pan with its lid on until one discovers its decomposing contents a few days later. If this happens always boil up the water in the pan for some while before throwing it down the drain and washing the pan. Then the bacteria which have been multiplying in there are killed.

Non-stick Pans

Non-stick pans and tin-lined omelette pans should only be washed with soap and water. Scouring them ruins the very surface which makes them worth using. If food is stuck on, soak it in hot water until it will come off easily. No metal utensils should be used in cooking or in cleaning the pans.

As non-stick pans must not be scoured the only way to remove stains is to boil up the water and cleaners in the pan. For each $\frac{1}{2}$ pint (250 ml) of water add $\frac{1}{4}$ pint (125 ml) of vinegar and 2 tablespoons of baking soda. Boil this up for 15 minutes and the stain should have vanished or at least be ready to wipe off. Rinse the pan well and rub in a little cooking oil and heat it.

PINE

Pine needs no more than a polish with a good beeswax polish. Once it has a good shine it needs an occasional wipe with a cloth damped with equal amounts of vinegar and paraffin. The easiest way is to put a spoonful of each in a jar with a clean duster and leave it closed until the liquid has been absorbed. This cloth is excellent for giving a quick shine to all polished surfaces. It needs to be kept in the screw-top jar between use so it stays damp.

PLASTIC LAMINATES

The plastic surfaces in kitchens need more care than some suppose. Using a cleaning powder, or any other abrasive, removes the shine and gradually converts a smooth easily cleaned surface into a rough troublesome one. Using the surface as a cutting board is just as bad. Only liquid cleaners should be used and cutting should be done on a separate board.

Although these surfaces will stand temperatures as high as 310°F or 154°C, a pan put on them straight from the oven or the hob will leave a mark. So will a cigarette. There is no way a burn can be removed.

Bleaches, dyes — including food dyes — acids and strong alkali can all cause stains. They should be wiped up before they do. Stains from tea or coffee come out if left to soak in a solution of washing soda and water. Pure lemon juice should remove ink stains from food packaging which has been left on a damp surface.

PORCELAIN BASINS

Rust marks on basins can be removed with a paste of Cream of Tartar. Leave the paste on the stain for a while to work before rubbing it off. Borax and lemon juice is another mixture which removes rust, though this is better on the surfaces of baths.

SMELLS

If a pan holds the smell of something which has cooked in it, such as fish, fill it with water, add a good dash of vinegar and boil it up. The smell will vanish.

Normal cleaners can make the smells which cling in refrigerators and plastic containers seem even worse. To get rid of them, use 2-3 good teaspoons of bicarbonate of soda in about a pint (500 ml) of water. Use this whenever you wipe out the refrigerator, and fill plastic containers with it and leave overnight. Another method is putting loose charcoal in the fridge to absorb the smell – good if you are going away leaving the fridge on, and the air may get stale. You can still use the charcoal on the barbecue afterwards.

STEEL

The cutlers of Sheffield, I'm told, used to dip steel in lime water to stop it rusting. Once rust has formed on steel, paraffin is very good for removing it. Soak small items in a dish of paraffin for 24 hours and wrap larger ones in paraffin-soaked tissue, then rub up. It won't, of course, remove the pitting which the rust has caused.

Emery powder on half a potato was once the best way to rub up steel, but powdered pumice or steel wool are more easily come by. Sometimes these work best when lubricated with equal parts of paraffin and turpentine. Though the most effective cleaner I have ever seen was a steel link pad which my mother, somehow, acquired from the household cavalry when she had to bring up a dreadfully rusted steel fireplace after the war.

STEPS

I have been told that at one time sour milk would be scrubbed onto steps to make them white. It sounds odd but it may have worked. What certainly does work is putting some salt or methylated spirits in the rinsing water to stop it freezing in cold weather. Use a tablespoon of either in a pint (500 ml) of water. Though for myself, I think it makes even more sense to leave the steps unwashed if there is a danger of ice forming.

Greasy marks from milk bottles which won't come out with washing may respond to a paste of Fullers Earth put over them and left to dry.

STONE FLOORS

The porous stone floors in cottages were never washed with soap and water because the stone would gradually have absorbed the soap and become slippery and dangerous when wet. It is far safer to use a solution of water and washing soda or ammonia, the way they always used to.

SWEEPING

Sprinkling moist, used tea-leaves on a wood floor before sweeping was once as natural to housewives as breathing. But even by the time I was at school, and did it when sweeping the classroom, it was considered old-fashioned and silly. A pity, because it really is worth doing if there is a lot of dust, as there can be when one moves house, for example. Tea-leaves, old coffee grounds, or grass clippings are all equally good at preventing the dust rising.

TEA STAINS

Washing soda, bicarbonate of soda and salt, each remove tea stains from crockery and plastics. Any of them can be used for small marks but if the inside of a tea pot has become brown, washing soda will do the best job. Leave it to soak overnight in soda and water and the stains will wipe off in the morning. Soda should not, however, be used on china which is decorated with gilt, as it will damage it.

Marks on plastics and laminates can either be covered with a solution of washing soda and water and left to soak, or covered by a tissue soaked in this mixture; then thoroughly rinsed.

UPHOLSTERY

Wiping gently with a clean cloth damped with 1 dessertspoonful of vinegar in $\frac{1}{2}$ pint (250 ml) of lukewarm water will remove most spots from Dralon velvet upholstery. This mixture is also very good for removing the shine from other upholstery on which people have rubbed their hands.

If upholstery is dusty and there is no vacuum attachment to suck the dust out, lay a slightly damp cloth over it and beat it. The cloth will then hold the dust instead of it being spread to all the other furnishings.

In my grandmother's recipe book there is a recipe entitled 'To all Fair Lovers of Needlework'. It tells you to clean embroidery with a mixture of '$\frac{1}{2}$ lb soft soap, $\frac{1}{2}$ lb honey, 1 pint of English gin' by sponging it on and rinsing with cold water and drying 'with little cloths'. It says 'the brightest colours will be unimpaired'. I was extremely sceptical about this mixture but found it in so many old books I felt it might not be as foolish as it sounded. To my surprise I discovered it can bring up the colours on needlework, especially on old tapestry, better than modern cleaners. Though obviously it will cause long term harm unless the honey is very thoroughly rinsed off.

VERDIGRIS

The green verdigris deposit which sometimes forms on brass and copper cannot be shifted by ordinary household cleaners but wipes off immediately with neat household ammonia and salt. Rinse well, and dry.

VINYL

Cleaning
A little known fact is that strong alkali can gradually extract the plasticiser from vinyl and make it liable to shrinking, brittleness and cracking.

Some proprietory floor cleaners are alkaline enough to cause this damage — especially if no rinsing is needed. Using 2–3 drops of a neutral washing-up liquid and a final rinse with a dash of vinegar in the water will get the floor just as clean without this risk, and this is what manufacturers recommend. But don't be heavy handed, more than 2–3 drops will just mean that soap will lie on the floor, making it sticky and slippery when wet.

Surface marks can be removed with a plastic scourer but once a stain has penetrated vinyl there is really no way to remove it. Food colourings, on their own or in food, are the worst culprits. Anything which might contain colouring should be wiped up immediately. Bleach, hair dye, photographic chemicals, paint thinners, fabric dyes, nail varnish and its removers can mark vinyl permanently, and in some cases dissolve it, if not removed quickly. On grime use a fine-gauge soap-filled metal scouring pad.

Polishing
This is one of those areas where the lazy score higher than the zealous. Two coats of acrylic polish a year are, according to the manufacturers, enough to give a protective coat. Four is overdoing it, and more than that will give a dirty yellowed look. Only the first coat should be taken right to the edges. After that it is best to stick to the areas which get the wear if you don't want a yellow rim to the room.

When the polish does become too thick and starts to yellow it can be stripped off. Use ½ a cup of household ammonia in 1 gallon (4 litres) of cold water, plus a few drops of washing-up liquid. Give the mixture 5 minutes to work before mopping it up and attacking stubborn patches with a nylon saucepan scourer. As vinyl could be damaged by the alkali of ammonia the floor must be rinsed with a cup of vinegar in 1 gallon of water to neutralise it.

WALL CLEANING

Painted Surfaces
It sounds topsy-turvy but all painted wall surfaces should be washed from the bottom upwards. The reason is that if water trickles down over a dirty wall it can leave a line which no amount of washing will remove. But if it trickles down a washed wall this doesn't happen.

In old books there are a multitude of recipes for cleaning walls. Onion water is often advocated, so is block soap and a loofah. But the best cleaners are those based on washing soda and ammonia. A good basic mixture is ½ cup of ammonia, ¼ cup of vinegar and ¼ cup of washing soda.

The balance can be changed to suit the particular wall you are cleaning. Another recipe gives 1 cup of ammonia, ½ cup of vinegar and ¼ cup of washing soda. Both these mixtures are to go in a gallon of water. Either way it's a powerful mixture which will bring up very dirty glazed tiles or prepare a wall for painting. A fraction of this quantity can be used to keep walls routinely cleaned. Whatever the strength wear rubber gloves, as it dries the skin.

Wallpapered Surfaces
Using bread to clean wallpaper really sounds like ye olde worldiness for its own sake – but far from it. Nothing else has just the right amount of moisture without a trace of wetness to damage the paper. Bread will take marks off which nothing else will shift. The easiest way to use it is to slice all the crusts from a loaf and work with these.

Some marks will also come off with a soft eraser, but great care has to be taken not to leave a pale patch. If this starts to happen make feather-like strokes radiating out from the centre. These will be less noticeable than a firm edge.

A grease mark on wallpaper will sometimes come out if blotting paper is put over it and a hot iron applied. How successful this is depends on the type of wallpaper.

Vinyl papers can be washed with the mixtures given for walls. But if a very alkaline cleaner is used they should be rinsed with a water and vinegar solution afterwards. It is also important not to let the seams get wet.

WASHING UP

By Hand
'Never put away plates, knives and forks uncleaned, or a sad inconvenience will arise when the articles are wanted,' instructed a women's magazine of a hundred and thirty years ago. The trouble is that 'sad inconvenience' is only avoided by the dreaded task of washing up. It is probably the one household task which everyone thinks they know how to do. It is also the one most often made more difficult than it need be.

The easiest way is not the 'pile 'em all in' system. It is the one once dinned into the heads of scullery maids, which ensures that nothing is ever dirtied by something dirtier than itself. The order of washing is glass, silver, china, dishes, pans. The glasses are done one at a time, with nothing else in the basin, to avoid chipping, and everything is washed in order of cleanliness, cleanest first. On all but the most modern knives the handle fixing is vulnerable to heat and wet. So the blades should be washed without putting the bolster in the water. Ideally everything should be rinsed in water, with a dash of vinegar added, to remove the alkali of the soap, then most things will come up shiny even if you don't dry them — knives and glass excepted.

Written down, this sounds a bother. But since things must be washed one after another anyway they might as well be done in the order which makes least work. This method is not half as troublesome as getting the grease off the glasses that were thrown in to soak with the frying pan the night before.

By Machine
When an efficient washing-up machine stops working well it is often because of trouble with the rotary arms which spray the water out. Gritty food stuck behind them can stop them rotating. Wiggling them usually clears this. Also pieces of food can build up inside them and block the holes the water thrusts through. It is normally a simple matter to remove these arms and get the food out, even if the manual doesn't show you how. Look for a pin or a screw holding each in place and remember the screw may well turn in the opposite direction to normal – so it won't undo as the arm spins.

WASTE DISPOSAL UNITS

The way to keep a waste disposal unit from becoming coated and smelly is to pour washing soda dissolved in hot water down it from time to time. Debris that builds up round the edges can be removed by simply feeding it a number of ice cubes which will scrape the sides as they go round.

WINDOWS AND MIRRORS

Printing ink has a marvellous effect on glass. Damp a piece of newspaper and use it to clean windows and mirrors and it will bring them up faster, and with less mess, than anything else: unless, of course, they are dusty or gritty. In which case wash the dirt off first and use a dry newspaper to polish up the glass afterwards.

Methylated spirits or vinegar in the rinsing water will improve the shine on windows if you prefer to clean them with detergent.

If glass is very fly-spotted use plain hot water and put a dash of paraffin on the cleaning cloth. Paraffin removes fly marks on glass faster than any other cleaner and some say it also stops the flies returning — though it would be hard to prove that. Whatever the cleaner, a final rub with chamois leather gives the best finish to glass.

The exception to the use of chamois leather is in the bathroom. Here the aim is to stop the glass steaming up. The way to do this is to put a little glycerine on the rinsing cloth. This doesn't leave the glass looking quite as good as the other rinse aids, but it will keep the mirror from steaming up, and make it possible to use it while someone is bathing.

WOK CARE

Woks are very prone to rust. The Chinese way of caring for them is to wash and dry them then put a drop of oil in the wok and heat it well. Then rub the hot oil into the surface of the wok with a piece of clean paper and this completely stops it rusting. Once oiled and cool it should be stored in a large plastic bag, or the oil will acquire an unappetising coating of dust.

WOOD FLOORS

I've tried numerous floor polishes but never found one which did not develop ugly marks if someone walked across it with wet feet. Linseed oil, on the other hand, will work up a polish which resists almost anything and needs a minimum of upkeep. Small wonder it was so popular with Victorian housekeepers.

Use a soft cloth to rub it onto an unsealed dark wood floor which is clean and dust free. Leave it for an hour or two and then wipe off the surplus. Repeat the process the next day and then leave it. After that use a mop which has been standing in a very little linseed oil, to wipe the floor whenever it needs cleaning. The shine will gradually develop as the oil oxidises.

Occasionally wood floors, and other unsealed wood, may develop a dark stain. The best treatment for such stains is to pour on a spoonful of neat lemon juice. Left on for a few hours this will usually bleach out the stain. If it fails try again with lemon juice and salt. It makes no difference whether the lemon juice is fresh or out of a bottle.

WOODEN SALAD BOWLS

There are two troubles with salad bowls and both stem from the wood being porous. The first is that if you accidentally leave the salad in it overnight there may be nasty stains in the morning. Try lemon juice on these if they are dark, oil them if they are pale. The other trouble is that washing with soap and water gradually takes the oils out of the wood: as a result it becomes dry and cracks.

The best treatment for a wooden salad bowl is to empty it as soon as you've used it and wipe it out with soft paper. If it still isn't clean enough brush it out under lukewarm running water, dry it thoroughly and rub on a very little salad oil.

FINE THINGS

In most areas a little bit of 'by guess and by God' doesn't matter, and if you are beguiled by the blandishments of the manufacturer into using the latest lipstick or aftershave it does no harm. This is not so when it comes to caring for beautiful things. The wrong use of old methods and the wholesale adoption of new ones hold equal hazards. So this chapter covers the best way to care for all the major types of fine furniture and ornaments. Though some of the methods in this section go back centuries, they are all still used and recommended by people who make a profession of caring for fine things.

Of course there are always special cases, and queries on these can be taken to the conservators at one of the major museums who can tell you where to get unusual ingredients. Advice from minor museums may not be so helpful, as expert conservators are thin on the ground.

BOOKS

Leather Bindings

Far too many beautiful leather bindings become dry and neglected for lack of a polish to clean them. Yet the mixture which is needed is extremely simple. One of Britain's top book restorers recommends equal quantities of plain lanoline and neatsfoot oil. The neatsfoot oil can be bought at any saddler and the two should be mixed together over warm water until they form a smooth cream.

Once a year put a very small dab of this mixture on a soft cloth, rub it into any new leather binding and polish it off with a fresh cloth. Old books may need to be cleaned more often, especially if the atmosphere is dry. A dry leather can also be given a deeper treatment with this mixture. Simply apply it more thickly and leave it for several days before rubbing off. This polish brings up the leather, and any gilding which may be on it, to a beautiful soft shine. To keep it like this use the polishing-off cloth to rub the books whenever they are being dusted.

This mixture is also excellent for leather belts and handbags, provided it is rubbed well off, but I wouldn't recommend anyone to follow the example of one conservator at the British Museum. He used the mixture on a fabric-bound volume and produced a greasy, and irreversible, stain. Fabric-covered books should only be wiped with a dry duster.

Storage

Books like a cool dry atmosphere and their main enemies are heat and damp. People are another major enemy, and good books can do with protection against them. If valuable books are stored amongst others, a discreet tape, to match the binding, can be put round each and tied at the spine. This makes it easy to exempt these books from the attention of visitors and children. It also makes it easier to remove them from the shelf without pulling on the spine.

If good books are stored in a cabinet it is wise to put a block of wood, the thickness of a book, at each end of the shelves. Nobody ever opens cabinet doors fully and if there is a book at the end of a shelf it will be scraped on the doors as it's removed. Another form of scraping to avoid is that of metal clasps on neighbouring books. The book with the clasp should have a fabric cover, for all but the spine, so it can safely be slid in and out.

Very large books put an enormous strain on the binding with their big heavy pages. The only way to ease this is to store them in low stacks laid on their side, even though this is not recommended for other books.

BRASS AND COPPER

Once the most popular way of cleaning really tarnished brass and copper was to use hot vinegar and salt, either immersing the metal in it or wiping it on. This is so powerful it took me just five minutes to remove twenty years of black untouched tarnish from a window latch, but it carries two risks. As the metal dries the mixture may create far worse stains than the original ones. The only way to avoid this is to rinse it off very thoroughly as soon as a shine appears.

The other danger is that it has recently been found that using any chloride — whether washing soda, salt, or one of the others — can sometimes set up bronze disease. This is a very rapid corrosion which destroys the entire structure of the metal, making it fall to pieces. So although salt and vinegar may be fine, if carefully used, for door knobs and copper kettles, it would be madness to use it — or any other mixture containing chlorides — on Uncle Arthur's treasures from India. For though bronze disease is rare nobody can predict when it will strike.

It is safer for the metals, but more hazardous for the person cleaning, to use citric, tartaric or oxalic acid in water to clean off major tarnish. Just how much you use depends on the state of the metal and the temperature of the water used with the acid. All these work faster in hot water than in cold so you would need to use less of them. Try ½ oz to 1 pt (15 g to ½ l) in warm water and add more if need be. Swab it on the metal and give it time to work before you rinse it off, remembering to protect the skin, avoid breathing it in, and keep it away from children.

The above methods remove tarnish but put no lustre on the metal. For that there used to be a multitude of recipes, most of them employing abrasives like rottenstone and powdered bathbrick — plus, I suspect, a quite phenomenal amount of elbow grease. For there really is no old recipe which is better than the modern polishes. Though there is one exception. Intricate brass comes up best rubbed with a wedge of lemon because this gives a good shine without the powdery residue which normal polishes leave. Rinse the metal and rub it with a chamois leather after applying the lemon.

If modern polishes run out, whiting and methylated spirits will bring up a respectable shine. The old idea of putting a light coat of beeswax polish on these metals is also a good one. It helps them keep their lustre for longer.

Brass on wood

Brass on wood, or inlaid into it, presents difficulties because any metal polish will gradually bleach the wood. Two old methods can be safely used on inlaid brass. One is to polish it with powdered charcoal, the other is to use whiting mixed with a little fine oil. If it is very tarnished the only remedy may be 000 wire wool. All of these should be used with infinite care on the end of a cotton bud. As none of these are quick, it is well worth a swift rub with a clean duster each day to maintain the polish.

Brass handles look best if removed each year for a good polish and simply rubbed up with a clean duster from then on. On antiques a good clean means leaving a carefully calculated amount of dirt, or they will look like reproductions. Number each handle and chalk the same number inside its position — there is no guarantee they are all identical.

If you want to use polish more often take a piece of sheet plastic or cardboard and cut a hole in it the exact size and shape of the metal. Mask the wood with this and avoid liquid polish which may run down behind it.

BRONZE

As it's in the nature of bronze to be dark, all it needs is dusting, though very dirty bronze can be wiped with a soft cloth wrung out in soap and water, rinsed with a soapless cloth and carefully dried. The exception to this would be a Victorian bronze with a coloured patination, which should only be dusted.

CLOCKS

If a clock stops because of dirt in the works one of the best ways to get it going again is to use paraffin. Simply put a rag soaked in paraffin on a saucer in the bottom of the clock and wait. The vapour from the paraffin gradually loosens the dirt, and the clock returns to working order. The wait may be a long one, though. I have known a clock take several months to return to normal. But even that may be faster than finding a first class clock-mender — which is, of course, what experts recommend.

CLOISONNÉ

Cleaning cloisonné is unfortunately a matter of elbow grease. Metal polish must not be used because if any liquid seeped behind the enamel it could make it lift. Rub the cloisonné with a chamois leather instead.

GILT

To appreciate the fragility of gilt one has only to realise the gold leaf used is so thin that viewed edgewise it is invisible. To make matters worse there are two main kinds of gilt: oil-based and water-based. The oil-based kind is damaged by spirit cleaners, the water-based one by water and unfortunately there are no firm rules for telling which is which. Even some museums leave their gilt uncleaned rather than risk the wrong assessment.

Two old gilt cleaning methods which are particularly to be avoided are those using the water from cooking onions, or a dash of ammonia. Either could improve the gilt at first, only to cause real damage in the long run, as the chemicals eat into it.

The only safe way to clean gilt is to wipe it with a dry cloth, preferably a silk one. (Continued overleaf.)

Modern gilt on picture frames is a different matter. It is usually copper alloy and a damp cloth will do it no harm.

GLASS

The composition of old glass varied greatly at different times and places, and this can make it unexpectedly vulnerable. Quite ordinary, modern, cleaning agents may harm it, and some glass may even be marked by water left standing on it. One chemical which is always to be avoided is ammonia, as it can cause glass to go cloudy. Denture-cleaning tablets — which some recommend — may do the same. I ruined a decanter testing them.

As there is no easy way to tell the vulnerability of the glass you are cleaning, the safest method is pure soap, not detergents, and hand-hot water. Rinse it in water, with a dash of vinegar added, to improve the shine, and use a warm cloth to dry it. The way professionals dry fine-stemmed glasses without twisting them off their stems is to hold the cloth still and turn the glass against it.

As glass stains easily, dregs shouldn't be left standing in it; but if this has happened a soak with 1 part vinegar and 2 parts water should remove the stain. A very old stain in a decanter, though, may resist even neat vinegar. Dealing with such a stain is a matter of trial and error because what works depends so much on the composition of the glass. The newspaper method is often one of the most successful.

Put a folded newspaper in the bottom of a bucket. Tear some more newspaper into pieces no larger than a coin. Drop plenty into the decanter and push them down the neck. Put it in the bucket and fill first the decanter and then the bucket with hand-hot water and leave it to soak for 24 hours. (Beware of using water so hot it will crack the thick glass.) Rinse out the paper and wash the decanter in warm soapy water. Then dry it as thoroughly as possible with twists of tissue paper pushed down inside it and leave it open for a day or so with a bag of silica gel in the neck to absorb the last hint of moisture. Even a small amount of water closed in a decanter can taint it with mustiness.

There is something in printing ink which usually brings glass up beautifully, but if it fails after two nights, try one of the other old-fashioned methods — potato peelings, nettles, or tea leaves in water.

IRON

Citric acid in water is the cleaner to use on rusted iron, or simply brush it with a wire brush or wire wool, plus paraffin, and oil it lightly.

IVORY

My grandmother always insisted methylated spirits was the only cleaner which should be used on ivory. She was quite right. Ivory is extremely vulnerable and meths is one of the few things which won't harm it. When dirty, piano keys, hairbrushes, and so on can simply be wiped with it. Carved ivory should be blown on rather than dusted, for fear of catching and breaking it on the duster, then very gently cleaned with meths on a cotton bud or soft bristle toothbrush. On intricate carving this needs patience — anyone short of it should leave it to experts.

Water cannot be used because it seeps into the hairline cracks and increases them. Strong sunlight and extreme cold also cause cracking.

The temptation to bleach ivory must be avoided. Bleach, peroxide and lemon juice will all 'burn' ivory. At first there may seem to be an improvement but gradually the ivory will lose its patina and become powdery and dull. So leave it the colour it is, mellowing with age is accepted as one of its qualities.

Clean ivory-backed brushes by patting them in warm water containing a dash of ammonia, without wetting the ivory. Rinse in the same way and dry bristle down. Methylated spirits on dental floss is the best cleaner for an ivory comb.

JADE

Jade is not at all fussy. It can be washed with any soap, but avoid abrasives as they will cause fine scratches and destroy the sheen.

JEWELLERY

Basic Cleaning
Most jewellery can easily be cleaned at home, but there are some major, and costly, pitfalls. It is not, as some people say, simply a matter of brushing it over with gin — which, in fact, could harm it badly.

If it's worn a lot jewellery should be cleaned each month, but if it's seldom worn once a year is enough. How it should be cleaned depends on the type of setting and the type of stone. Whatever method you use stones may fall out in the process. So, if you don't want to chase lost gems through the drains, the cleaning must be done in a bowl, not a sink, and the water tipped away through a very fine sieve. It is, in fact, a good thing if stones do fall out during washing, because otherwise they would almost certainly have come out in wearing and been lost.

Watch out for antique jewellery with a closed back to the stones. In a lot of such jewellery these stones were backed with foil. Contact with liquid can permanently discolour the foil and ruin this type of jewellery. The only safe home cleaning for foil-backed settings is a rub with a dry chamois leather.

The basic method of cleaning jewellery is with warm water and wash ing-up liquid in a small bowl. Hot water could damage stones and loosen settings. Soak the jewellery for a while and then brush it clean with a soft bristle toothbrush. A wooden cocktail stick can be used to pick dirt gently out of the crevices. Rings which are clogged with soap can be cleared more easily by using methylated spirits instead of water. Rinse the jewellery well and dry it with a hair dryer or fan heater set on cool. Even this gentle treatment could be too much for some stones (*see* below).

Gold Jewellery
Unlike silver, gold always seems bright and beautiful, but it is amazing how much better it looks after the dirt from the atmosphere has been removed. Professional jewellers have two ways of cleaning pure, unset, gold. Either they wash it in hot soapy water, or they soak it in neat household-strength ammonia for 5–10 minutes. Intricate pieces should be brushed well with an old pure bristle toothbrush, to get every scrap of dirt out of the crevices, before rinsing and drying. Ammonia is especially good for removing the old soap and body oils which can build up in gold chains which are worn continually, but it should not be used when anything is set in the gold. (*See* above for the cleaning of stones.)

Platinum Jewellery
Platinum can be treated like gold.

Silver Jewellery
Plain silver, or silver set with stones which are not fragile (*see* below) is best cleaned in commercial or home-made silver dip as there is then no problem of polish lodging in the cracks. If the stone is fragile rub it up with a silver-polishing cloth or chamois leather instead.

JEWELLERY WITH FRAGILE INSERTS

The fragile stones most often found in jewellery are opal, turquoise, pearl, coral, jet, amber and, surprisingly, emerald. All of these, except emeralds, can be cleaned with soap and warm water, but all other chemicals should be avoided.

Acrylic Jewellery
Acrylic inserts or plain acrylic jewellery should be treated like a fragile stone and kept away from strong chemicals.

Emeralds
Emeralds present a special problem. Emeralds are more prone to flaws than other precious stones. So in the countries where they are found quite a few dealers soak the emeralds in warm green oil which penetrates the cracks and fills them. Once full of oil the flaws become so invisible that even a jeweller may be unable to detect them. The danger is that home cleaning— or indeed wearing an emerald ring while doing the washing up — may draw out the oil and expose the flaws in a previously 'flawless' stone. So although cleaning with cold water and a soft toothbrush may do no harm, thorough cleaning is best left to professionals.

Opals
Opals are especially fragile. Being basically silica and water, they craze and lose their colour if they become dry, so they have to be kept away from heat. If they become dull and scratched professional polishing is the answer, but nothing whatever should be rubbed into them — certainly not glycerine which, though recommended by a well-known advice column, would damage the colour of the opal.

Pearls
One of the nice things about pearls is that anyone can tell the fake from the real thing. Just rub it against the flat of your front tooth. If it feels smooth it is a fake, if it is slightly rough it is real. Though this won't tell you whether it is natural or cultured. There isn't a simple test for that so you just have to trust the jeweller.

Opinions are divided on whether pearls strung in necklaces should or should not be washed in warm water and soap. Some say it does no harm, others that it weakens the thread. If they are rethreaded as often as they should be, which is every six months to a year if worn a lot, they may not need cleaning. Whatever else you do to them, never leave pearls in contact with any acid, it could dissolve them.

LACQUER

Really good lacquer is so extraordinarily fragile that even fine white flour can scratch it and a drop of water can eat into its surface. The only way to clean it is to dust it lightly with a scupulously clean silk cloth. As it gets old the surface may become tacky. There is no way of preventing or reversing this. Clean cheap modern lacquer with a damp cloth.

LEATHER

It is often said that leather chairs should be oiled. This is what gave Edwardian chairs that heavy black look. But if you don't want that look, don't oil them. Unsealed leather should be left as it is. Sealed leather should be cleaned occasionally with a cloth wrung out in warm water and a dash of vinegar, then dried and polished with a good wax polish. Even a well-used chair needs this no more than once a month. Old leather which is in poor condition can be treated with the mixture for leather book bindings.

Leather desk tops can either be wax polished or treated like book bindings.

MARBLE

The point to remember with marble is that, being porous, it absorbs whatever is put on it — whether ink or cleaning agent. So when anything is spilt on it action must be taken fast to prevent a stain.

Cover ink spills immediately with salt and when it has taken up the ink brush it off and cover any remaining mark with sour milk. It may need to be kept moist with sour milk for a couple of days before the stain goes completely.

Brown rust and grey iron stains can be bleached out with repeated applications of lemon juice and salt, although sour milk also removes them, in time.

Red wine, tea and coffee, which are all very common on mantelpieces, will come out with repeated applications of hydrogen peroxide. Salt and lemon can also be used on red wine.

The porous nature of marble also means that if soap is used on it too often it may build up a soapy surface. So the best general cleaner to use is water and washing soda, though on really grimy marble this old-fashioned paste may work better. Take $\frac{1}{4}$ lb (125 g) of whiting, a little laundry blue (for white marble only), 1 oz (30 g) of washing soda, and $\frac{1}{4}$ lb (125 g) of pure soap. Put them all in a pan with enough water to make a cream and boil them for $\frac{1}{4}$ hour. Brush the paste onto the marble and leave it on for $\frac{1}{2}$ hour before washing it off.

MARQUETRY

The special feature of marquetry is that being a thin layer of wood over a thicker base it is dreadfully vulnerable to changes in heat and moisture. This can cause one layer to expand or contract faster than the other, so small pieces of marquetry often lift out of place. When this happens they should be stuck back immediately, before they are broken off and lost. Use a minute amount of PVA adhesive on the end of a cocktail stick. Because of this problem marquetry should never be put near fires or radiators and it is very much better to dust it with a soft brush rather than with a duster, which could catch on any raised corners.

Light is another danger. Many of the colour variations were obtained with wood stains and some of these stains fade extremely easily. So anyone lucky enough to have a piece which has kept its colours should make sure it stays in the shade. Polish it like any other wood, but more carefully.

MOTHER OF PEARL

Mother of pearl has its own sheen and needs no polishing, just a rub with a soft cloth. It should certainly not be oiled, as some old books suggest. If it's really dirty wash it with pure soap and water. Detergents and washing-up liquids could harm it.

PEWTER

One of the great, and largely forgotten, delights of pewter is its ability to hold its temperature and keep a goblet of wine chilled no matter what the temperature of the air. This may well have been what made it so popular with the ancient Romans. Today the secret of a really cool drink on a hot day is first to chill your pewter goblets in the refrigerator with the wine.

In the old days, when pewter was more popular, there were a host of different recipes for polishing it; soap and whisky, wood ash and turpentine, and so on. None except the wood ash would have had much effect. And pewterers say that pewter, being basically a mixture of tin and other metals, was never meant to be shiny and it is quite wrong to try to make it look like the bright metals.

The dull sheen which it ought to have is best achieved by washing it in soapy water and polishing it occasionally with good silver polish. The whiting and water mixture given for silver is ideal, but methylated spirits should not be included as pewter, being porous, absorbs strong smells. When polishing something like a goblet, polishing round it will produce a sheen which shows it off to best advantage. If the pewter is being displayed a little furniture polish will give it an extra lustre.

If, heresy though it is, you prefer a brighter shine, or simply want to remove bad marks, 000 guage wire wool is the answer — 00 produces scratches. The softness of pewter means this must be used with extreme care, and it may be a job best left to experts. Be especially careful not to polish or rub near touch marks showing the date and maker of the piece. A candlestick, with touchmarks proving its considerable age, recently fetched £1,400 more than an identical one of a later date.

Pewter-lovers say it enhances whatever is drunk from it. However, drinks don't improve pewter. Acid fruit drinks should never be drunk from it, and other dregs should be rinsed out straight after use.

SILVER

The old ethic of applying lots of elbow grease is totally wrong for silver. Rubbing slowly wears away the silver and the hall marks which date it. Plain silver, with nothing set in it, is most easily cleaned with silver dip. Make your own with a plate-sized sheet of aluminium foil and 1 tablespoon of salt to $\frac{1}{2}$ pint of water.

Drop the silver in, leave it a minute or two, and remove it as soon as it looks clean. Then rinse and dry it and give it a quick rub with a chamois leather. Used the day after it is made, this dip is just as effective as the bought variety and has the advantage that it can be made in any quantity. But beware of dipping non-silver parts, such as ebony teapot knobs, or plate which is at all worn.

If you have aluminium pans an even simpler method is to dissolve a handful of washing soda in a large pan of hot water and drop the silver in, removing and rinsing it as soon as it looks clean. Both these methods will remove tarnish, but only polishing will give it a sheen.

Puritans can set their consciences at rest: dipping is not the lazy way to remove tarnish, it is the professional way. When it comes to polishing, professionals also use an old method which knocks spots off any of the branded polishes on sale today. Put a tablespoon of whiting in a bowl — it is still sold by good ironmongers for a fraction of the price of silver polish — mix the whiting to a cream with water and add a drop or two of household ammonia. If you have no ammonia use methylated spirits instead of water. Simply wipe this mixture onto the silver and off again. It is as easy as that. There is no need to rub unless it is exceedingly dirty. Finish with a chamois leather, first rinsing any cutlery.

Black acid stains which fail to come off can be removed by rubbing with salt and lemon. Salt stains should be rubbed hard with the whiting mixture plus salt. I know those treatments sound too much like 'a hair of the dog' to work, but they do.

For intricate silver — chased cigarette boxes, trays with dragooned edges and so on — the way to prevent polish lodging in the dips is to use very little polish and put it on and rub it off with soft bristle shoe brushes.

Another quick and easy way to bring up intricate silver boxes is to rub them with a wedge of lemon, rinse the juice off and rub lightly with a leather. This is especially useful if you want to keep your hands clean and suddenly discover dirt on something you want to use.

Just how far you should go in getting every bit of tarnish out of the cracks is a matter of debate. Some museums believe in bringing silver up so it looks as if it had just come from the silversmith's bench. Other experts say that to make any antique look like new is to remove the very qualities which lend it charm and show the design to advantage. It is really a matter of looking at each piece and seeing what suits it, not polishing away like an automaton.

Silver-Polishing Cloth
It's convenient to have a silver-polishing cloth ready to give a rub to anything which is looking tarnished. To make one, mix together 4 teaspoonfuls of whiting, 3 cups of water and 2 tablespoons of ammonia. Soak a piece of towelling in this mixture, wring it out, let it almost dry, and store in a polythene bag.

Storing Silver
Before silver is stored for any length of time it should be well cleaned to remove any substance which might eat into it while in store. Salt, ink, and rubber bands are particularly harmful, so is any form of acid. Cotton gloves should really be worn for the final leathering and packing because even a seemingly dry finger can have enough acid perspiration on it to produce a nasty mark on stored silver. For the same reason silver should be stored in acid-free tissue paper.

The more that light and air can be excluded from the silver the less tarnished it will become. A close wrapping of dark tissue paper and a plastic bag with as much air squeezed out as possible make the best protection. Some people say it also helps to put a piece of camphor in the bag, but not touching the silver.

SILVER GILT

The great advantage of silver gilt, for those who can afford it, is that as the top layer is gold it does not need cleaning. Just wash it by hand or even in a dishwasher.

SILVER PLATE

As silver plate is only a thin layer of silver over base metal it is far more vulnerable to all forms of cleaning than solid silver. Only if it's in perfect condition can it be put in silver dip, and it should never be left standing in it. The whiting mixture given for silver is the best cleaner to use.

TORTOISE-SHELL

Tortoise-shell can be damaged by direct sunlight, water, and oils of all sorts. Any of these can cause clouding. When this happens the only cure is professional scraping and burnishing. If it has become dirty the best way to clean it is to put whiting on the heel of your hand or on a piece of leather and rub the tortoise-shell against it. It isn't a quick method but it is one which will safely bring the tortoise-shell to a good sheen.

WOOD FURNITURE

Caring for fine wood furniture is far less work than most people imagine. Contrary to popular belief it does not need to be polished all the time 'to feed it'. In fact, wood cannot be fed. All wax does is to protect the wood from changes in humidity by making it harder for moisture to get in and out. Experts on antiques say once a piece has a good shine it only needs to be polished two or three times a year. The rest of the time all it needs is a rub with a clean duster and an occasional cleanse to remove the effects of the atmosphere.

Cleansing

If polished furniture develops a slight bloom or has finger marks, wipe it over with a cloth well wrung out in warm water and a good dash of vinegar. Then rub it with a clean dry duster. If a velveteen duster is used for routine dusting the furniture is less likely to develop this bloom.

Reviving

If antique furniture does not have a good sheen or has patches with black greasy-looking deposits, it needs reviving. This is a process of gradually taking off the build-up of dirt and wax. The mixture which top conservationists use for this is 2 parts pure turpentine, 2 parts methylated spirits, 2 parts vinegar, 1 part raw linseed oil. Put all the ingredients together in a bottle and shake it well.

The mixture separates easily so it must be re-shaken each time more is taken. Put a little on a cotton wool ball and work first on a test patch somewhere unnoticeable. If the piece has been finished with shellac or French polish a shine should gradually show through. If this happens the mixture can safely be used. If, after working right through the dirt, no shine appears the piece is only beeswaxed. In that case it is safer to give it to an expert to revive. Without the protective layer of French polish there is a danger of working the dirt into the grain of the wood if you do it yourself.

When using reviver, work a small area at a time and keep changing to a clean piece of cotton wool or the dirt will simply be shifted from one spot to another. The whole piece must be looked at, as you work, to see the effect. The aim is *not* to bring it up like new but to bring it up to the point where the dirt and old polish which remain simply add to the feel and charm. There will always, on an old piece, be a difference between the edge and the flat and it is important to retain this difference. It is very much better to do too little than too much. Finish off by rubbing with a dry duster.

Carefully used furniture reviver will not harm shellac or French polish — if it did it would not be used in major museums — but if left in drops or pools on the surface it can eat into it. It should not be used at all on the plastic or bakelite inlays which occur on some Victorian pieces, such as musical boxes, or on very early furniture, such as dark oak chests. The almost black patina which very old furniture acquires through centuries of polish is a vital part of its appearance.

Furniture reviver cannot clean oxidised linseed oil — this is a finish which needs professional cleaning.

Polishing

With furniture only needing to be polished two or three times a year there is really no case for using those 'time-saving' silicone sprays, and there is much to be said against them. In time they perish and discolour and when that happens they require expensive professional attention as they are extremely hard to remove. Even before that happens they look wrong on old furniture. Like polyurethane seals, which should be avoided, they reflect back light in a quite different way from traditional finishes, giving the furniture a hard modern look which is out of keeping. This is because the shine comes from light passing through the polish, not simply bouncing off it, and the light is affected by the type of polish it passes through.

Any first-class wax polish can be used, but the following mixture attracts dust less than the usual beeswax polish. Heat 2 parts carnauba, 2 parts paraffin wax, and 1 part beeswax over a *flameless* heat until they melt — if it were near a flame it could catch fire. When all the ingredients have melted mix in 4 times their combined volume of pure turpentine to make a thin cream.

This polish should be applied very sparingly and left for 5–6 hours before polishing very thoroughly. The commonest fault in polishing is to use too much polish and too little elbow grease. The housemaid's trick of using soft brushes, instead of cloths, to polish carved areas is still a good one. It is by far the easiest way to prevent polish building up in the cracks.

Positioning Wood Furniture

The two enemies of fine wood furniture are sunlight and dryness. Antique furniture was not made for a dry atmosphere, and central heating is always liable to crack it. Houseplants in the room, not on the furniture, help considerably, so do saucers of water tucked out of sight under the furniture — provided you remember to top them up — or humidifiers. That does not solve the problem of positioning the furniture. The counsel of perfection is to keep it out of the sunlight, which will bleach it, and away from radiators. But in many rooms avoiding one of these dangers means approaching the other and it has to be a matter of assessing the susceptibility of the piece to either hazard.

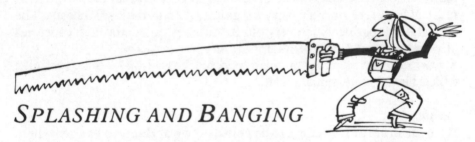

SPLASHING AND BANGING

Ask any experienced carpenter or painter to tell you his tricks of the trade and you will find he uses a whole host of little touches to make his job easier. They go a long way to explaining why he will do the job in half the time of the average amateur, though an old hand at do-it-yourself may equally have a very useful set of his own. A complete collection of tricks of the trade from amateurs, professionals, and do-it-yourselfers would fill a book — and most would only be used once in a blue moon. So instead I have selected only those which seem to me, as a seasoned do-it-yourselfer, to have a place in the repertoire of anyone who ever has to pick up a paintbrush or wield a screwdriver. I make no apology for the fact that some may seem so simple as to be scarcely worth bothering with. Making things simple is just what it's all about. More often than not it's the small touch which makes the difference between doing a job quickly and well, or struggling through it slowly and badly.

ADHESIVES

On fine gluing jobs a wooden cocktail stick makes the best applicator and the more sparingly the glue is used the better the job usually looks at the end. Surplus adhesive needs to be wiped off as you go along. If you wait, and go back to it, it may already have hardened.

When a mending job goes wrong, or needs to be re-done, getting rid of the old adhesive is usually the biggest problem. Each type of glue needs a different solvent. Clear adhesives like Bostik No. 1, and contact adhesives such as Evo-stik, soften with acetone or amyl acetate. (*See* Stain Removal for hazards.) Epoxy resins need cellulose thinner or a strong paint stripper such as Nitromors. Soft glues like sticky tape should respond to methylated spirits. However, it may be worth getting the glue manufacturer's own solvent before you even start on a tricky job.

Rubbery adhesives evaporate so easily that one can put away a full tin and return to find it almost empty. The trick to avoid this is to give the lid an extra firm close and store it upside down. If you overdo the tightening on the lid of any glue it needn't remain unuseable: running very hot water over it should loosen it.

CHINA MENDING

Epoxy resins have made it marvellously easy to mend china, but perfect results take trouble. The temptation is to start gluing immediately. It's far safer to check the position of every piece first to avoid mismatches, and if there is even a hint of dirt on the surface it should be cleaned with methylated spirits and left to dry.

Missing chips can be built up invisibly if the resin is mixed with a little kaolin, from a chemist, or with dry modelling clay.

The firmest way to hold the pieces in place is with gummed brown paper tape. I know this sounds very old fashioned, but its great advantage is that it shrinks slightly as it dries, giving a firmer hold than any other tape. Wipe any surplus glue off with a tissue moistened with methylated spirits before applying the tape — when the tape is removed it will be too late.

When leaving the mended object to set, give it plenty of support. Handles can be supported with plasticine, clay or — at a pinch — even a thick flour and water dough. With bowl-shaped objects enlist the laws of physics to help you, and invert them. I find the faster a mend dries the less likely it is to ease out of place. The ideal way to speed things up is to pop the mend into an oven which has just been turned off after use. It will set very much faster, so keep an eye on it and when the glue is firm, but not yet glassy hard, damp the tape and remove it. Then use a very sharp razor blade to pare off any glue which may have oozed as the tape tightened.

CLAMPING

A marvellous system of clamping which I learnt from a cabinet maker needs no clamps at all. Instead it uses inner tubes. Cut an inner tube to make a broad 'rubber band', and put it round whatever needs to be clamped. The pressure can then be adjusted by slipping wedges of wood between the inner tube and the part you are clamping. As inner tubes come in a wide range of sizes it's not hard to find one close to the size you need and garages are usually glad to give them away.

Of course some mending jobs may be better suited to metal clamps. The snag is they can easily mark a polished surface. Use an inner tube once again, but this time put a pad of it under each part of the clamp to protect the wood. It does an excellent job and gives a better grip at the same time.

DENTS

I have seen it said that the way to remove dents from furniture is to put a thick pad of damp brown paper over the dent and put a hot iron on the paper. That *is* the way to get rid of a dent, but there is a drawback. If it's done properly the dent should go, but the polish will be ruined.

This is a method which should only be used on stripped furniture. Unfortunately there is no way to raise the dent on a polished surface without harming the polish.

DOORS

After the squeak of chalk on a blackboard the next nastiest, and most aggravating squeak is a squeaking door hinge. There are three possible cures — oiling, puffing in powdered graphite (sold by locksmiths), or squeezing in washing-up liquid of the gluggy sort. Different squeaks respond to different treatments and where one of these fails another will work perfectly. Graphite can also be used to cure the squeak in piano pedals without harm to the piano.

When a lock which once used to catch stops doing so, it's usually a sign that the door has sagged slightly and the two parts of the lock are out of true. It may be possible to correct the sag, but if it isn't the lock socket can easily be filed to allow the tongue of the lock to go fully home once more.

If a door is sagging the trouble usually lies in the hinges. The screws may have worked loose or the hinge may have bent slightly through being too weak for the weight of the door — a common problem with cost-paring building.

Hinge problems can also cause doors to stick, but a more likely reason is that the wood has swollen or over-thick painting has filled what was once a gap. The easiest way to find the point of sticking is to repeatedly shut the door with pieces of carbon paper ranged down the lintel. The part that comes up black can then be planed or sanded down.

If a block is needed to prevent a door swinging back and damaging furniture a cotton reel is the perfect answer. Simply put a long screw through the hole and screw it to the floor. If it's somewhere where it won't be tripped over, glue covering to match the floor over it and it will be almost invisible. If this could be a hazard it's wiser to paint the reel a contrasting colour, to go with the room, before screwing it down.

DRAWERS

One of the first household hints I ever learnt was when my mother showed me how to stop drawers sticking by rubbing the runners under them with a cake of moist soap. It is still the easiest and best way unless it's the sides which are causing the trouble. If soaping the bottoms doesn't work, test the sides. Rub chalk all over the sides of the drawer and slide it in and out a few times. The marks on the chalk will show which parts need attention. Soap can be tried on any part which looks badly rubbed, but sanding the wood down may be the best answer.

The lower edges of sliding cupboard doors can also be given the soap treatment. But check first that the real problem isn't dirt or wet in the groove. Those soap won't cure.

DRILLING

It is often assumed that the speed at which an electric drill should be used depends entirely on the type of material which is being drilled. Unfortunately it isn't quite as simple as that. It depends on both the material which is being drilled and on the size of the bit. Wood and steel can be drilled at the higher speed with bits of up to $\frac{1}{4}$ inch (0.6 cm) in diameter. Wider bits, or masonry with any sort of bit, usually need the lower speed.

On a shiny surface, such as a glazed tile, drills have a nasty habit of skidding off the spot to be drilled and embedding themselves somewhere quite different. The way to keep them where they ought to be is to put an X of transparent tape over the spot. With a masonry drill used at a very low speed this will hold the point in place till it gets below the shiny surface of the tile.

FLOOR BOARDS

Creaking Boards
If floor boards creak like a haunted house the cause is usually a split in the wood. Sometimes puffing French chalk into the split will cure the creak. If it doesn't the only answer is to nail the loose sections firmly to the joists.

Filling the Gaps
It's tempting to ignore gaps in floor boards, but if they're of any size they'll allow an unpleasant amount of dust and cold to rise, so it can be well worth filling them. The simplest way to do this is to mix a quantity of wallpaper glue to a *very* thick paste with water and shredded brown paper. Plug the gaps with this, being careful not to push the paper down too far or it will just fall into the cavity below. If the floor is going to be sanded leave the paste a little proud, so it can be sanded perfectly level when fully dry, and stained and sealed with the floor.

Filling the gaps can be a very cheap procedure as quantities of brown paper can usually be had for nothing when shops throw away wrappings. Or, if the floor is to be painted or fully carpeted, old newspapers can be used. Failing wallpaper paste, the old formula of $\frac{1}{2}$ lb (500 g) of flour, $\frac{1}{2}$ teaspoonful of alum, and 3 pints (1.5 l) of water can be substituted.

GLASS

There's no need to throw away a good glass just because it has a chip in it. A small chip can be smoothed off completely with very fine wet and dry abrasive paper. A big chip on a fine glass is better dealt with by returning it to the shop which sold it. They should be able to have the rim recut to remove the flaw.

If glass is broken rather than chipped it can be mended with epoxy resin, but on clear white glass the resin will show up as a yellow line.

If your glass or tile cutter isn't working too well, dipping it in paraffin or turpentine should improve its performance considerably.

GLUE RESISTANCE

One of the odd features of teak and afrormosia is that they are so full of resin it can be impossible to get glue to take on them. The cure for this is to brush the surfaces which are to be glued with carbon tetrachloride, or a similar dry-cleaning fluid. If this is left on for a couple of hours it will break down the resin and make it possible to glue the wood in the normal way.

HARDBOARD

If hardboard isn't conditioned before it is laid it can buckle in the atmosphere of the house. The way to condition it is to thoroughly wet the back, using about a pint of water on a sheet 4 feet square (3.7 sq m), then leave it lying in the room where it will be used, for four to five days. If there isn't time for all this, at least leave it for a couple of days in the room to get used to its atmosphere.

When laying harboard as a base for flooring, the way to cut it out accurately is to make an exact pattern, of the floor and its fittings, in newspaper. Stick this on the hardboard, draw round it and cut it out. As an underlay hardboard should be laid rough side up. The exception to this is when it will be under thin vinyl tiles, then it needs to be smooth side up. Stagger the joins for a better finish, and screw or nail down through the board, not up into it.

HEAT SAVING

A great deal of heat escapes into walls. So a good way to save heat and money is to put foil behind the radiators. The foil reflects heat back into the room, where you want it. Sheets of sticky-backed foil can sometimes be bought for the job, but ordinary kitchen foil is cheaper and just as effective.

HESSIAN

Old fashioned hessian, the sort sacks were once made of, is just as good a wall covering as the modern paper-backed version — and a fraction of the price. Hanging it just takes a little more patience, a sharper blade, and a bit of know-how. Allow about 2 inches (5 cm) extra at the top and bottom of each length, and iron it before hanging — creases will not come out by being smoothed onto the wall, as one might suppose. Glue the wall, not the hessian, and smooth the hessian in place with a dry paint roller,

41

making sure the threads lie straight. Seams should overlap by about 1½ inches (4 cm), the same must be left where the material meets door and windows — but don't cut off the extra at the sides or top and bottom.

The most important point about hanging plain hessian is that it shrinks as it dries, so nothing must be cut until it has dried out completely. How long this takes depends on the room and the weather, but a week is not too much. When it's very thoroughly dry use a metal ruler and a *very* sharp blade to cut through both layers of the seams and trim the edges. Peel off the excess very carefully, so as not to fray the material which is left, and glue and roll down loose edges very gently. It sounds complicated, but it isn't.

LAMINATE

There are only two problems with applying laminate — cutting it without chipping, and putting it on absolutely square. The way to avoid the first is to score the line slightly with a very sharp blade and cut it with the right side uppermost using a fine-toothed tenon saw.

To get the laminate accurately positioned, first stick drawing-pins all round the vertical edge of the surface it is being glued to. Their heads should just show above the surface. The laminate can then be positioned exactly against them.

If you forget to put in the drawing pins and find the laminate is slightly askew and stuck fast, don't despair. Put foil over the laminate and iron it until the plastic is warm enough to soften the glue underneath. It can then be lifted off quite easily and repositioned.

LEVERAGE

One of the nicer laws of physics is that by which the longer the handle the greater the leverage and the less the effort needed. If you haven't bulging biceps it's always a good plan to buy wrenches, spanners and so on with long handles and so cut down the labour of the job.

LIGHTING

I'm convinced a room stands or falls by its lighting. It does more for the furniture and the people in the room than any other single thing. Hard light not only makes people and furniture look their worst, it even kills conversation. To make light soft bounce it off some surface. This can be a wall or ceiling, or just the back of the light fitting itself.

Soft lighting doesn't necessarily mean low lighting. When planning working areas such as kitchens the rule of thumb is that you need 20 watts a square yard (sq m) with filament bulbs. (For fluorescent light this would be 10 watts — but fluorescent light is the cruellest light of all.) For the least eye strain the light should be in front of the person who is working, so light may need to come from the edges of the room rather than from the middle.

LOCKS

If a lock jams there is no need to send for a locksmith. It will usually clear if a little powdered graphite is puffed into it. But don't oil it. Oil is more likely to gum up the works of a lock than make it glide more easily. All locks should be given a puff of graphite once or twice a year to keep them running smoothly, and this is rather less trouble than fighting with one that has been neglected.

PAINTING

Paint Application
Experts always start near a window and work with the light in front of them, finishing each patch in the same direction to give an even grain.

Paint Choosing
The difficulty is trying to guess how it will look when reflected back at itself from the other three walls. If you are able to get a sample, don't try it out on a plain wall. Put it on the two sides of a corner. Then you can see how the colour changes with reflection and how it looks with the light falling on it from two different angles.

Paint Drips
To avoid paint running down your arms when painting a ceiling, cut a slit in a sponge and push the handle of the brush through it before you start. The sponge then catches the drips, and you don't. Even so, it's best to wear an old hat when painting ceilings. It's easier to work when not worrying about getting paint in your hair — and no one sees you looking silly in the hat, while everyone sees you looking odd with painty hair.

Painting Briefly
It's scarcely worth getting a roller-tray dirty for a small amount of painting. Instead, put the tray in a loose plastic bag, which shapes to the tray when paint is put on it. Secure the end of the bag when the paint is on it and simply throw it away when the job is done.

Painting Over Wallpaper

Wallpaper may well bleed into paint, if the chemicals in the paint affect the dyes in the paper. If you don't want to strip the paper, paint a test patch which includes all the colours in the pattern — some dyes may be more vulnerable than others. Leave it to dry. If it *does* bleed, the choice is between stripping the paper or painting it with a primer.

Painting Under Basins

Before painting the pipes under a basin or sink it is wise to loosen the rings which hold the trap in place. If they are locked solid, this is the time to clean off the paint which is holding them. If they aren't, loosening ensures that you won't lock them now. Tighten them only when the paint is dry.

Paint Skin

Prevention is much better than cure, and the best prevention is hammering the lids of paint tins well on, and storing them upside down.

When a skin *has* formed it is disastrous to try and ignore it, resulting in never-ending tiny bits to pick off the wall. The skin can be removed by sieving the paint through a piece of nylon stocking stretched tight, with a rubber band, over a fresh container. If you can't be bothered to do that, fix the nylon loosely over the top of the paint so that it hangs down into the tin. Then when you push your paint brush in the skin stays the other side of the stocking. The only drawback is that it's hard to get the last of the paint out of the bottom of the tin.

Paint Smells

One of the best, and oldest, ways of removing the smell of paint is to put dishes of water containing sliced onion in the room. Lots of dishes will be needed in a large room. The onions must not be eaten afterwards — and onion-loving children should be warned. Burning a mixture of charcoal and juniper berries in the room is another old method; so is a bucket of water with new hay in it, or putting a few drops of oil of lavender in the paint itself. I'm told this last is most effective, but so loathe the smell of lavender that I'd rather keep the smell of paint.

Paint Splashes

Splashes on a window can be prevented by wetting a sheet of newspaper and pressing it against the glass before painting near it. When newspaper won't stick to frosted glass the solution is paint the glass with neat washing-up liquid. Within twelve hours or so the paint will wash off with hot water. Hardened splashes come off glass with a razor blade.

Paint Tins

Few things are more maddening than an almost full tin of paint with its lid stuck fast when you want to use it (the shops will be shut that day). The cause is usually paint brushed off on the rim when the tin was last used. The need to wipe overloaded brushes against the rim is removed if a string is taped taut across the top of the tin before you start to paint.

Save yourself having to open old tins unnecessarily. Before you put them away, paint the tops of the lids with the paint inside (manufacturers lids are seldom exact), and mark on the outside the level of paint left.

PAINT STRIPPING

Caustic soda (sodium hydroxide) is usually the most effective and cheapest stripper for anything which can be taken outside to work on. As it needs very thorough rinsing it shouldn't be used for indoor fixtures, or by anyone stuck in a flat.

Fill a strong PVC bucket with hot water and, at arm's length, add $\frac{1}{2}$ lb–1 lb (250–500 g) of caustic soda. (NEVER *reverse this and add water to soda. The concentrated mixture which is created when the first water goes in can erupt like a volcano spewing the caustic solution towards your face*.) The temperature of the water, and the amount of caustic needed, vary with the toughness of the finish which is being removed. Varnish comes off far more easily than paint, and the hardest finish of all is a brown pseudo wood finish with a thick layer of white gesso under it. The hotter the water the more effective it is — but beware of inhaling fumes.

Professional paint strippers use tanks of caustic to dip furniture in but it works well when brushed on with a plastic washing-up brush. Leave it until the paint is bubbling, then hose it off with a strong jet of water. This may need to be repeated layer by layer, and obstinate patches can be treated with some of the solution mixed with flour or cornflour, to hold it. When all the paint is off the wood should be swabbed with equal parts vinegar and water to neutralise the caustic in the grain.

Caustic soda has no effect on plastic based on PVC but it should not be brought in contact with tin or galvanised iron. Beware of trying — as I once did — to kill two birds with one stone by using hardened paint brushes to apply it. It not only removes the paint, it removes the bristles.

The effect on those bristles is a fair indication of the effect prolonged contact can have on the skin. *Thick hole-free rubber gloves, Wellingtons, a* plastic mac and goggles are no more than basic protection — especially the gloves and the goggles. Any skin which is splashed should be liberally rinsed at once. Like all strong alkali THIS STUFF BURNS, but it does so very slowly. You may not feel any pain until there is a hole in the skin.

The working area should be well hosed down afterwards, especially if there are any animals about. Keep animals in while you are working. They won't know the liquid isn't water.

PAINTBRUSHES

Choosing

A bad workman may blame his tools but it is also true that bad tools make a bad job, no matter how good the user. It is worth buying the commercial quality brushes used by professional decorators if you intend to do a lot of painting. They apply the paint better and last longer. Look out for ones with split ends to the bristles, it's the sign of a good quality bristle.

Preparing

It is a good idea to drill a hole through the centre of each paintbrush handle just above the ferule. Then when the brush needs to be soaked it can be suspended in the liquid by pushing a skewer through the hole and resting it across the rim of the container. It also allows the brushes to be hung to dry in the same way, so the bristles are never pushed out of shape through repeatedly resting on their ends.

Some people like to soak new brushes in linseed oil for 2 or 3 days before using them. The method is to bind the bristles in a piece of paper secured with an elastic band, to keep them straight, and rest them in a little linseed oil. The oil gradually creeps up the length of the bristles. When the oil has soaked right up into the ferule, press the oil out of the bristles. Then rinse them in white spirit and brush them out on newspaper till the last trace of oiliness has gone. The advocates of this method say the oil which stays trapped under the ferule prevents the damage wet can do there. There are also those who say it is a waste of time because the oil washes out as the brushes are cleaned. In fact it all depends on how thoroughly the oil gets into the ferule and on how the brushes are subsequently cleaned.

Cleaning

If you have bothered to buy good brushes — or, at today's prices, have even bothered to buy bad ones — failing to clean them thoroughly the moment painting is over is an expensive mistake. Turpentine, white spirit and branded cleaners all do a good job, but the cleaner which has the edge is paraffin. Paraffin gets the brushes equally clean and unlike the other cleaners it has the ability to separate from the paint afterwards. Overnight the paint and colouring will fall to the bottom of the jar leaving clear paraffin which can be poured off and used again even if the next paint is a totally different colour. Which is why old-timers in the decorating trade always use it.

After cleaning a brush in paraffin wash it in soapy water and dry it on a clean rag. If a brush is left standing in water, the water will get under the ferule and swell the wood, thereby making the bristles loose. Then the brush will moult onto the walls as you paint.

Keep changing your paintbrush every few hours. If the same brush is used all day the paint will harden in it and be difficult to clean off.

Brushes which have gone slightly hard can be softened by boiling them in vinegar for a while. Really hard brushes need sterner treatment. Soak them in cellulose thinner in a glass jar — it is as effective as the products sold for cleaning brushes and much cheaper. To speed up the process use a skewer to make holes between the bristles so the thinner can get to the centre. When the paint is thoroughly soft rinse the brushes well and clean them in paraffin and then in hot soapy water. Dry them thoroughly.

Storing
Paintbrushes should be completely dry before they are put away and it is worth putting a piece of paper round the length of the bristles to keep them straight. If they are real bristle put a few mothballs with them to prevent moths and woolly bears eating them.

PLANING

How smoothly a plane glides depends on the amount of friction which is set up. For a really smooth glide apply candle wax frequently to the underside of a steel plane. If you are lucky enough to possess a cabinet maker's wooden plane, use linseed oil instead.

PLASTIC COVERINGS

If the self-adhesive plastic shelf coverings in the flat you have just moved into are too hideous to bear, iron them with a sheet of paper over. Then peel them off while they are still hot. This method will also remove sellotape from walls without taking the paint off too. The sticky residue comes off with methylated spirits.

POLISH REMOVAL

Surfaces which are going to be painted, varnished or re-polished need to have the old surface entirely removed. French polish comes off with methylated spirits, and white spirit removes wax and silicone polishes — but silicone can be a tough job. Whatever the finish, use lots of small rags and keep taking a clean one otherwise the softened polish is just being re-spread and any dirt is being worked into the grain. For finishes other than these *see* Paint Stripping.

POLISHING

New wood which is going to be wax polished should be given two coats of the shellac-based polish, often sold as 'white polish', to fill the grain. Smooth each coat down to almost nothing with flour paper to give the perfect surface for applying the wax. Like all abrasives the flour paper must be worked with the grain.

An alternative to this gives a finish which, in my experience, withstands heat and wet better than any other. It is to rub one coat of linseed oil well into the wood and give it a week or two to sink in before applying a good wax polish. This is not a method to use on valuable antiques or on light woods but it is excellent for a plain mahogany dining table of no great worth which has just had old French polish removed.

PUTTY REMOVAL

Putty will often break away quite easily if a strong blade is slid behind it. But if it's set solid it can be softened with a strong paint stripper, taking great care not to strip the surrounding paint or varnish. Dab the stripper on and leave it for 10–15 minutes to work on the putty. Scrape off the putty as it softens and repeat as necessary, finishing off by cleaning the area with white spirit or turpentine.

RATCHET SCREWDRIVERS

It is possible to oil ratchet screwdrivers to keep them moving smoothly, but they will last longer and work better if powdered graphite is used instead of oil.

ROUGH WALLS

The standard advice to those who have rough walls is to cover them with anaglypta paper so its rough surface will conceal the problem. Now, I only have to see such a paper to wonder what trouble is underneath it. Yet there's seldom any need to go to such extremes. If a wall is cross-papered with a lining paper, before the top paper is put up, it will conceal a lot. Choosing a wallpaper with a strong and very informal pattern will do the rest. The papers to avoid are those with strong lines, which will appear to zig-zag as they go over humps.

SANDING

The names of the abrasive papers do nothing to suggest the jobs they are intended for. Just to uncloud the issue sandpaper is also called glasspaper and is intended for wood. Emery paper is intended for metal, and flour paper is an extra fine paper which can be used on wood or fine metal. That said, anything can be used for anything if it gives the effect you want.

Any abrasive paper works best on a flat surface if it is wrapped round a rectangular block of cork. Cork is very much better than a wood block because it is slightly softer than the surface below it. If the sandpaper and its debris are sandwiched between two surfaces of equal hardness the debris becomes trapped and tends to roughen the very surface you are trying to smooth. It is important to brush the sawdust off very frequently.

Once the paper becomes clogged the dust can be freed by rubbing the back of it to and fro in a curve over a square edge. This, of course, only works if the surface which is being sanded is dry. Damp surfaces clog the paper completely.

The most vital point of all is always to work *with* the grain on wood not across it. It is so easy to get fed up with the same arm movement and do one sweep in the other direction. Be warned — the marks from a single stroke across the grain can take hours to remove.

SASHCORDS

The sashcords on sash windows will run more smoothly if a moist cake of soap is rubbed along the part of the cord which passes over the pulley wheels.

49

SAWING

In most homes planes and saws are not as sharp as they should be. They can be made to cut more easily by rubbing a little wax furniture polish on the blade. If the wood is at all damp it is worth putting polish on sharp tools too. It prevents the damp in the wood holding the blade.

When sawing a long cut the two sections of wood tend to squeeze the blade. To prevent this put a wedge of wood in the cut, to hold it slightly wider than the blade.

When sawing through thick timber the simplest way to be sure of making a vertical cut is to clamp the timber against a thick guiding block along the cutting line and keep the saw against this.

If the wood is veneered on both sides — as it can be when cutting the bottom off a door after laying a thick carpet — mark the cutting line on the underside and score through it with a sharp blade before sawing. Then splinters of veneer won't be broken off by the saw teeth.

SCREWS

Ideally brass screws should be used in any good woodwork. They will go in more easily if the tip of the screw is dipped in pure beeswax polish. They will also be easier to remove if you need to. If no beeswax is around a touch of almost any grease from butter to vaseline will do the trick on screws or nails. I have even seen old carpenters running a screw through their hair — and if you have hair that greasy it may as well be put to good use.

Screwing Oak
No cabinet maker will ever use steel screws in oak. The tannic acid in oak reacts with the steel and causes a blue stain to appear on the wood round the screws. On the other hand brass screws aren't strong enough to be screwed into a wood as hard as oak without great risk of them breaking. A cabinet maker taught me the way out of this double bind. It's to screw a steel screw fully home, then remove it and screw in an identical brass screw.

Screw Tightening
A screw which has become loose can often be tightened by the simple expedient of glueing a wooden matchstick into the hole and screwing the screw back in again.

Screw Removal

There are a number of ways of removing screws which seem to be stuck fast. If the screwdriver can stand it, a few blows to the end of it with a hammer will often get a screw moving, but the blows must be hard enough to slightly shift the screw in its bed. Or, if you have such a thing, hold the tip of a red hot poker against the head of the screw till it heats and expands. It should then come out when it's cold. I'm told the tip of an iron set on maximum will have the same effect, but mine doesn't get that hot. A vertical screw will sometimes loosen if paraffin or vinegar is poured round the top and given time to sink in. When all else fails, the head of the screw can be drilled off.

SHARPENING TOOLS

I've heard that in Suffolk in the old days the farm lads would visit the local graveyard when they needed to sharpen their tools. The sandstone gravestones did an excellent job on the blades and to this day bear the marks to prove it. Failing such a graveyard a carborundum is the answer.

The best lubricant to use when sharpening tools on a carborundum is a mixture of neatsfoot oil and paraffin, in equal parts. Any cabinet maker will tell you that mineral oils should never be used because being sticky they gradually adhere the iron filings to the stone and make it useless. If you have a stone to which this has happened put it on a sheet of blotting paper in an oven which has just been turned off. The warmth should make the oil and old filings run off.

If the problem is more wear than clogging, the carborundum can be re-ground very easily. Simply put a paste of silver sand and water on a piece of glass and rub the stone on this until it regains its surface.

SHEET FLOORING

Cold sheet floorings are likely to crack when rolled or unrolled. It is wise to leave them in a warm room to 'relax' for 24 hours before trying to unroll and lay them.

Old fashioned linoleum and modern sheet vinyl behave quite differently. Lino stretches a little after it's laid, but vinyl, when not held down by glue, shrinks slightly.

When buying vinyl allow 4 inches (10 cm) more than the room measurement all round and lay it leaving an overlap for a few days before trimming.

The laying of the flooring should be planned so seams don't hit areas of heavy wear, such as doorways or just in front of the sink or stove. It is a simple precaution but it makes a big difference to the life of the flooring.

TILES

Fixing

As nobody is guaranteeing that any wall is straight, floor tiling should be started from straight lines at right angles across the middle of the room. The easiest way to get a straight line is to rub a string liberally with chalk which contrasts with the floor, hold it taut across the room, and snap it so it hits the floor sharply shedding a line of chalk. On wide rooms it is best to snap sections of the string, holding it down at points along its length.

Wall tiles also need to be fixed from right-angled lines marked on the wall. However firm fittings like soap dishes seem to be, they need a couple of strong strips of sticking plaster to hold then in place till next day. As the surrounding tiles may not be any too firm themselves the first day it is safer to leave the exact space for any heavy fitting and fix it the day after the other tiles.

The best implement for smoothing grouting at the end of any tiling job is the most unsophisticated tool of all — the rounded end of a stick.

Tile Removal

One of the advantages of a tiled floor is that if a tile is stained or damaged it can be removed and replaced. This is easily done by putting a sheet of foil over a vinyl tile – so there is no risk of it melting onto the iron – then ironing it until the glue underneath is warm and soft. If it is then pierced in the centre it can be levered up without damaging the edges of the surrounding tiles.

Glazed and quarry tiles which are damaged come out quite easily when thoroughly broken up with a hammer. Wear goggles or glasses for this job as the pieces are apt to fly.

TOOL STORING

Few home tools are used daily, so they need to be protected against rust. A very light coat of vaseline is a possibility, but the very best protection is a smear of 3 in 1 oil. Incidentally, either of these can be used for gardening tools as well as on those for carpentry.

UNEVEN TABLE LEG

The swiftest cure for a wobbly table is to put some sawdust mixed with wood glue onto a piece of paper in a small heap. Put this under the leg that appears to be shorter and press down until the table is perfectly firm and level. When the glue has set trim off the excess so the addition is invisible from above.

WALLPAPERING

Papering Over Grease

Everyone knows wallpaper should all be stripped off before putting up a new lot. Everyone who has ever been so perfectionist in an old house also knows that layer upon layer of wallpaper can sometimes be applied with no very dire results. But there can be problems if there is grease on the wall because it will gradually seep through to the surface of the new paper. This can be prevented by putting a coat of paint over the grease spots and giving the paint time to dry thoroughly before papering over it. In a kitchen, where there may be almost imperceptible small spots, it is a lot safer to strip the old paper – chore though it is.

Wallpaper Stripping

The easiest way to strip wallpaper is undoubtedly to hire a steam stripper. If there is no steam stripper available cut plenty of diagonal slashes in the paper with a sharp knife and apply hot water, containing a good dose of detergent, on a sponge or paint roller, until the glue loosens.

Wallpaper Hanging

It is never safe to assume that even a door is vertical. Doors, windows and corners of rooms can all be out of true. So the best start is a vertical line drawn with a plumb line. Just hang a pen knife, or a kitchen implement with a hole in the handle, from a piece of string and you have a perfect plumb line.

I am always tempted to work my way round a room. But if one does this, sure as fate, the worst seam in the room ends up right above the fireplace for all to see. Instead, the first piece should be centred on the middle of any wall and the following strips worked away to each side of it. A beginner may find it less nerve-wracking to do the very first strip in the most inconspicuous place in the room, then move to the centre for the next strip.

Before carrying a long strip of paper flip-flop it into a curvey zigzag till it becomes small enough to hold easily. The top can then be placed in position and each 'zig' pulled down in turn and smoothed into position. Very slow workers should keep checking that the zigzags are not sticking neatly and immoveably together.

When papering in awkward places — round radiators, light switches and so on — a lot of trouble is prevented by glueing the wall not the paper.

Then the paper doesn't stick to the obstruction. At the tops and bottoms of walls the secret of a perfect fit is to fold the paper very carefully exactly where it meets the ceiling or skirting and then cut it a touch longer. Cutting exactly on the fold line leaves a tiny gap. Fortunately, very few papers are sold with a selvedge, but those that are should be trimmed with a sharp blade and a steel rule before being hung.

To make the whole job easier tie a piece of string taut across the top of the glue bucket. This can be used to take excess glue off the brush and, more importantly, to rest the brush on when you want to take a break. Then glue doesn't get half way up the handle.

WIRING PLUGS

An electrician once taught me the golden rule he used when teaching apprentices how to wire a plug — Red with an R to the Right, bLack with an L to the Left. By a happy chance it works equally well with the new colours — bRown to the Right, bLue to the Left. The third wire always goes in the centre. Beware of using this rule for anything more complicated than a basic plug, as the wiring positions may be different.

CUT FLOWERS

Every good gardener knows that plants, like people, have their preferences and that one which will thrive on a south wall will sulk and shrivel if put facing north. The far simpler tastes of flowers cut for the house are less well known, though as amputees they need a little care, and the price one pays for ignoring their needs can be an arrangement ruined by drooping heads and twisting stems. Here there is only space to cover the likes and dislikes of the flowers most often picked from the garden or bought from flower shops. Once you know those, it is easy to experiment and to work out what suits almost anything you care to bring in.

GENERAL CARE

The trouble with treating flowers properly is that it makes for unpopularity with one's friends. No one who arrives bearing a gorgeous bouquet takes kindly to seeing it dumped in a bucket and put in the broom cupboard or lavatory. Yet that is the best thing to do for the flowers. Whether they come from a garden or a florist, flowers are thirsty after a journey. So they must first be conditioned and given a long overnight drink in the cool and dark, if they are to last well in a vase.

The first step with flowers is to re-cut all the stems which will have become dry and unable to take up water. I am told the ancient Japanese tradition was to do this under water, so no airlock could form in the stem and prevent water reaching the flower head. Stems which bleed white sap must then be seared with a flame, and woody stems (except roses) hammered. Most flowers then need a drink right up to their necks in lukewarm water in a cool dark place. The biggest problem here is often finding a container tall enough. Tall spaghetti jars and bread crocks may need to be commandeered.

Some of the flowers I mention need their stem tips dipped in boiling water. This should be done with the water off the heat and the flowers themselves well protected from the steam.

ARRANGING

When you are out of chicken wire, pinholders, or Oasis, the next best support for flowers is, surprisingly, sellotape. Fill the vase with water, to avoid wetting the tape later, and over the top make a noughts and crosses grid with the tape, running it well down the side for firmness. It may not win the prize at the flower show, though in skilled hands it might, but it does allow flowers to be arranged not dumped. If a glass vase is used, having no visible means of support makes the flowers look marvellously light and airy. So I find it the perfect way to arrange informal cottage garden flowers.

In a small bowl it is often most practical to arrange flowers in moist sand. For dry arrangements plasticine, wire or brown Oasis are the answer — green Oasis crumbles when dry.

LIFE EXTENDERS

Conditioning alone extends the life of flowers considerably, but how they are treated once in the vase also makes a difference. Spring bulbs should stay in the same water, as they lose too much sap if the water is changed. Other flowers benefit from having the water changed daily and a tiny piece cut from the bottom of their stems. Of course, nobody has time to do this with every vase, so a great mythology of life extenders has grown up — bleach, aspirin, salt, starch, copper coins, lemonade, and sundry chemicals are all candidates.

Starch doesn't do much for flagging flowers, but put in at the start it does seem to hold on heads which drop easily. Salt is best for reviving spring flowers. Lemonade revives most other flagging flowers amazingly, almost certainly because it's sweet; research suggests flowers have a sweet tooth and nothing keeps them going like sugar. Copper reduces the growth of fungus and bacteria in the water. Aspirin can revive sagging flowers but does harm to healthy ones — it looks as if flowers and people are more alike than we suppose.

PICKING AND BUYING

The early morning and the evening are the best times to pick flowers. Flowers picked when the sun is full on them die more rapidly, so do those picked wet with rain.

If you are buying, the days to do it are Tuesdays and Thursdays, when most florists have just been to the market. Monday is the day to avoid. It's the day for selling Saturday's leftovers. Whatever the day, you need a street market approach to get the best from a flower shop. Take nothing on trust. Having such a perishable commodity, a florist naturally wants to get rid of the oldest first, and these are just the ones you don't want. Instead go for the bunches still in bud, and even then look to see if the stems look fresh below the water. The signs that flowers have been too long in the shop are dark, slimy stems below the water-line, a lack of sheen on the petals, and pollen that falls easily. It is never worth buying a bunch with any of these signs, however lovely it looks.

PRESENTS OF FLOWERS

Flowers, or pot plants, which are waiting to be given away should be given water and put in the coolest room in the house until they are needed. They keep far better like this than put in a warm room where you can see them.

WRAPPING FLOWERS

If you want to give a bouquet a sauna bath, put it in cellophane. Undoubtedly it looks glamorous but it dehydrates flowers and can halve their life. Florists only use it because they feel the public wants the initial glamour more than anything. So anyone who values the flowers more than the wrapping should ask for paper.

When carrying flowers from the garden for any length of time it is a good idea to cut down the amount of moisture they lose through their flowers and leaves. Wrap the bottom of the stems in moist tissue and tie them loosely together in a plastic bag, to prevent drips. Then put a large, well-perforated plastic bag right over the flower heads. Like this, if they are kept reasonably cool they will arrive looking as fresh as when they were picked.

FLOWERS NEEDING SPECIAL CARE

ANTHURIUM AND STRELITZIA

These exotic flowers are prone to air locks and are likely to do much better if cut under water and conditioned in very deep water before arranging. They particularly benefit from being recut every few days and put in fresh water.

BULLRUSHES

Being seed heads, bullrushes, and some grasses, need to be sprayed with a firm hair lacquer soon after picking. It takes very little warmth to bring bullrushes to a point where they explode like gigantic dandelion clocks, so this is not a job to put off till tomorrow. Once sprayed they can be used immediately or hung upside down in a plastic bag with holes in it, to dry without getting too dusty.

CARNATIONS

Carnations are loners and last longest by themselves, but they look so good with other flowers it can be worth sacrificing a day or two. Ideally they should be bought when the buds are full and firm and just showing colour. They can then be opened for arranging by carefully pulling back the green calyx and gently blowing on the petals.

All too often only open flowers are on sale. These need to be carefully checked. Ignore the florist's fury and gently press the centres of the flowers. One just out will feel firm and almost crisp, but petals which feel soft are old and a bad buy.

If they are really fresh carnations can be kept for up to a week in the bottom of a fridge, if well encased in newspaper. This makes them one of the most convenient flowers to take as a gift. The only special treatment they like, apart from a long drink, is being broken at a joint rather than cut, because they take up water best this way. But they'll endure a diagonal cut without much protest if it's necessary to make them the right height.

CHRISTMAS ROSES

As one might expect of a flower which blooms in a British winter, Christmas Roses, or hellebores, need a lot of water. To help them drink deeply, their stems should be pierced several times below the water line, or a pin scratch should be made down the length of the stalk. The way to make them last longer is then to dip the base of the stems in boiling water for a moment or two, give them an overnight drink in water up to their necks, and arrange them in the deepest water possible.

CHRYSANTHEMUMS

Chrysanthemums are often sold when past their best. Look for crisp green foliage, and flowers with very crisp petals and a dark very tightly packed centre. The bottom of each stalk should be thoroughly hammered and put in boiling hot water for a couple of minutes before standing the flowers up to their necks in cool water. The leaves rot easily, so any that would come below the water line in the arrangement must be removed and the stem rubbed *completely* smooth so there is nothing left to rot. These are flowers which really do need their water changed every day, or the bacteria which build up will soon kill them.

DAFFODILS AND NARCISSUS

Daffodils and tulips may seem like natural companions, and are often combined in bouquets. In fact they are natural enemies and shorten each other's lives. The only way they thrive together is in Oasis.

Any white part on daffodil or narcissus stems should be cut off, as it will not take up water properly, and the cut should be straight to keep bleeding to a minimum. Because bleeding shortens the life of these and other spring flowers they should not be re-cut once they are arranged, nor should their water be changed. They also prefer to be arranged in shallow water, which makes them ideal for Japanese-style arrangements.

DAHLIAS

Dahlias have a short vase life but need little attention. Just sear the ends of the stems or dip them briefly in boiling water before giving them a long drink. They will last longest with a little sugar.

FLOWERING CURRANT

In Lancashire there is a superstition that it is unlucky to bring flowering currant into the house. Whether or not it's unlucky, it certainly is unpleasant. Once in the house this innocent-looking shrub gives off an overpowering smell of cats.

FORSYTHIA AND ALMOND BLOSSOM

In many springs the forsythia opens only to be battered and bruised by wind and rain. To have it at its best, pick it before the flowers come out and allow it to open in the house.

In a warm room it will open fast and can be brought on some while before it flowers in the garden. Put to open in the dark it will come on more slowly. Either way, give it one day in the cool as a transition from garden to house.

Almond blossom can be picked at the start of the year and brought on in the same way but it needs a couple of days in the cool, to acclimatise, before being brought into the warm. It should then develop a marvellous display of flowers.

GERBERAS

Gerberas, the South African flowers like giant daisies in bronzy lipstick colours, need very special treatment. Their stems rot extraordinarily fast under water. So instead of giving them a long drink and arranging them in the normal way, put them in a jug with a $\frac{1}{2}$ inch (1 cm) of boiling hot water in the botton. In a couple of hours the stems will have stiffened. They should then be arranged in water which comes no more than a quarter of the way up their length. This way the rotting is at least kept to a minimum.

GEUMS

Geums are just the shape and size one often needs in a vase but the trouble is they have a nasty habit of hanging their heads. The only way to stop them doing this is to take a jug with an inch or two of boiling hot water into the garden with you. If they are put in this the moment they are picked they should stay stiff — but it's no good waiting till you get indoors to give them this treatment. It won't help then. Once indoors give them a drink of cool water right up to their necks before arranging them.

Some may still insist on drooping. If they do the only solution is to cut them much shorter and re-dip them in boiling water.

GLADIOLI

Gladioli are very easy-going flowers. All they need is to have their stems cut under water, and re-cut every 3–4 days. Nipping out the top bud and removing the lower blooms as they wilt helps gladioli to open.

In the garden they have an annoying habit of all coming out at once, giving you a glut of them for the house. The way round this is to pick them when the buds are just showing colour. They can then be left without water in a cool dark place for as long as a week. This allows them to be held over for a special occasion and spreads the length of time you can have them in the house. After that treatment all they need to revive them is a long drink of warm water.

HEATHER

During the cold months heather is often the only flower to be picked. Arranged in water it can be a menace, dropping its bells almost as soon as it is in the warm. But if you take half a potato and stick the stems straight into this, as if it were Oasis, the heather will last for weeks without dropping a bell. If the stems are thin make holes for them in the potato with a fine skewer.

IRISES AND LILIES

I have seen it suggested that lilies should be sprayed with hair laquer or have their stamens cut to prevent the fall of pollen. It would be a shame to do either. Lacquer would mark and disfigure the petals and there seems little point in having lilies at all only to destroy the delicate balance of line and colour between the stamens and the petals. But do keep them away from soft furnishings as the pollen will mark what it touches. Both these flowers should be bought in bud, and need their stems cut at a slant and any wilting flowers removed to encourage new buds to open. Lilies foul their water rapidly so it should be changed as often as possible.

LILAC

Lilac is quite unable to take up enough water to support both flowers and leaves, and if it's a battle between the two the leaves win. So the only way to keep the flowers looking good is to strip off every single leaf and add leaves to the arrangement on separate stems. To get the maximum uptake of water strip the bottom two inches of bark off the stem and hammer it well. Give them plenty of water and never let it expose the barkless stem to the air.

LILY OF THE VALLEY

These are not fussy flowers but they do prefer their water to be hand-hot, not cold.

LUPINS AND FRIENDS

Lupins, delphiniums and other hollow-stemmed flowers need special treatment or they soon drop their petals. Cut the tip of the stems and stand them overnight in water up to their lowest blooms. This is especially important for lupins as they keep on growing in the vase, and without this treatment they will twist as they grow and spoil the lines of the arrangement.

The next day dissolve a dessert spoon of sugar in 1 pint (500 ml) of warm water. Cut each stem to the length for the arrangement, fill it with the mixture and plug the end firmly with cotton wool. Treated like this these flowers can sometimes live for as long as two months. A weak starch solution is also said to be good, but seems to me more troublesome.

MIMOSA

The conditions which mimosa likes, and which keep it fluffy and delectable, are precisely those inside a plastic bag. Which is why it is sold in plastic bags, and why no wise florist ever takes it out to show to you. So, if the conditions in your rooms are those of a plastic bag you may have problems, but you can also have beautiful mimosa. If not, mimosa is a bad buy. Though spraying the air around it — not the flower itself — every few hours may, with luck, keep it looking good for a day or so.

NASTURTIUMS

Nasturtiums are killers which destroy any other flowers put with them. The only safe way to arrange them is entirely by themselves.

ORCHIDS

I have heard people say the best way to preserve an orchid is to put it in the fridge. But, in fact, domestic refrigerators are too cold for such flowers and would freeze them to death. The way to keep such an exotic buttonhole fresh is to put it in the coolest room in the house — even if this is the lavatory — keep it dark and lay a ring of damp cotton wool lightly round its throat to refresh it. The *cymbidium* branch of the family are exceptions to this. Damp would mark the front of their petals, so a cushion of damp cotton wool should be used behind the flower instead. Buttonholes of camellias or gardenias can be treated like *cymbidiums*.

POPPIES

All the members of this family, from the dainty Shirley poppies to the blowsy Orientals, will shed their petals almost immediately if the stems are allowed to bleed. The way to prevent this is to sear the ends in a flame as soon as they are cut and sear them again if they are trimmed to fit an arrangement. After that never re-cut them.

PROTEAS

Proteas need no more attention than an extra good hammering to the stems and a daily change of water.

ROSES

All roses like special care, and florists' roses are extremely touchy. The way to please them is to cut their stem at an angle while holding it under water, and slit the bottom inch — roses last less well if their stems are hammered. Then protect the blooms from steam while you plunge the ends into boiling hot water for a minute or two, and stand them overnight in cool water up to their necks. To arrange them re-slit any stems which are shortened, remove any leaves below the water line and top up the water daily. They do not last well in Oasis.

If a rose hangs its head it is probably suffering from an airlock, especially if the stems have been hammered. There are three possible ways to make it perk up. Either re-cut and 'boil' the tip of its stem, or make a pinhole through the neck at the point where it bends, or re-cut the stem and remove any excess leaves on the lower half before rolling it closely in newspaper with its head smoothed upright and standing it overnight in warm water up to the neck. I personally use belt and braces and combine piercing with one of the other two.

STOCKS

Stocks are some of the most beautiful killers in the business. Lovely though they look with other flowers, they have a reputation for killing almost anything arranged with them. This is probably because the stems and leaves rot so quickly under water and foul it for all the rest. To cut this fouling to a minimum scrape every bit of leaf from the stems, put a copper coin and a teaspoonful of sugar in the water, and change it daily. They need to be prepared for the vase by cutting and hammering the stems, dipping the tips in boiling hot water for a minute and giving them a very long drink.

TULIPS

The trouble with tulips is that they go on growing in the vase and contort themselves as they grow. The way to stop this is to cut the stems straight across, roll the whole bunch tightly in newspaper and stand it overnight in warm water up to the necks. Having had this treatment open tulips, but not those in bud, can be persuaded to adopt almost any position. The secret is to hold the stem and *gently* caress it into the curve you want it to have in the vase.

Tulips can also be changed into unrecognisably exotic blooms by simply reversing their petals. To do this take a newly opened tulip and gently stroke each petal between the finger and thumb, reversing the upcurve at its base until it turns backwards from the centre to reveal its brilliant inner markings. I am normally against tampering with nature, but the effect created when red tulips expose their black markings is so sensational I am prepared to make an exception.

Whatever the arrangement, pricking the stem just below the water line extends their life and discourages twisting. They also like a little sugar in the water and dislike the company of the daffodil family, or having their water changed.

VIOLETS

Violets are strange drinkers, for flowers — they use their faces. The way to make them last longer is to first put them in a cool place upside-down with their faces in water overnight. After that they can be arranged as usual, although they do better in moist sand than in water. A daily spray with cool water will extend their life even farther.

None of this applies to African violets, which would positively dislike such treatment.

DRIED FLOWERS

A great mystery is often made of drying and preserving flowers, but nothing could be easier. Ferns dry beautifully between newspaper, under any well-trodden rug. Some of the most effective — honesty and teazles, for example — grow like weeds, dry themselves on their stalks, and only need to be gathered before wet and wind destroy them. Then rub off the outer seed-cases of honesty between the fingers, and hang the sprays up until you need them. Flowers like hydrangea and helichrysum, grasses, and the flat seed heads of fennel and cow parsley only need to be picked at their prime and hung upside down to dry in the warm. Among the few which need special treatment are *Iris foetidissima* which needs to have its orange berries fixed with clear nail varnish just as they show, and *physalis* which must be picked when its first Chinese lantern turns orange. The rest will turn as it dries. If you wait till they all turn, the first will have been ruined by weather.

Even preserving in glycerine isn't hard. A mixture of 1 part glycerine to 2 parts water needs to come about 5 inches up the well-hammered stem of a woody plant. Leave it until it looks saturated, which will be about three weeks, wiping the same mixture on any leaves which look about to curl.

This is a job for the early summer before insects have damaged the leaves. The preserved leaves can then hang in a paper bag till they are needed in autumn. It is worth experimenting with any attractive trees or shrubs, but mahonia and beech can be relied on to be effective.

Your Stomach

FOOD AND DRINK

I have had a life-long love affair with food but I sometimes wonder whether some cooking books should be classed as fact or fiction. For many I suspect the answer must be fiction. They assume the cook, like the fictional detective, has every technique mastered and can handle every situation — the cakes always rise, the sauces never curdle, and the onions never make anyone cry. This chapter is quite the opposite. It won't teach a complete novice to cook but it is designed to fill the gap many cooking books leave by providing some of the quick routes to success and some of the remedies to the disasters which strike all but the most impeccable cooks.

APPLES

When most people grew their own apples the divisions between cookers and eaters were far less rigid. Many varieties served for both, and some still can. The much reviled Golden Delicious are a far better cooking apple for any dish which needs firm slices than our revered Bramleys, and taste infinitely better cooked than raw. Try them in apple tart or simply peeled, sliced and tossed in butter with a touch of vanilla sugar.

A tradition which is dying is that of serving certain apples to complement certain types of cheese. Many of the old apples are no longer in the shops, but Cox's Orange can still be eaten with Cheddar cheese, and Worcesters with Double Gloucester. There is a marvellous harmony between English cheese and apples which makes it worth experimenting to find the right combination for each.

ARTICHOKES

People make a palaver of leaf artichokes, but they are wonderful just as they are — no leaf trimming, no choke removal, nothing. Just cut the stem level with the base, soak the head upside down in salty water for a while if you suspect insects, and cook in boiling salty water until a leaf pulls off easily. This will take about 45 minutes. If you absolutely must deform the beautiful double pointed leaves by snipping their ends off, rub each cut with lemon or equal parts vinegar and water as you make it, to stop it going black.

ASPARAGUS

I have seen people use some odd methods to prevent the tips falling off asparagus as it is cooked — standing the bunch in a coffee percolator for example — but a foolproof method is to use foil. Having trimmed the bottoms off the stalks and washed them, tie up a bundle for each person — it is much easier to sort them when cold than hot. Wrap the upper half of each bundle in a strip of aluminium foil which sticks out beyond the tips. Fold the tip end slightly so it encloses the tips but lets water in. Then lie all the bundles on their sides in boiling salty water and cook them until a skewer easily penetrates the stalk half way up. That way each stalk will be evenly cooked and the tips intact.

AUBERGINES

Aubergines seldom need skinning. If they do, grill them till the purply skins turn black and can be peeled off. If aubergines are being fried it is a good idea to salt them for an hour or so first as, oddly, drawing the water out of them seems to make them less greedy for oil and produces a better dish. It also removes the slightly bitter taste they sometimes have. Slice, cube, or halve and score them, and sprinkle on about a dessertspoon of salt per lb (500 g) and leave in a colander to drain for an hour or so.

AVOCADO PEARS

There is something in the stones of avocado pears which slows down the browning of the flesh. Leave the stone in any half which is left in the fridge, and cover it with cling film to reduce air flow to a minimum. Or, having made dips or salads of avocado, perch all the stones on top and cover with film. This won't keep the flesh green for ever but it will mean you can dress and have a leisurely drink without starting the meal with a brown mush. Rubbing or squeezing lemon on the surface also keeps it green, but I always regret the change of taste.

BAKING CAKES AND BISCUITS

Baking is like trying to catch a horse, if you show fear everything goes wrong. So courage is the first ingredient, but know-how helps.

Lighter Sponge
If your sponge cakes won't rise, adding a dessertspoon of boiling water to the mixture just before putting it in the tin may do the trick.

Inexpensive Sponge
If eggs are short, or expensive, a tablespoon of vinegar can be substituted for one of the eggs in a cake, with no ill effects, providing it contains a raising agent.

Unbroken Cakes
It is always the best and lightest cakes which break most easily in turning out. There is no risk of this if the tin is lined with greaseproof paper or, even better, baking parchment. Trace the shape of the tin on the paper and cut it out slightly smaller. The paper comes off most easily while the cake is still warm. Damping it also helps.

Unburnt Cakes
There is no help for a cake left in far too long, but a perfectly cooked cake won't burn where it touches the tin if the tin is greased with suet. This is because suet has a higher burning point than other cooking fats.

To prevent the outside of a large fruit cake overcooking, wrap the bottom and sides of the tin in several layers of a damp newspaper and place a baking tin of water in the bottom of the oven.

Cakes which Stick to the Tin
If a cake sticks in a tin which hasn't been lined run a knife round the edge and stand the hot tin on a folded wet cloth for a while. It may then come out quite easily. Tarts and biscuits which stick will come off if re-warmed in the oven or over a gas flame.

Flatter Tops
If a cake is to be iced, spread the mixture in the tin so it dips in the centre. When it rises it will have a flat top.

Tastier Baking
Plain sponges and biscuits are much more interesting when made with sugar which has had a vanilla pod stored in it. The pod is expensive but it lasts for ages. Failing that, add the grated yellow rind of a lemon — this make all the difference to cup cakes.

Timing Cakes
The biggest pitfall in baking was created by baking tin manufacturers in

the form of aluminium tins. Cakes cook much faster in these than in traditional tin ones, but recipe books never say which type their timings were based on. The only solution is to check the cake three-quarters of the way through the given time. If a skewer stuck into the centre of the cake comes out clean the cake is done, whatever the recipe says. If it has any cake mixture clinging to it close the door very slowly — slamming it can flatten the cake — give it the full time and test again, till done.

Cakes with Cherries

Unless a cake is jam packed with fruit, cherries tend to get a sinking feeling and end up at the bottom. There is no infallible way to stop this, but tossing them in flour or warming them a little in the oven before adding them to the mixture does help. These methods can be used for all dried fruit.

Cheaper Dried Fruit

Now that dried fruit has soared in price, family cakes may have to use it more sparingly. It tastes better and goes farther if it's soaked in a very little water overnight. This allows the quantity of fruit to be cut by half or a third. If flavour is more important than economy soak it in brandy, whisky, or a liqueur — it will taste wonderful.

Thinner Biscuits

I've found very thin biscuits tend to squeeze out of shape as they're moved onto a baking tray. The way to avoid this is to turn the baking tray over, roll the paste out on the back of it and cut the biscuits out there. All you then have to do is remove the paste from between them and bake them just as they lie there.

Icing

If you find your icing wants to slide off the cake, try dusting the surface of the cake *lightly* with flour before you ice it. This should hold the icing in place.

Sometimes the problem is not so much keeping the icing on the cake as the cake on the icing. When sandwiching a number of layers together keep them in place by pushing a wooden cocktail stick through the layers as you go. Remember to remove the stick, or someone may get a nasty mouthful.

Icing — in Emergency

Melted sweets are often advocated as an emergency icing. Melted marshmallows or peppermint creams certainly work, after a fashion, but unless you live above a sweet shop going to buy them would take more time than making a butter icing.

In a real emergency, with no time at all, just sprinkle on icing sugar, through a doily if you have one. However this does have its pitfalls. I once used it on my daughter's birthday cake, sprinkling the sugar over her cut-out initials, then removing the paper. All went well until she took a deep breath and blew her candles out — covering everyone around with flying sugar. So it's an icing to keep for non-birthday cakes.

Beating
If one has to beat or cream by hand it is a lot faster if the bowl isn't slipping about. It won't if it's standing on a damp cloth.

Making and Keeping Sponge Cakes
To be sure of success with a sponge cake all the ingredients should be at room temperature. This is especially important with a Victoria sandwich or the eggs may curdle instead of mixing with the butter and sugar. Dusting the greased tins with equal amounts of flour and sugar gives a sponge a nicer skin, and the top will be glossier and tastier for a sprinkle of sugar before it's baked.

Any sponge is at its best eaten the moment it's cool. Although one which has gone a little dry can be rescued (for family use, at least) by steaming it for a while. Alternatively, if you know you won't be able to eat a sponge up quickly, use glycerine to keep it moist. A dessert-spoonful, added with the flour, in a 3–4 egg cake will help it to keep moist a good deal longer, even though it won't be as luscious as when fresh.

BÉARNAISE SAUCE

If Béarnaise sauce separates despite being cooked very slowly in the top of a double saucepan, it can be saved. Add a teaspoon of lukewarm water for every 2 egg yolks already in the sauce, and beat it furiously till it comes together.

BEETROOT

Raw beetroots hardly bleed at all when boiled if they still have a couple of inches of stalk on and salt or vinegar is put in the water. Small round ones are even nicer baked in the oven. Simply put them in a covered dish in a low oven for 2–4 hours depending on their size. Whatever the method of cooking, they are done when the skins rub off easily.

BLOODY MARY

Unlikely as it may sound even the best Bloody Mary is improved by mixing in half a glass of dry sherry. Don't mock it till you've tried it.

BOILING FOWL

An old boiling fowl is said to be made tender by putting a ¼ teaspoonful bicarbonate of soda in the cooking water, but as tough fowls seem impossible to find in London I have not been able to test this.

BREAD MAKING

It is a pity a mystery has grown up round something as wonderfully easy and satisfying as breadmaking. If it were really half as difficult as people make out bread would never have become the staple food of peasants the world over.

Yeast is an organism with only one aim — to divide and grow. Once started it takes very considerable heat or cold to stop it. Snow and even ice have successfully been used in bread-making, and a night in the fridge does it no harm at all. Those stories about the slightest draught or cold killing it are pure fable, but what it really likes is gentle warmth, especially at the beginning of the process.

Preparation of Yeast
Yeast's tendency to multiply is checked by the suppliers so it can be sold neatly. Like a car on a cold morning, it needs a little warming up before it runs smoothly again.

Wash the mixing bowl out with hot water to warm it and use flour which has been in the airing cupboard for a while.

The yeast itself should be mixed with water at 98°–108°F (37°–42°C). Always add dried yeast to water while stirring fast, to keep the globules apart. Adding liquid to the yeast, or failing to stir, creates a solid gunge which dissolves with great difficulty.

Dried yeast needs a pinch of sugar in the water — but only a pinch — too much sugar hinders rather than helps. It also does better if it is allowed to stand until it has worked into a froth on the surface, before being added to the flour.

Fresh yeast is the exact opposite of dried yeast. It dissolves most easily if the water is gradually added to it, and it does best without sugar. Unlike dried yeast it can be added to the flour as soon as it has dissolved.

Recipes are normally based on fresh yeast. If dried yeast is used halve the quantity: 1 oz (28 g) of dried yeast equals 2 oz (56 g) of fresh yeast.

Kneading

Dough won't stick to oiled or buttered hands, and if a little fat works its way into the dough in the kneading it will be all to the good and make for a moister loaf. When kneaded enough the dough will feel slightly springy to the touch.

Proving

The best place for a bowl of dough is inside a large plastic bag. This will stop the surface from becoming dry. What happens then is a matter of timing. Contrary to what most people believe, bread does not need a lot of heat while proving. Temperatures above 85°F (30°C) are positively bad for it and so is strong heat from a single direction. So standing it on the television, as I have seen suggested, is not a good idea.

Heat does speed up the process, but the texture and flavour of bread depends on how long it has taken to prove. The best bread is proved slowly at room temperature — 65°–70°F (18°–21°C). So if the cook feels comfortable in shirt sleeves the temperature is just right for making bread — and if proving takes all day the result will be worth waiting for. Incidentally, bread needs less yeast if it proves for a long time. So if you haven't quite the amount of yeast the recipe suggests, simply leave it to prove for longer and all will be well.

Salt acts as a check on yeast, while Vitamin C speeds it up. So very salty bread will take longer to rise, but for a quick loaf dissolve 25 mg of Vitamin C with every ounce (28 g) of yeast. Unfortunately flavour is sacrificed to speed here and I confess if I'm in that much of a hurry I prefer the even faster, and much tastier, soda bread.

Bread For Better Keeping

A teaspoon of glycerine added for every pound (500 g) of flour when making bread should make it stay moist for longer.

Bread — Final Stages

Bread is cooked if it sounds slightly hollow when the base is rapped with the knuckles. Left to cool in the tin the crust will become soggy. Lay it on its side either across the top of the tin or on a wire rack. If a soft crust is wanted wrap the hot loaf in a clean tea towel until it is cold. This is especially important with soda breads which often have an unpleasantly tough crust if left to cool in the air.

Bread — in Emergency

When the bread runs out just as teenage hordes descend, or one returns ravenous from a holiday to find the larder bare, the shops closed and the bread in the freezer rock-solid, the solution is one familiar to every Indian grandmother. It's the fastest easiest form of bread known to man: the chappati.

Hot and fresh it is delicious with butter and jam, or cheese, soup or anything else you might normally eat bread with. Mix ½ lb flour (250 g) with ½ teaspoon salt and enough water to make a pliable dough. Knead it a minute or two, roll it into ping-pong sized balls between the hands and then flatten each with the hands or a rolling pin until thin, before frying without fat on a very hot griddle or in a frying pan. Each side is cooked when it takes a touch of brown in places — which is in under a minute. Wholemeal flour is traditional, but self-raising flour works well and plain will do at a pinch.

Bread Refreshing

The taste of hot fresh bread is one of the great simple delights, but one which is seldom available at meal times. Fortunately bread, buns and croissants can be re-heated to almost the same deliciousness if they are passed rapidly under a running tap before being put in the oven at gas mark 2–3, 300°–325°F (150°–165°C). It is the steam rising which makes the bread as light as when it was new, so it is vital that the bottom is damped as well as the top. Croissants need rather less damping than buns or loaves and take as little as 3–5 minutes to heat, while a large loaf takes about 20 minutes. Deep-frozen bread must be thawed before heating.

BROAD BEANS

When our grandparents grew broad beans they had different recipes for them in each of their three stages. The most delectable has always been when the pods are no thicker than a woman's finger and the whole pod can be cut in lengths like a French bean. The simplest way to serve them is boiled till just tender and tossed in parsley butter. The middle stage is the familiar one when the beans are shelled and cooked. Later, when even the skins of the individual beans become leathery, they can be boiled in the usual way and sieved (not liquidised) to leave the skins behind. The soft purée, seasoned with salt, pepper and a little butter or cream, is a delicious alternative to mashed potato. My grandmother always boiled a pod or two with the beans and said it improved their flavour — and maybe it does.

BROTH CLARIFYING

The clarity of broth is not something we set as much store by as they did in the time of Mrs Beeton but if aspic is needed there is nothing to touch the home-made variety. The way to clarify broth for aspic is to chill it and remove every speck of the solidified fat. Then take 1 egg white for every 1–2 pts (500–1000 ml) of stock and beat them to a froth before adding them to the cold stock. Heat the stock until it just boils, beating gently all the time. Simmer it for 10 minutes, without stirring, before pouring it slowly through a fine sieve lined with scalded muslin. The liquid should be allowed to drip through the froth and the muslin without pressing or squeezing.

BUTTER

If unsalted butter is unexpectedly needed, simply pour boiling water over salted butter which has been cut into small pieces. Once melted put it to chill. When set the salt will be in the water not the butter.

Clarified Butter
It isn't hard to clarify butter, but it is a bother. It's far simpler to buy the Indian clarified butter, called ghee, or substitute equal quantities of butter and good tasteless oil.

CABBAGE

People may tell you that to stop the foul smell of cabbage cooking you should place a piece of bread on top, or put a walnut or a bay leaf in the water. There is in fact a much simpler solution — don't overcook the cabbage and don't cover it. Cabbage only smells if it is overcooked or has a lid over it, and the same is true of the rest of the tribe — sprouts, cauliflower and broccoli.

All these vegetables, with the exception of red cabbage, not only smell better but taste better when cooked so there is just a hint of crispness left in them. This may mean sprouts only take 4 minutes or so to cook. The old stories that lightly cooked vegetables are bad for you are complete fiction. The less they are cooked the more they retain their goodness, and all this tribe are really at their best lightly stir-fried the Chinese way.

Those who find cabbage difficult to digest should take a leaf out of the German tradition and cook caraway seeds with it. Caraway has a special affinity with the flavour of cabbage and at the same time makes it more digestible and less likely to cause wind.

CARROTS

There is a natural sweetness in young carrots fresh from the garden which is lost with age and keeping. Some of that flavour can be recaptured by adding a teaspoon of sugar to the water the carrots are cooked in.

CAULIFLOWER

Cauliflower tastes very much better, especially if it's being eaten raw, if it is soaked in fairly strongly salted water for several hours. Of course the salt also kills any creepy crawlies which may be lurking in the curd.

Cooking cauliflower in milk and water is sometimes recommended to whiten it. This is not a tip I rate. The whitening effect is variable but it invariably makes the saucepan boil over. Squeezing lemon juice on the florets, on the other hand, does stop the cauliflower going grey and goes some way to killing the peculiar yellow colour which spoils some cauliflowers today.

CAVIAR

Those who perpetually serve cold toast can take heart. If they were serving caviar it would be correct. Hot toast must never be served with caviar because it melts the eggs and makes them slurp.

CELERIAC

Peeled celeriac develops an unappetising greyish tinge unless it is treated with lemon juice or dropped in water with vinegar added. Some recipes call for it to be blanched. If so there should be vinegar or lemon juice in the water.

CHAMPAGNE

If the end of a champagne bottle is left over the problem arises of how to keep the champagne from going flat. A bit of diligent paring with a sharp knife will cut the cork down to size, but a simpler way is to use a silver spoon. For some odd reason dropping the handle of a silver spoon into the neck of a champagne bottle keeps the champagne fizzy. Not that it lasts for ever like that. A day is about the limit — but then who could resist drinking it for longer than that. What the spoon won't do is keep out fruit flies which adore champagne, so a piece of cling film over the top is a good extra.

76

CHEESE

Crumbly English cheeses cut like butter if you use a hot knife.

For very large cheeses a wire may be better. There is no need to buy one. Simply take a length of heavy-gauge fuse wire, fix a large coat button to each end and smooth it out straight.

A wire is a useful gadget for cutting through a whole Stilton. For, contrary to popular belief, a whole or half Stilton should be cut, not scooped. The saying among Stilton-makers is 'cut high, cut low, cut level'. Which means cut a slice right across the top a couple of inches down and leave this disc-shaped slice on top of the cheese. Then cut wedge-shaped sections out of it as if it were a cake. This exposes the minimum surface to the air and creates the least wastage. Stilton-makers are so proud of their product they are among the few manufacturers who don't want to make money out of the quantity consumers throw away.

Whatever the cheese, it needs to be out of the fridge for 2–3 hours before it is eaten. Very cold cheese has far less flavour. If it is put under a cheese bell the bell must have an air hole in it — a lot of fancy cheese bells don't, and the cheese suffers.

Grapes and ripe pears are the perfect accompaniment for soft French cheeses, apples and celery complement the English cheeses. Port is better drunk with Stilton, rather than poured over it.

CHEESE FONDUE

If cheese fondue curdles, as it unpredictably can, the solution is to mix a couple of teaspoonfuls of potato flour (*fécule*) with water — or even better white wine — and stir this in with a loop whisk till the fondue comes together once more.

CHERRIES

If stoneless cherries are needed for a garnish the stones are easily removed, provided the cherries are ripe enough. Scald a hairpin, poke the U of the pin through the stem hole, scoop it round the stone and pull.

CHESTNUTS

There are those who say chestnuts should be boiled before shelling — a quick route to mushy chestnuts, broken nails and a frayed temper. Instead, use a very sharp knife to cut a slit *across* the hump of each chestnut (not up towards the point) and put the nuts in a moderate oven.

In about 15 minutes the slits will be widening into a smile. Take out each chestnut as soon as it smiles and shell it while it's still hot by squeezing the corners of the smile between finger and thumb. At this stage they will be slightly underdone and perfect for boiling up for stuffing or cakes. If they are to be eaten as they are, with a touch of salt to bring out the flavour, give them a few minutes more.

CHICKEN

Chickens are a bit short of flavour nowadays but one way to give broiler birds a little of the savour of free range ones is to cook them with tarragon. On its own this herb neither smells nor tastes like chicken, but it does add a chicken flavour to the bird. Mash a tablespoonful with a large nut of butter and seasoning and put this in the cavity of the chicken. As this runs out in cooking spoon it over the bird.

A chicken normally takes 20 minutes to a lb (500 g) at gas mark 6, 400°F (200°C), but to test if it's done push a skewer deep into the thickest part of the thigh. If the juice which runs out is completely clear the bird is cooked. If it is at all pink it isn't.

CHICORY

It is fortunate that these elegant white cigars are seldom dirty because washing them makes them bitter. The most cleaning they can stand is a wipe with a damp cloth just before they are used. Of course this care will be no help if your greengrocer has managed to palm off some green chicory which has already gone bitter. Any chopping must be done with a stainless steel knife as chicory is discoloured by ordinary steel and given an unpleasant metallic taste.

Recipes which call for it to be blanched or boiled are fairly rare, but if it is being cooked in water a squeeze of lemon juice and a crust of bread in the water will help to prevent it turning an unappetising grey, and a teaspoon of sugar will improve the flavour.

CHRISTMAS PUDDING

The blaze of brandy over the Christmas pudding is too often a faint flicker. For a really good burn up put the cooked pudding on a *hot* plate and warm the brandy in a soup ladle over a flame before lighting it and pouring it over. Warming the alcohol and keeping it warm on a hot dish is the secret of getting any flambé to work, and provided you keep shaking the dish, to fan the flames, it will keep burning while you carry it to the table.

COFFEE

I have a reputation for making the worst coffee in the world. My method will remain a secret to all but my worst enemies. However, a friend of mine has a way of making perfectly delicious coffee with no equipment at all. He puts a few spoonfuls of coffee in a warm jug with a pinch of salt, pours on boiling water and leaves it to stand for a few minutes. The grounds are then sent to the bottom by dropping in a tablespoon of very cold water, and it is done. How much coffee and how much water depends on the variety of coffee and the fineness of the grind.

CORN ON THE COB

Fresh corn on the cob is one of the few vegetables which should be cooked without salt. Salt toughens the skin round the grains. Some people find that putting a few of the inner 'leaves', which sheath the corn, in the cooking water improves the flavour of the corn.

CRABS

The way to open a crab is to stand it on its flat edge and give a swift karate chop to the edge that is uppermost. Non black belts should wear an oven mit to do this. The top half of the shell should now lift up like a lid.

Once a crab is open the only preparation it needs is the removal of the dead men's fingers — the grey frond-like parts which are folded over the lower body. Served just as it is, with a good mayonnaise, it's one of the simplest and best summer meals imaginable.

CREAM SAUCES

Cream sauces aren't difficult to make but they *are* tricky. Most cream sauces, whether hot or cold, have an acid element in them, such as wine, lemon juice or vinegar. The acid will never curdle the cream if both are the same temperature and the cream is stirred very hard as the acid is added.

It is almost impossible to get the average gas flame to remain low enough to slowly thicken a cream sauce without it going out. The answer is either to use a heat-reducing mat over the flame, or to raise the pan higher by resting it on a couple of inverted bread tins.

If time runs out before the cream has thickened an emergency remedy, despised by some gourmets, is to thicken it with a little cornflour or arrowroot. Mix either to a thin cream with a little milk and add it teaspoonful by teaspoonful, stirring well as it goes in and cooking the sauce after each addition, until the perfect consistency is reached. Provided you don't add too much, and turn a cream sauce into a gluggy white sauce, only connoisseurs will detect the ruse.

CREAM WHIPPING

Cream which is to be whipped should be cold. Warm cream whips less well and is more likely to separate and become buttery. It whips faster if about $\frac{1}{2}$ teaspoon of lemon juice is first rapidly stirred into each $\frac{1}{4}$ pt (125 ml). Equal quantities of double and single cream will whip as well as double but taste less rich. Whereas folding beaten egg white into beaten cream extends and lightens it without diminishing the flavour.

When a large quantity is needed and cream is expensive an excellent substitute is $\frac{1}{2}$ pt (250 ml) milk, $\frac{1}{2}$ lb (250 g) unsalted butter, and 1 teaspoon powdered gelatine melted together, liquidised in a blender for a minute at the highest speed and left to cool. This tastes far more like fresh cream than any other substitute and can be whipped, but it won't take heating.

CUCUMBER

It is a myth that leaving the skin on cucumber makes it indigestible. It is both better for the digestion and prettier to leave it on. However, some people do find cucumber itself disagrees with them. Sometimes slicing and salting it for an hour can make it agree with such people.

CURRANTS

Stripping currants from their stalks with the prongs of a fork lacks the sensuous feel of hand stripping but it does save time.

CUSTARD

If a real egg custard is cooked in the top of a double boiler it shouldn't curdle. But if it does accidentally get slightly too hot and separate there are three ways of curing it — give it a quick whizz in a food processor, or put it in a bowl and beat it very hard, or put it in a clean jar and shake it till it comes together.

Once cooked custard rapidly forms a skin unless it is given a protective layer. This can be a moistened circle of greaseproof paper, a thin layer of milk trickled on with a spoon, or at worst a thin scattering of castor sugar.

Baked custards are smoothest if the milk is brought almost to the boil before mixing in the eggs, and cook most evenly standing in a baking tin of water which comes half way up their sides.

DRIED BEANS

The wind-producing power of beans is legendary. It wouldn't be if people put them into cold water and then boiled them for 20 minutes before throwing away the water and starting again. Most of the flatulence-producing elements seem to be thrown away with the first water.

Some dried beans can be eaten raw as sprouting beans, some cannot. The larger beans all tend to be indigestible, the red bean in particular. It is poisonous unless thoroughly cooked and must be boiled hard for at least 10 minutes to change the poisonous elements in the bean into edible ones. Ironically, slow cooking makes red beans even more poisonous than they are when raw. So it is vital that they are well boiled before being added to a slow cooking dish like chilli con carne.

All but the smallest dried beans need overnight soaking.

DRIPPING

One of the great treats of my childhood was roast beef dripping, with its luscious jellied juices, on hot toast with plenty of pepper and salt. It was an early lesson in the special flavours of meat fats and I wince when I see them thrown down the sink. There is no better fat than beef fat for pre-frying a beef stew, for example.

All fats, except beef fat for toast, should be cleared of debris. To do this put the fat in a pan with plenty of water and bring it to the boil. Mutton fat will need a good dash of vinegar with it to remove the muttony taste. Let the fat simmer a few minutes, then cool and chill it. Lift out the solid block of fat and scrape any bits carefully off the underside before melting it down. It can then be stored in a jar with fat of its own kind — different fats should never be mixed.

Fat from birds is especially good for frying liver and potatoes and, best of all, in the delicious Jewish chopped liver.

Raw fat, such as the casing of kidneys, can be made into dripping by cutting it up very small and putting it in a tin in a low oven till it runs to liquid.

DUCK

Roast duck should have a thin crispy skin. The way to achieve this is to set it on a grid in the baking tin and sprinkle the skin with salt. As it roasts keep *repeatedly* pricking the skin all over to let the fat run out. By the time it is cooked all the fat under the skin should have melted and run away leaving only the crisp skin. (For timing see Chicken, page 78.) Cook goose exactly the same way.

EASTER EGGS

The original Easter eggs were just hardboiled eggs and in Switzerland they have a tradition of colouring them for Easter. Grass is tied tightly round each egg in bands and crosses and then the eggs are boiled with onion skins until they are a beautiful deep yellow. When the grass is removed the children have golden eggs charmingly patterned in white.

EGGS

Beating Egg Whites
Dishes which include beaten egg whites, soufflés and meringues for example, have a reputation for being difficult. They aren't, but egg whites are fussy. They beat more slowly when cold and won't go stiff at all if there is the slightest bit of grease in the bowl — and 'grease' includes any trace of egg yolk. So the secret is to use a very well washed warm bowl and an immaculate, room temperature, egg white.

Adding a pinch of salt helps the white to snow and adding just under a tablespoon of warm (not too hot) water for each egg white increases the volume. So does standing the bowl over simmering water while beating. Whites are fully whipped when they will stand firm with a point sticking straight up. They must then be used quickly before they fall.

In the old days round-bottomed copper bowls were always used for whipping eggs in big kitchens, and chefs still use them. If one has the muscles for hand beating they feel marvellous to use but I'm told there is no evidence that they really do the job any better.

Boiling Eggs
The way to boil eggs without ever having them burst is to first pierce a small hole in the round end with a fine skewer or darning needle. (There

are also gadgets to do this.) The hole lets out the air which would have cracked the egg as it expanded in the heat. If the egg is already cracked this won't help but putting a good dollop of salt or vinegar in the water should contain the problem, so will wrapping the egg in foil.

Odd though it may sound the secret of a good boiled egg is not to boil it. At a little below boiling point the albumen in eggs changes and becomes rubbery. So the best boiled eggs are only simmered, and all other egg cooking should be done gently.

How long it takes to boil an egg perfectly depends on its age, its temperature, and its size. New laid eggs take longer than old ones. But a medium sized, recently bought, shop egg, straight from the fridge, put into boiling water and simmered for $4\frac{1}{2}$ minutes will have a white just set and a runny yolk.

Oeufs mollets — the shelled soft boiled eggs the French serve with sauces — need 6–$6\frac{1}{2}$ minutes.

Hardboiled eggs take about 10 minutes, but a more subtle result is produced by simmering them for 5 minutes and leaving them in the water to cool. This gives a firm white which is set but creamy as it nears the yolk, and a yolk cooked through but not dry and floury. It is a good idea to make a habit of boiling onion skins in the water in which eggs are to be hardboiled. The skins dye the shells yellow, without affecting the taste, so a hardboiled egg is instantly spotted in the fridge.

Testing for Freshness
Among the many old tests of a fresh egg the best is to put the egg in about 4 inches (10 cm) of water. If it lies flat on the botton it is fresh. If one end tilts up, less so. If it floats to the top it is either bad or at that slack shapeless stage when it is impossible to fry without breaking it. Shining a light through the egg also works — if you can read the signs the light reveals, which isn't easy. But testing if the round end feels warm or cold against the lips is, despite its advocates, no test at all.

Omelettes
Omelettes are lightest if a dessert-spoonful of water, not milk, is added for every egg. The eggs should then be beaten no more than will just mix them — over-beating makes them rubbery.

To cook the omelette use half oil half butter, it burns less easily than butter but tastes better than oil.

Poaching
Half the secret of perfect poached eggs is to have really fresh eggs, the other half is to put a dollop of vinegar in the water to hold the white

together. Have the water really hot and stir it into a whirlpool at the centre. Using a cup slide the egg into the centre of the water and turn it down to simmer till the white is cooked but the yolk deliciously runny. Drain the eggs on absorbent paper before putting them on toast.

Scrambling

At one time scrambled eggs were usually called buttered eggs and butter is the key to scrambled eggs. Add seasoning and a dessertspoon of milk for each egg in the bowl and beat no more than will mix the eggs completely — over-beating makes the eggs rubbery. Melt $\frac{1}{4}$–$\frac{1}{2}$ oz (14 g) butter for each egg and pour in the eggs when the butter is *just* foaming. Immediately turn to a gentle heat and stir constantly. Stop cooking when the eggs are almost, but not quite, done — they will cook a fraction more as they are served.

Separating Yolk from White

Anyone who dislikes washing-up should learn the knack of juggling the yolk between the two halves of the shell and letting the white trickle out between. Failing that the easiest way is to crack the egg carefully onto a plate, cover the yolk lightly with an inverted glass and tip the white into another container.

If a yolk is left over it can be slipped into a pan of boiling water and poached till firm for use as a garnish or in sandwiches. This is also a useful trick when sauces require only the hard boiled yolk of an egg, as it leaves the white useable for another course, which normal hardboiling does not.

Shelling

Eggs are easiest to shell if they are plunged in cold water as soon as they are cooked. Even a soft egg can then be shelled without breaking if it's handled gently. Tap it all over with the back of a spoon until the shell is crazed all over. Then with the egg cupped in one hand run it under cold water, letting the water flow in under the shell, while peeling the shell off in small sections.

Shelled eggs cut most easily with a wet knife — it saves the yolk clinging to the blade. Use a sharp but old knife so the rough surface will hold the water.

Recognising a Hard-boiled Egg

If you can't remember which of the eggs in the rack was hardboiled spin each of the eggs in turn, on its side, on a flat surface. A raw egg has a lolloping spin and looks oval from above as it spins. A hardboiled one spins evenly and looks circular from above.

Eggs — Not From Chickens
Eggs from birds other than chickens should be treated with a certain amount of caution. The shell on a duck's egg, for example, forms late and ducks are messy creatures, so there is a risk of a duck egg being contaminated with harmful bacteria. For safety duck eggs should always be well-cooked. For the same reason gulls eggs, small as they are, should be cooked for 15 minutes.

EVAPORATED MILK

Evaporated milk, as it comes from the tin, will not whip, but it can be made whipable. Pierce the tin and stand it in a saucepan with water halfway up it. Boil the water for 20 minutes before removing the tin and chilling it. It may then be so thick it has to be scraped out of an opened tin rather than poured, but it will whip well. Though, unlike fresh cream, it will gradually return to liquid if it is left some while.

FAT REMOVAL

The best way to remove every speck of fat from liquid is to put it in the fridge until the fat is firm enough to lift off. If there is no time for this, and skimming with a spoon has failed to remove enough, put some ice cubes in a piece of kitchen roll and skim them across the surface. Keep renewing the paper as the fat clings to it.

FISH

Scaling
There is no need to do anything complicated to remove the scales from a fish. Just rub firmly from the tail towards the head with the back of a knife. Some say you should soak the fish first but all this does is reduce the flavour of the fish.

Skinning Fish
Fish skins most easily if an incision is made at the tail end and the skin pulled off from the tail up.

On Dover soles the incision should be made at an angle at the tail end and the skin pulled diagonally up off the body.

Plaice and lemon sole are exceptions. Make a slit above the gill and along the top fin. Then peel the skin off in a downward diagonal.

It may be easier to get a good grip on a fish skin if you damp your fingers and dip them in salt first.

FIZZY DRINK REVIVER

When tonic water, or any other fizzy drink, becomes tired and flat it can be somewhat revived by adding a pinch of bicarbonate of soda and shaking very gently. Be warned — more than that, or too brisk a shake, will make it fizz right out of the bottle. Hold your thumb over the top, rather than put a cap on it. Then a fountain is the worst that can happen. Tightly capped it might explode. Use at once.

FLAVOUR

The way to draw the flavour out of food, for a broth for example, is to cover it with cold water and slowly bring it to the boil. To keep the flavour *in*, use a high temperature to start with. A roast should go into a very hot oven at first, and very hot liquid should be added to stews and casseroles and boiling chicken.

FRENCH DRESSING

French dressing can be made and stored in the refrigerator ready for use, though it must be admitted that it never tastes quite as good as when freshly made. Making it in a food processor produces a thick creamy sauce half way between French dressing and mayonnaise. Though it sounds odd, substituting milk for half the oil in the recipe produces a dressing which doesn't taste of milk but has a softer flavour ideal for cucumber, or a lettuce and walnut salad. As using milk halves the calories it's an excellent compromise for slimmers.

FRUIT

Skinning Fruit
The skins of peaches, apricots and tomatoes will all come off effortlessly if they are plunged into boiling water for a minute or two, then into cold water. The timing depends on the ripeness of the fruit — the less ripe they are the longer they need in hot water. Grapes also respond to this treatment but some varieties put up a fight.

If there are young children around it's worth applying the same method to oranges. Pop an orange into boiling water for a few minutes then into cold water and the skin and pith will come away cleanly and easily. Just how long you leave it in hot water depends on the size of the orange and the thickness of the skin. If you've got it right even young children should be able to leave the adults in peace and peel their own.

Food and Drink

Fruit Salad

The best fruit salads are those which are made in stages. Citrus fruit comes first because the juice which runs from it will stop other fruit going brown in the air. When enough juice has run from it, and from the sugar, slice in the apples, pineapple, and any other firm fruit except pears and bananas. Pears, bananas and any soft fruit should be added at the last minute or they will go mushy in the juice. The whole thing must be kept cold but not too deeply chilled or some of the flavour will be lost.

The other way to prevent apples and pears from browning is to squeeze lemon juice over them or drop them in water with lemon juice or vinegar in it.

If, as can easily happen at a party, a fruit salad is in a warm room for some time fermentation may start — nature has a penchant for making alcohol. The signs are that bubbles appear and the fruit feels slightly prickly in the mouth — like eating champagne. If there is no sign of mould and the only ingredients are fruit, sugar, and possibly alcohol, it is quite safe to eat — though its effects may be laxative. Add some alcohol and eat it immediately. If you don't like the prickle it can be liquidised and drunk, or added to yogourt.

Enhancing Fruit

From the time when the crusaders brought a taste for them back from the east, spices were an important part of British cooking. Some were found to have a special affinity with certain fruit. Apple pie is scarcely apple pie without some cloves, but other traditional spices have become neglected. Cinnamon warms the flavour of apples, peaches and bananas. Pears are improved by cloves, cinnamon or vanilla. While melon sprinkled with ginger is quite different from melon alone.

Fruit enhancers don't stop with spices. Honey brings out the flavour of all fruit — try honey and strawberries for a taste of paradise. Lemon strengthens the taste of paw-paw. Certain liqueurs also bring the best out of other fruit. Everyone knows about kirsch with pineapple and rum with bananas, fewer know peaches are wonderful with Cointreau, bananas with Tia Maria, and blackberries with Drambuie. Or that gooseberries stewed with elder flowers taste wonderful.

Cutting Fruit

It used to be said that only a silver knife should be used to cut fruit. Those not born with a silver knife between their teeth shouldn't feel they are missing anything. This was in the days before stainless steel when using ordinary steel gave fruit a nasty metallic taste.

FRYING

If the heat's too low food absorbs fat and goes greasy; if it's too high the outside overcooks before the inside's done. Start hot, and moderate the heat as necessary.

Deep Frying

Nothing wet should be put in deep fat because the moisture makes the fat seethe up. So, no pan of deep fat should ever be more than half full. If it seethes up, lift the basket of food out of the fat and the fat will subside. Don't try to move the pan off the heat — the fat could spill and start a fire.

Lard, dripping, and vegetable oils can all be used for deep frying and the way to test if they have reached the right temperature is to drop in a cube of bread. If it floats and turns a good brown in about a minute the fat is right for most things. Though as different foods need different heats this is not necessarily right for everything.

However carefully the cooking is done, pieces are always left in the fat. So it should be strained through a muslin laid in a fine sieve or the debris will appear as black specks on the next lot of frying.

Oil which has the taste of the last food fried in it can be cleaned by frying a few pieces of raw potato in it.

There are those who find they get a better result with breadcrumbed dishes if they leave them in a refrigerator for a while before frying, as the crumbs cling better after a spell in the cold.

Frying in Salt

Get a fairly heavy pan really hot and sprinkle across it ½ teaspoon of salt. When the salt is really hot put in the food. For steak and hamburgers this is next best to a charcoal grill — and it puts fried food back on the slimmer's menu.

GOOSE

Goose suffers from the same fattiness problem as duck and should be cooked in just the same way — see page 82.

GOOSEBERRIES

A pinch of ground ginger added to gooseberries when they are being stewed takes the edge off them. However, it doesn't, as some people claim, make them need less sugar. Nor does it make them taste of ginger.

HADDOCK

Haddock tastes less salty if it is poached with a tablespoon of vinegar in each pint (500 ml) or so of water, or in milk.

HAGGIS

The skin on haggis bursts very easily. At one time cooks used to wrap haggis in muslin before cooking it. A wrapping of foil is more convenient today.

HAM

The saying that the nearer the bone the sweeter the meat was never truer than where ham is concerned. A certain Italian Contessa, who would eat nothing but the best, is reputed never to have eaten any ham but that nearest the bone. If she arrived at the grocer before he had cut the ham down to that point then she bade her chauffeur drive her round and round the square till the right cut was reached. That is taking things too far but whether the ham is boiled, baked or smoked the meat nearest the bone is more tasty and less salty — even if the slices may be a little less elegant.

Ham is said to taste sweeter when boiled with a handful of hay. If there is no hay to hand, as in my part of London there isn't, a good spoonful or two of dark brown sugar does the job. A ham normally takes 20 minutes to cook per lb (500 g). By that time the skin should come off very easily — if it doesn't the ham is not cooked. It will be moister and tastier if left to cool in the stock.

The traditional way to finish a ham is to stud the fat with cloves and sprinkle it with brown sugar before baking it in the oven. Almost better is the coating of coarse dark marmalade used by one of London's most expensive grocers.

Having cut into a ham, cover the cut face with a butter paper to keep it moist.

HOLLANDAISE SAUCE

Like all egg and cream sauces this sauce, which is so good with fish or asparagus, takes time. Hurrying means turning up the heat, which means trouble. All the ingredients should be at room temperature to start with and not even the water over which it is cooked in the double boiler should be allowed to boil. If all is well it should thicken slowly. If the thickening suddenly speeds up it is probably heating too fast. If so turn down the heat and add half a teaspoon of very cold water, to cool it.

If the worst happens and the sauce separates it can be rescued by putting a fresh yolk in a bowl resting over the lower half of the double boiler. Then with a lower flame very gradually work the curdled sauce into the yolk and continue making the sauce as before. However, even this is no help if the sauce becomes so hot it forms grains — what you have then is a rather nasty form of scrambled egg fit only for an omnivorous dog.

HOT CROSS BUNS

Surprising as it may sound, a grind or two of black pepper does a lot to bring out the spices in home-made hot cross buns. This is not really as outlandish as it sounds. Pepper is, after all, one of the spices and is used quite often in spiced cakes and biscuits in some other countries.

ICE CUBES

When there are a lot of drinks to be made, the fastest way to put herbs, or a twist of orange or lemon, in a drink is to have it ready frozen in an ice cube. Put whatever ingredients you want to use in the ice cube sections and just pour on water and freeze. Try borage and orange zest for Pimms and chopped mint for Bloody Marys or vodka and tonic. Herbed ice cubes can also be prepared for adding to cold soups.

If you want really elegant ice cubes make them with water which has boiled for 10 minutes or more. The ice will then be clean as a glacier mint — for a day or so at least.

Large ice cubes last far longer than small ones for packing round bottles at a party. Fill well-rinsed waxed fruit juice containers with water, freeze them and peel off the carton.

JAM

The most delicious jam recipes are those in which the fruit and sugar are mixed together and left overnight for the juice to run, so no other liquid is needed. They are also the least economical, being heavy on fruit and sugar for the amount of jam produced. Whatever the recipe, melting a good lump of butter in the pan before cooking the jam (or chutney) makes it much less likely to stick.

Set Testing
Fruit varies enormously in its setting power but under-ripe fruit always sets best. As fruit ripens pectin, the setting agent, diminishes and changes. It is easy to test and see how much pectin is present. Once the fruit has been well simmered, but before the sugar is added, put a teaspoon of the juice in a glass and let it cool. If there is plenty of pectin a thick clot forms when 3 tablespoons methylated spirits are added and the glass gently shaken. A moderate amount of pectin will produce several clots, but if no clot forms the jam will need added pectin — which can be bought, or made from apples at home. The test for setting is that a spoonful is cooled quickly, and the cold surface wrinkles when touched. For speed, test hot jam on an ice cube.

Crystallisation
A common problem is jam crystallising in the jar. This won't happen if the sugar is totally dissolved before the jam is brought to the boil and the jam is not over-stirred. But if it does crystallise, heat it in a moderate oven until the crystals melt, and let it cool again. Or use it in jam tarts.

Rich Jams
Rich jams, such as raspberry and plum, are improved by a lump of butter stirred into them near the end of cooking.

Marmalade
Marmalade is clearer if a dessert-spoonful of glycerine is added for every 8 lb (4 kg approx.) of jam half way through boiling.

Stone Fruits
Jam from stone fruits is twice as good if the stones are tied in a piece of muslin and cooked with the jam, especially if some of the stones are cracked and the kernels put aside and added to the jam at the end of cooking.

Rising Fruit
Fruit which rises to the top — cherries and strawberries for example — will distribute evenly if the jam is cool before it's potted.

JELLY STRAINING

In the days when most homes made their own jams and jellies jelly bags were far from universal. A common substitute was to invert one chair upon another, put a bowl on its seat and fasten a square of doubled muslin above it by tying each of its corners to one of the legs. Provided the knots are tight the jelly will drip through the muslin into the bowl as happily as through any expensive jelly bag.

JERUSALEM ARTICHOKES

In contact with the air Jerusalem artichokes go a nasty greyish pink unless each is dropped in water with lemon juice or vinegar added as soon as it's peeled.

Like potatoes, they taste particularly good when flavoured with nutmeg. Even a simple artichoke and milk soup can be a real delight if this is used to flavour it.

KIDNEYS

The flavour of kidneys is improved by cutting them in whatever manner is needed for the dish, then soaking them for a couple of hours in warm salted water or in water and milk.

LEMONS

When only the yellow zest of the lemon is needed a potato peeler will pare it thinner than a knife; while a warm lemon, or one which has been rolled firmly to and fro for a while, gives slightly more juice.

LETTUCE

Lettuce which has gone limp crisps up fastest if a peeled and chopped potato is put in the cold salt water with it.

LIVER

The vast army of liver haters may be surprised to hear that liver doesn't have to be dry, rubbery and boring. In Italy they have a way of cutting it as thin as an ice–cream wafer. They then season it with salt, pepper and lemon juice and let each side no more than kiss a hot, very lightly oiled, frying pan. Served with a wedge of lemon to squeeze over and a sprinkling of fresh chopped parsley this is a real delight. As butchers are at first incredulous and then annoyed when asked to cut liver this thin it is usually easier to take a firm chilled chunk of lambs liver and a sharp knife and slice it oneself. But if you value your fingers don't try to slice it this thin when it is thawed and flabby. If thick liver is your delight the way to make it tender is to soak it in milk for a couple of hours.

MAYONNAISE

It is possible, with luck or an electric blender, to make mayonnaise using a fridge-cold egg yolk and warm oil — but it is spitting in the eye of fate. To blend easily and without curdling, both need to be at room temperature. Then, with the yolk well mixed with 1–4 teaspoons vinegar or lemon juice and the oil really put in drop by drop while stirring hard, there should be no problems. Adding a touch of mustard to the yolk and stirring with a loop whisk increase the chances of success.

If mayonnaise does separate it is one of the easiest sauces to recover. Put a fresh egg yolk in a clean bowl, season it slightly and add a touch of vinegar before very gradually beating in the curdled mixture.

MERINGUES

Where meringues often fail is that having baked beautifully they stick like limpets to the tin and have to be broken off in pieces. The old way to avoid this was to put them onto a hot baking tin and, when the upper surface was just firm, turn them carefully on their sides with a spatula to expose the gooey bottom to the warmth. This works, and those who like totally dry meringues can let the bottom dry and then break it with a spoon so the inside dries too. If, like me, you think half the joy is in the gooey centre the answer is to line the tin with vegetable parchment. This is absolutely foolproof. The meringues don't need to be turned on their sides and they peel off perfectly every time.

Some say a little cornflour should be added to a meringue mixture to help it stand. But I find it spoils the texture. If the whites have been whipped to a peak to start with, half the sugar beaten in till very stiff, and the remainder folded in, the mixture should need no such prop. Though what can be added is $\frac{1}{2}$ teaspoon vinegar for every 2 egg whites. This makes the centre more marshmallowy, which is especially good for large meringue cases, which often seem to be dry.

MINCE

Adding salt to mince dishes, such as spaghetti Bolognese or shepherd's pie, early in the cooking tends to make the mince rubbery. It is best to add the salt when the dish is almost cooked.

MUSHROOMS

It is odd the way so many useful practices in the home have been lost yet some quite useless ones retained. Peeling mushrooms is one of them. It stems from the days when if you had mushrooms at all they came from a field and were far from clean. Today's cultivated mushrooms need no peeling at all, just a rinse under a tap to get any grit off.

The older a mushroom is the more it loses moisture and becomes soft. When soft they drink up fat and easily become greasy, so the softer the mushroom the less fat should go in the pan.

If they have to be sliced and left for later a covering of lemon juice on the cut surface will keep it white, but at the price of a slight change of flavour which doesn't suit all dishes. Slicing mushrooms is so quick it's often better to simply slice them at the last minute.

MUSSELS

You may have noticed that the mussels in good restaurants always seem to be bigger and plumper than the ones you buy yourself. Well it isn't just a matter of expert buying. The secret of plump mussels is to give them a feast of porridge before you cook them. Put the mussels in water and for each gallon of water add 2 cupfuls of porridge oats. Leave them to gorge themselves for a day *or* night, not longer, before cleaning and cooking.

NETTLES

Eating nettles has all the pleasure of converting a vice into a virtue, and there's the bonus that they come at a time when other vegetables are expensive. For it is the young shoots which should be picked, with rubber gloves, cooked like spinach and eaten with a good bonus of butter or cream. Unlikely as it may sound they really do taste good and are very popular in Ireland where this culinary tradition was never forgotten.

However I wouldn't go along with those who say they can't tell nettles from spinach. Nettles are similar but no more than that. Incidentally, this is not a vegetable to try when it's older. Old nettles taste vile.

NUT SKINNING

The quick way to skin almonds, walnuts, pecans and pistachio nuts is to pour boiling water over them and leave them for a few minutes. Add a pinch of bicarbonate of soda to the pistachios to make them greener. Nuts must be left for no longer than the water takes to loosen the skin, or they become soggy. For this reason it's best to do them in small batches, for the skin is only easy to remove just after you take them from the water.

Hazelnuts don't respond to water and need to be toasted gently under a grill for a minute or two, shaking the grill pan to make them grill all over. Then pop them in a paper bag and shake it so the skins rub off against one another.

ONIONS

Unless an onion is extra strong, or the cook extra sensitive, an onion doesn't cause tears till it loses its roots or is chopped. So tears can be delayed by peeling onions down from the top and leaving all the roots on till last. If this fails, peel the onions under water and keep them submerged till the job is done.

Putting onions in boiling water or in the freezer for a while before peeling them stems the flow of the oils which cause the tears. Unfortunately both methods give a slightly softer texture to the onion, which is no good if the onion is to be eaten raw or pickled.

It is chopping onions which is the real tear-jerker. But the method I was once taught by a chef makes a quick job of it and shortens the agony. Stand the onion on its root end and cut down in a series of slices which don't quite sever the under-side. Cut another set of slices cross hatching the first lot. Cut the last slice right through. Lie the onion on this flat side and cut it down in slices ending with the root end.

If only half an onion is needed cut it in half with the skin on. The left-over half will keep for several days with its skin on but rot rapidly without it. Don't believe those who say butter should be rubbed on the cut surface. Far from making the onion keep better it actually speeds up the rotting.

There is no need to peel onions which are being put in broth or the stock for gravy. Just wipe them clean and cut off the roots. The skins will give a good golden brown tone to the liquid.

OVEN TEMPERATURES

Obviously the most economical way to use an oven is only to cook an individual item where the oven is hottest. There is usually considerable difference between the temperatures at the top and bottom in a gas oven, so check your oven manual. The most thrifty way of all is to cook a number of dishes needing varied temperatures in different places in the oven. In war time when fuel was scarce housewives brought this to a fine art.

The exception to the rule about always putting a single item in the hottest place, is a fruit cake. A large fruit cake should always cook in the centre of an oven.

OYSTERS

Unfortunately there is no way to tell if an oyster is going to disagree with you until it does. But the chances of trouble are increased if you have been drinking whisky.

PANCAKES

Pancakes don't have to be limited to times when there is plenty of milk. Cream soda can be used as a substitute for all of the milk in sweet pancakes and beer can be used instead of some or all of the milk in savory ones. Both these variations taste extremely good. In fact beer pancakes are traditional in the north of France. However, don't believe anyone who tries to tell you they are much lighter made this way; it won't necessarily make any difference.

Any pancake batter will be lighter if it stands for an hour before being cooked. It should then be used up entirely as it goes off overnight.

PASTA

When I first went to Italy I was amazed at the amount of salt which went into the pasta water, yet it's one reason why it always tastes so good there. The other thing they always do is put a little oil in the water, to stop the pasta sticking together, and give the pasta a quick stir as it goes in.

Lasagne needs special attention as the large flat surfaces stick fast very easily. Be generous with the oil and put the strips in one at a time.

The Italians cook all pasta 'al dente' — so it still has a slight bite at the centre. Cooking it like this means keeping a very close eye on it towards the end. It rapidly changes from underdone to soggy and overcooked. Re-heat pasta by pouring boiling water over it, stirring it well and draining it after 2 minutes.

PASTRY

One reason why some people are natural pastry cooks and others aren't is that pastry likes to be cold and some hands are colder than others. The marble slabs of old fashioned kitchens were a marvellous help to the pastry maker, especially to the hot-handed. Now the easiest way to cool pastry is to fill a bottle with iced water and use it as a rolling pin.

Pastry is so much a matter of touch that no two people produce the same results with the same recipe. There are those who find using half water and half vinegar as the liquid for shortcrust makes it lighter — for light pastry the liquid should always be really cold — but in my experience pastry is only as light as the handling it gets.

The traditional way of baking a pastry case 'blind' without a filling, was to line it with crumpled greaseproof paper and fill the paper with dried beans to hold the pastry down and stop it bubbling. The beans can be stored and used again for this, but they are no good for eating. A cheaper way is simply to rest a slightly smaller baking tin on the pastry. If a pie or tart is not baked blind the way to stop the inside pastry going soggy with the liquid from the filling is to paint it with lightly beaten egg white.

If the top of a pie burns it can be rescued, if the filling is sweet, by scraping off the burnt pastry and brushing it well with a thick syrup of sugar and water. Return it to the oven and watch it carefully till the new top turns golden. If, incidentally, you have trouble remembering which is a tart and which a pie there is a slightly puritanical mnemonic, 'tarts go topless', which should help.

PEAS

Fresh peas are almost one of the lost vegetables, appearing in the shops for little more than a blink and often scarcely looking worth buying when they are there. But if you find good ones try cooking a few of the younger pods in the water with them to bring out the flavour.

Frozen peas are not totally beyond redemption. Cooked in the French country way for fresh peas they taste almost like them — instead of using water cook them in butter with the chopped outer leaves of lettuce, a very little chopped onion, and salt and a touch of sugar.

Pea soup is a nice example of old-fashioned thrift and wisdom. Traditionally it includes bacon rind to flavour it, at no cost to the cook, and mint which counteracts the wind-producing tendency of peas as well as helping the flavour.

97

PEPPERS

Even the Italians haven't found an easy way to skin sweet peppers. The only method is to put them under the grill or hold them on a skewer over a flame until the skin blackens and can be pulled off under cold running water. I always think there has to be a better way but this seems the only one which works at all.

Peppers can go bitter if they are left with water on them for any length of time before cooking. So it is always safest to leave any washing till just before they are to be used. When stuffed peppers refuse to stand upright and threaten to spill their stuffing into the sauce take a leaf out of my greengrocer's book. Make a ring of crunched up foil and stand them in that.

PICKLING

I have seen it suggested in books that hot vinegar should be poured onto pickled onions. But in the farmhouse kitchens of my early childhood no one would have countenanced hot vinegar for crisp pickles such as onions or red cabbage. The vinegar and spices were always heated and allowed to get completely cold before they went over the vegetables, because hot vinegar partly cooks them and takes away the crispness.

PINEAPPLE

There is a good excuse for being extravagant and serving pineapple at the end of a meal. Not only is it less work than a pudding, it is also meant to aid the digestion. Culinary tradition has it that it should be thickly sliced and sprinkled with kirsch. I think there is a strong case for nonconformity. Thinly sliced it is pleasanter to eat, looks prettier, and it is far easier to cut the edge off without leaving eyes. And though kirsch is fine with a very ripe pineapple fresh from the fields it does little for the acid fruit which have ripened on their way to Europe. These taste best with a touch of salt in the sugar to bring out their flavour, and rum or one of the softer fruit liqueurs.

The tuft, with a small dome of pineapple attached to it, can be potted and grown as a houseplant. But at Christmas an excellent way to use it is to ask any children present to guess how many leaves it contains. Then leave them to pull it apart and count them. The number is astonishingly large and should give the adults time to have at least one cup of coffee in peace. There must of course be a prize for the closest guess.

PIZZAS

For years I struggled to cut the strong undercrust of pizzas with a knife. I realised my mistake when I saw a friend in Italy pick up the kitchen scissors and cut through a pizza like butter.

If you like a crisp outside to pizzas, or quiche, try taking the bought ones out of their cases and putting them directly on the oven shelves to heat — always assuming the shelves are clean.

PLUCKING

Any bird plucks more easily while it is still warm. This is an excellent excuse for persuading whoever killed it to also pluck it. This can't, of course, apply to game which is always hung for a while in feather.

PORK

One of the chief delights of roast pork is crisp crackling. To achieve this brush the skin with olive oil and place the joint on a grid in the baking tin so it doesn't sit in the juices from the meat. When pork skin gets moisture on it, it becomes tough and leathery, so this is a joint which should not be basted.

As there are health risks in eating underdone pork it must always be cooked till the flesh is white. Test for this by pushing a skewer into the thickest part of the joint. When cooked it should let out a clear watery juice without a trace of pink in it. This usually takes 20–25 minutes for every lb (500 g) in a hot oven, 30–35 minutes a lb (500 g) in a moderate one.

Pork keeps less well than other meat and should be eaten rapidly, especially in thundery weather when it can turn in a matter of hours.

POTATOES

The way we constantly eat them today you would scarcely think the British once regarded these strange South American imports with suspicion, thinking them poisonous and possessed of alarming aphrodisiac properties. Slimmers and lovers alike may wish that they were, but what they really offer are taste, Vitamin C, minerals and bulk. The flavour, texture, and Vitamin C are all at their best when potatoes are cooked with their skins on. Which makes a nice excuse for saving work. New potatoes can be eaten just as they are, well scrubbed and still in their skins. The skins taste delicious and are excellent roughage for the digestion. Old potatoes can be peeled while still hot; which loses none of the elements which are concentrated just below the skin. Of course, eyes and damaged parts must be cut out first, so must any green areas. Green areas and sprouting eyes contain concentrations of a slightly toxic substance. It would take a great deal of it to harm you but it is wiser to avoid it, especially when cooking for young children.

Jersey Potatoes

Jersey potatoes have a flavour all their own which merits special treatment. Hold in every bit of flavour by putting them in a parcel of foil with a lump of butter, a sprig of mint and a touch of salt. Close the foil tightly and put it in a moderate oven for half an hour or so. This is a modern version of the old French way of cooking them in paper cases.

Boiled Potatoes

Oddly enough boiled potatoes shouldn't be boiled: they should be simmered. Boiling encourages them to fall apart. They are improved by being left in cold salt water for an hour or two before cooking and this is one vegetable which should be put into cold water and brought to the boil.

The blackening which happens with varieties like Home Guard and Pentland Ivory can be prevented by adding a dash of lemon juice or vinegar to the water.

Once cooked the texture is improved if they are shaken gently over a low heat in a dry pan for a moment or two, with a clean dry cloth over the top. This absorbs any extra moisture. This is also the remedy for over-cooked potatoes, which can then be mashed using butter but no milk.

Mashed Potatoes

When mashed potatoes go gluey it is usually because cold milk has been added to them. Some varieties react this way to cold milk so it's always safer to heat the milk before adding it. For the best mashed potato of all, season it with pepper as well as salt and try adding grated nutmeg, or chopped onion or parsley.

Baked Potatoes

The skin on a baked potato ought to be the best part, but it seldom is. To make it delicious scrub and dry it well, rub it with butter and sprinkle it with salt. The texture of the skin is spoilt by putting it in foil; the potato tastes far better put directly onto a baking sheet.

For a floury texture in the potato cut a nick in the skin to let the steam escape.

If there's a hurry there are two ways to speed up the cooking of jacket potatoes. Thrusting a metal skewer right through the potato, and leaving it in, carries the heat to the centre of the potato and cuts the cooking time by almost half. Another way to shorten the time is to boil the potatoes for 10–15 minutes before putting them in the oven. If you do neither a 7 oz (200 g) potato takes about 1–1½ hours at gas mark 6–8, 400°–450°F (200°–230°C).

Chips
Chips are very much better if they are soaked in cold salt water for a while before cooking. It takes off the excess starch and makes them crisper. But they need very careful drying afterwards. If damp chips are put in the pan the fat can react to the water and seethe up dangerously.

Potatoes always absorb the taste of the last thing which was cooked in the oil. If the fat wasn't last used for potatoes throw the off-cuts of potato in and let them absorb the taste in the fat before throwing them away and cooking the chips. If you don't you may have more fish with your chips than you bargain for.

Small quantities of chips cook better than large ones which lower the temperature — and temperature is critical. Too low and the chips absorb the fat, too high and they are burnt on the outside and raw inside. Test with one chip before adding the rest.

Roast Potatoes
A friend of mine once returned from a restaurant claiming she had discovered the secret of making the best roast potatoes in the world. The chef's method was to half boil them, then put them in plenty of very hot dripping and baste them continually, until golden brown. What the chef might have added is that the quality of the dripping is important. It must be pure. Beef or lamb are fine. But if the potatoes are to go with a bird nothing is as good for potatoes as duck or goose dripping. In old kitchens this was just one of the reasons why goose fat was highly prized.

PRUNES

Tea is the answer to good prunes, tea and some zest of lemon. Any type of tea can be used to replace water for stewing them. The most economical way to use it is to put the prunes in a wide-necked thermos and simply pour boiling tea over them. Add the zest of lemon and close the flask till next day. Some prunes will then be fully cooked, others within an ace of it, depending how dry they were. Dried apricots can also be treated this way, but with China tea rather than Indian.

RABBIT

Rabbit tends to be a dry meat and the cottagers' way round this is typically thrifty and practical. When roasting a rabbit, left-over bacon rinds would be threaded through the back. This both moistens the meat and gives it extra flavour.

RHUBARB

To prevent rhubarb disintegrating into imitation seaweed do as the Danes do. Dissolve the sugar in the water and thicken it with potato flour — sometimes sold under the French name *fécule* — before adding the chopped rhubarb. The *fécule* has to be mixed to a cream before being added to the liquid and boiled. It should make the liquid thick but translucent, before the rhubarb is poached in it. Zest of lemon or a touch of root ginger are both traditional aids to the flavour of rhubarb.

RICE

A squeeze of lemon in the water gives rice an elegant whiteness. A spoonful of oil helps to keep the grains separate. Having cooked it till the centre is firm but no longer hard, rinse it in hot water to remove the surplus starch. Covering the rice with a cloth to absorb the steam while it waits to be served will stop it clumping.

SAFFRON

The traditional way to draw the colour out of the little threads of saffron is to pound it slightly and pour over it 2–3 tablespoons of the liquid from the cooking — or boiling water. Then leave this to steep until the liquid is a strong orange before straining it into the dish. Leaving it till the colour is too deep can produce a bitter taste, so can putting the threads directly into the food.

SALADS

Salads which include lettuce or other green leaves soon become mushy and wilted once the dressing is on them. The dressing is best put on at the last minute. The reverse is true of salads made with potatoes, rice, cooked dried beans and pasta. All these benefit from absorbing some of the dressing while still hot.

SALMON

I have heard people say they couldn't ever cook salmon, even if it was given to them, because they lacked a fish kettle. A salmon may not come one's way too often, but if it does that is a very bad reason for turning it down. Salmon is one of the many foods which cooks as well in foil in the oven as in liquid on the top. Simply butter a large sheet of foil and enclose the salmon in it, like filling in a pasty, closing it tightly at the edges. Bake it for about 30 minutes to the pound at gas mark 1, 275°F (135°C).

Many fish are at their best cooked this way whether whole or in pieces, and herbs and vegetables can be tucked in the foil with them.

SALTINESS AND SWEETNESS

On cook's duty at a Girl Guide camp I once mistook the salt for the sugar when cooking gooseberries. That size of error cannot be put right but slight over-salting can be. A remedy for soups, stews and gravies is to add a chopped raw potato and cook it for about 15 minutes. By which time it should have absorbed some of the salt and can be fished out. Adding some sugar is a better solution for French dressing and sauces which can take a hint of sweetness.

If food is too sweet a pinch of salt or a dash of vinegar, according to the type of food, may put it right.

SANDWICHES

The essence of a good sandwich is a generous filling, well seasoned if it is savoury, on thin tasty bread. This rules out plastic wrapped, plastic flavoured, pre-sliced loaves, but real bread is easily sliced if buttered first and cut with a hot sharp knife. Heat the knife over a flame or dip it in boiling water and dry it. Only egg sandwiches break the buttering rule. The filling stays together best if the eggs are mashed with the butter, though mayonnaise or salad cream can also be used to bind them.

SARDINES

As an old age pensioner showed me, there is no need to wrestle with those dreadful keys. Just turn the tin over and open it with a tin opener. Once out of the tin sardines taste far less oily if well sprinkled with vinegar.

SCONES AND SODA BREAD

My friends always laugh at the bottles of sour milk they find in my fridge — proof, they think, of my lack of organisation. No one familiar with the Scottish and Irish traditions of scone and soda bread making would find it odd. For there is nothing like sour milk for making light scones. The acid in the milk reacts with the alkali in the raising agent and they froth up, taking the rest of the ingredients with them. A fairly acid plain yoghurt is almost as good. But don't do as I once did and use very sour cream or the taste will be quite awful. With sour milk there is no odd taste at all.

The way to produce a softer crust on soda bread is to wrap it in a thick soft cloth as soon as you take it from the oven. Or, for the softest crust of all, bake each loaf in the oven in a heavy well buttered casserole with the lid on.

SHELLFISH

The French tradition is to open shellfish by sliding the knife in near the hinge of the two shells. The British one is to slide a knife in at the point opposite the hinge. Either way no mollusc will let you *lever* it open. Slide the knife in close to the flatter of the two shells and swing the blade so it will cut through the point where the creature is attached to the shell. It will then open easily. If it opens easily as soon as you put the knife in, and before you cut anything, it is dead or dying and should be thrown away. Shellfish must be alive until the moment they are eaten or cooked. This means they will clamp shut when tapped.

SHORTBREAD CUTTING

In Scotland there is a pretty and very practical tradition for the cutting of shortbread which has been cooked in a round tin. Shortbread, like biscuits, must be cut while still hot. The first 'cut' is made by pressing an inverted glass into the centre. Then lines are cut radiating out from this. Each piece looks like one of the gores of a petticoat — which is how the name petticoat tails came to be associated with shortbread. This method can be used for any similar confection. Its great advantage, as the thrifty Scots housewives realised, is that it makes a central piece out of the points which would otherwise have crumbled off and been wasted.

SOUR MILK

A pinch of bicarbonate of soda and a pinch of sugar added to a pint of milk which is just on the turn, but not yet truly sour, makes is possible to use it in cooking without it separating as it heats or tasting sour.

SPICES

The spices which we, in the West, think of as Indian — curry powder, turmeric, cumin, and coriander — give a fuller flavour in cooked dishes if they are fried a little to start with.

STRAWBERRIES

Colette writes of how her mother would rise at dawn to gather strawberries, then spread them on cabbage leaves till they were to be eaten. In France the curious ability of cabbage leaves to strengthen the flavour of strawberries is so well known that the porcelain manufacturers once made cabbage leaf plates — though the magic is certainly not in the shape of the leaf. Fortunately even punnet strawberries gain something from the touch of cabbage. Put the leaves under and over the strawberries and cover them with cling film for a few hours. But if you cannot gather the strawberries at dawn you will never quite taste perfection.

If the strawberries are being served on the stalk leave them on a cabbage leaf. The glaucous blue of the cabbage is an infinitely lovelier foil to the red of strawberries than the sharp colours of china or the edgey green of vine leaves.

Sprinkling ground black pepper on strawberries makes them taste almost like some oriental fruit. But to get this effect you must slice them. Putting pepper on the outside of the fruit does nothing for them.

Strawberries are even better with sour cream than with sweet cream. Buy it soured or add a little lemon juice to sweet cream while stirring hard — though this isn't as good as the real thing.

However you are serving them, strawberries should only be washed at the last minute, and then with their stalks on. If they are washed with the stalks off they go soggy much faster.

SYRUP

When short of sugar golden syrup can be used instead in many recipes. Try using half the quantity that you would use with sugar, as syrup is almost twice as sweet. If syrup is used instead of sugar in buns it gives them a different texture and can produce a slightly sticky top which children love.

TENDERISING

When marinading was developed, centuries ago, it was mainly to prevent the meat going bad. An excellent side effect was that the acid in the marinade made the meat more tender. Wine, lemon juice, or vinegar can all be used to tenderise and flavour meat in combination with herbs and spices to improve the flavour; it's interesting to experiment.

The most remarkable tenderiser of all is paw paw. It contains a powerful enzyme which breaks down the protein in meat. So spreading paw paw pulp on meat, or wrapping it in the skin of a paw paw for a day, makes meat more tender than any other method.

THICKENING

When a sauce or stew fails to thicken there are two emergency remedies. The first is the one the French call *beurre manié*. You take rather more butter than flour and work the two into a paste. Small pieces of this are dropped into the simmering liquid until it reaches the right consistency. This mixture can be made and stored in a jar in the fridge against the day when it is needed.

If a sauce should look clear, arrowroot or cornflour are the best thickeners. Mix a teaspoonful of either with a tablespoon of cold water. Pour this into the sauce, off the heat, while stirring hard. Once it is mixed in simmer the sauce, stirring all the time until the right thickness is reached. They thicken fast, so it's easy to keep making and adding a little more till the sauce is just right.

When the flour runs out a stew can be thickened the old Scottish way, with a handful of oatmeal. You'll get the best results if you put it in at the start and give it a long slow cook.

Curries from Sri Lanka are especially good and a friend from there once taught me that part of the secret was to thicken the curry with a handful of grated coconut. Given a long slow cook it melts into the sauce, improving the texture and the flavour enormously.

TINNED MEAT

The easy way to slice tinned meat really thinly is to chill it, open both ends of the can, and push it out slowly cutting it as it emerges.

TOMATO KETCHUP

When narrow-necked bottles of ketchup, or any other sauce, refuse to release their contents the deadlock can be broken with a drinking straw. Hold your thumb over one end while you thrust the other to the bottom of the bottle. Remove your thumb and the ketchup will pour out quite easily with never a splat.

TOMATOES

As shop tomatoes have lost much of their natural sweetness before they reach us they need a sprinkling of sugar to bring out their true flavour. This is why Italians often add sugar to tomato sauces. They also add basil, the herb which most perfectly sets off the flavour of tomatoes. A salad of newly picked tomatoes and fresh basil is so good I would choose it for my last meal on earth.

TRUFFLES

Having a spare truffle is not one of life's commoner experiences, but it's a luxury worth making the most of. An old French method is to put the truffle in a box with half a dozen or so fresh eggs, uncooked and in their shells. Seal the box tightly and leave it in a cool place for 24 hours. By then the eggs will have absorbed the scent of truffle, and you can enjoy the luxury of superb truffle-flavoured boiled or scrambled eggs and still have the truffle to put in another dish. A neat case of having your truffle and eating it.

TURKEY

One of the less great British traditions is that of turkey ruining. Every year scores of noble self-sacrificing housewives get up at dawn on Christmas Day to start the turkey on its long ordeal by slow cooking. Their labours are so routinely rewarded by a dry bird that the myth has grown up that turkey simply *is* like that. Far from it. There is a far better, and lazier, though less well known, tradition which produces a moist and succulent bird which really is a treat for the Christmas table. When I was a child the village baker would cook the outsize turkeys in his bread ovens. The best were those wrapped in well buttered greaseproof paper before going in the baking tins lying on their sides, so the potentially dry breast meat was bathed in butter. He would cook them for about 15–20 minutes to the lb, turning them on the other side at half time. The paper would be removed and the bird set breast uppermost to brown toward the end of the time. Being bread ovens they were set at a low to moderate heat. Lacking a helpful village baker the same result can be produced by cooking a turkey at gas mark 3, 325°F (165°C). In a small oven it is safer to use foil — which can't burn — rather than greaseproof paper. Like this a 10 lb (5 kg) stuffed bird takes only 3 hours to cook. Sleep in till 10 am, it will still be ready by lunchtime. Allow 15–20 mins. per lb for other sizes.

VODKA

Vodka is served very cold. Keep it on ice until the moment it is poured. In Russia they make a fiery vodka by steeping chillies in it. It is easily copied at home, but go easy on the number of chillies. The true Russian version is only for masochists and those who have shifted the iron curtain to the roof of their mouth.

WALNUTS

Walnuts for pickling are usually ready by about the end of June. The old test to see if they are still soft enough is to push the eye of a darning needle into them.

Their juice is a deep brown stain which no amount of scrubbing will wash off, which is why it's a traditional stain for wood. Hole-free rubber gloves are essential when handling them or you'll look like a half-washed black and white minstrel.

WEIGHING

Cooking books usually tell you to flour or wet the scales before weighing sticky substances like treacle or honey. There are far easier methods. The simplest is to put the mixing bowl or pan on the scales, note its weight, and transfer the treacle straight into it from the jar till the scales have risen by the required amount. If the pan is too big for the scales use the subtraction method. Put the jar of treacle on the scales and spoon it out into the pan until the scales have gone down by the right amount. Even a child can use these methods tidily — which is more than can be said for flouring the scales!

WHITE SAUCE

When I was newly married a plump Swiss concierge at a Geneva concert hall taught me the secret of making white sauce, while in the hall my husband recorded Ernst Ansermet conducting Stravinsky. There are now better recordings, but the sauce was part of a long culinary tradition and has stood the test of time.

Use plenty of butter so the flour is totally absorbed into it. Cook the butter and flour over a moderate flame till they are white and fluffy. This gives a glossy-looking sauce and means the flour is part cooked before the milk is added, which saves a great deal of time and prevents it tasting floury. But beware, cooked too long or on too high a flame it will change colour and there is then the basis for brown sauce, not white. The second secret is to use a loop whisk to stir it – no other type will do. Beat the sauce hard with it as the milk is added and keep stirring until the sauce is thick. It would take a magician to make lumpy sauce with a loop whisk however fast or slowly the milk is added.

If the sauce has to stand it will form a skin — and this will make lumps. Prevent this by trickling spoonfuls of milk over the surface till it is completely covered, and putting the lid on the pan.

WINE

Recently many of the conventions which were once observed, about what to serve with what, have been overturned. All the same claret goes best with light flavoured meat, Burgundy with stronger flavoured meat, and a white wine is the best foil for fish.

If friends arrive bearing a fine bottle it may be worth asking if they would like it opened then or would rather drink it on their next visit. For a good wine ought to rest for 24 hours after travelling or it will be less than its best.

Opening Wine Bottles
The only openers which shouldn't be used are those which apply air pressure. They could cause an explosion if there was a flaw in the glass or the wine had formed its own gas. A very old cork may be impossible to remove. In this instance one of London's top wine merchants recommends breaking the neck of the bottle below the bottom of the cork. To do this you insert the corkscrew. Wrap a cloth round the neck of the bottle and give a sharp blow to the ridge at the mouth of the bottle, with the back of a large knife. Presumably you pour through muslin, to catch any fragments of glass.

Wine Decanting
Any wine tastes better for the right treatment — cheap wine needs it, cru classé deserves it. The most vital thing of all is to let a red wine breathe.

Red wine ripens rapidly when air gets to it and this makes an enormous difference to the taste. In our grandparents' time wine was always decanted, and decanting isn't an affectation. It's a very good way of getting air right through the wine. Another good way is to pour it into a clean glass jug and then back into the bottle. If you are tempted to pour yourself a glass on the way, do so, it will do everyone a favour by leaving a larger surface exposed to the air.

A good mature red should have sediment in the bottom of the bottle. To avoid decanting the sediment the wine needs to be poured very slowly, in a continuous stream, with the light behind the bottle. If it is to be returned to the bottle rinse the bottle well and shake it thoroughly dry. The sediment can be strained and used for cooking. It won't make a fine dish, but it will do a lot for a family stew.

Preparing Wine

Once opened a good bottle of red should stand for 2 hours and a poor one for 3 hours. The ideal place is fairly high up in a warm room such as the kitchen. On top of a tall fridge is ideal. But standing it on the stove, or dunking it in hot water — as I have known restaurants do — destroys rather than helps the taste.

White and rosé wines need to be chilled for 1–2 hours in a refrigerator. Give the shorter time to the better wine. Those bachelors who are always prepared, with a bottle in the fridge, are not doing the drinker much of a favour. Beyond a certain point coldness stops improving the flavour and starts to dull it, and wine does not like being stored indefinitely at that temperature. White and rosé wines can be drunk as soon as they are open, they don't need time to breathe.

Once open all wines should be drunk within 24 hours.

Pouring Wine

The Victorian adage 'hold a woman by the waist and a bottle by the neck' is correct, but largely ignored. Some other old rules of wine pouring are more worthwhile. The ideal wine glass should hold 6–8 oz of wine (180–240 ml) and curve inwards at the rim to hold the scent of the wine (it also chips less easily and takes less space on the shelf than an outcurving glass). This size looks enormous, but don't worry, it should never be filled more than ⅓ of the way up, so there's no risk that guests will double their intake.

For champagne the correct glass is a tall slim one. Those saucers on stems, beloved of caterers, which allow every bubble to rush up the nose are a relic of the champagne cocktail era of the 1930s, and should have died with it.

Brandy balloons might have been designed so even the 'merriest' guest could not spill his after-dinner drink. The correct measure is not more than will stay in the glass even if it is laid (or knocked) on its side.

Champagne

A radio show I am sometimes on doesn't just use champagne to warm up its guests, it frequently showers them with it. Not deliberately of course. It's just that the producer has no fridge in which to chill it, and there is no way anyone can open warm champagne without creating a fountain. The pressure in a champagne bottle is 96 lb (6.75 kg/sq cm) to the square inch — about as much as the tyres of a double-decker bus — and, as everyone knows, warm gas expands, bursting out at the first opportunity. If champagne is properly chilled there should be no problem, providing it isn't shaken, but covering the cork with a cloth as you ease it off is a good precaution against it flying into a light fitting.

Port

Port with cheese, especially Stilton, is one of the few great British contributions to gastronomy. The other tradition is always to pass port in a clockwise direction round the table.

YOGHURT

An Indian friend who makes the best yoghurt I have ever tasted says the secret is that she uses a $15\frac{1}{2}$ oz (440 g) tin of evaporated milk to every pint of ordinary milk. I have to admit that even made like this mine is not as good as hers. This may be because part of the secret of good yoghurt is developing a chain, in which one culture is made from a little of the previous one and it gets better as the 'generations' succeed one another.

All you need do is take a small carton of plain yoghurt and beat into it a pint of milk which feels just slightly hotter than your finger. Then put the mixture overnight in a closed thermos flask or in a casserole wrapped in a blanket in the airing cupboard. In the morning you will have yoghurt, but leave it in the heat no longer than that or it will grow sour.

BUYING
AND STORING

Buying food is an art. Each fruit, vegetable, cheese or creature has its own signs which will tell you whether it's fresh or stale, and whether it's a good variety or a poor one. Sadly these signs are now almost as forgotten as the spoors once followed by native trackers. To measure the scope of this loss you have only to go into any supermarket and see people rejecting plump tasty carrots in favour of thin elongated ones they imagine to be younger, or watch them buy fish so far past its best as to be scarcely worth eating. The complete art can only be learnt on the ground, but here are some of the tricks of buying and storing which may be useful to even the most discriminating shopper.

BROWN SUGAR

Brown sugar has an annoying habit of clumping together in a solid mass. This can be prevented or cured by putting a piece of bread in the bag or jar with it.

CAKE

The best way to keep a cake fresh for the longest possible time is to store it in an airtight tin with a slice of bread. The bread needs to be replaced as soon as it goes hard. Some people find a piece of apple is equally good. If the cake is iced place it on the lid and put the tin on over it. That way the icing is far less likely to be spoilt.

CAULIFLOWERS

I'm told an old gardeners' method of keeping cauliflowers at their peak was to cut them with 4–5 inches (10–13 cm.) of stalk. The lower leaves were then stripped off and the stalk thrust into slightly moist sand in a cool place.

CELERY

As a child I was taught only to buy dirty celery because celery begins to lose its flavour as soon as its washed. Dirty celery is hard to find nowadays but if you can get it and leave the washing to the last minute it still has the best flavour of all.

CHEESE

Cheese Buying

There is a world of difference between the farmhouse versions of the great British cheeses and the mass-produced vacuum-packed versions found in most supermarkets; this is partly because cheese dislikes vacuum packs. But nowadays, the presence or absence of rind is no longer any kind of a guide to a good cheese. The prizewinning farmhouse cheddar at a recent Bath and West show was made in a vast rindless block.

Now that the only guide is the flavour of the cheese, perhaps more and more retailers will return to the old practice of offering customers a taste before they buy. It's a service which can reasonably be expected if you are paying a premium price. Whatever the type, look for a moist surface. No cheese should seem dry or greasy.

Some of the continental cheeses are seasonal. The time to take a hard look at Brie and Camembert before you buy, is in the early spring. They may have a thick white slab at the centre of each slice and be a runny yellow round the edge. This uneven ripening is a danger signal. It usually means the cheese has been over-chilled in transit, and cheese like this will never ripen fully and evenly. If, however, there is a thin layer of white in the centre of a slice it should be perfect in a day or so — depending on how you keep it. Bear in mind that although Brie and Camembert are creamy right through when ripe, they won't necessarily run. A high fat Brie, 62% *matier gras* for example, will keep its shape even when very ripe indeed.

Among the most risky buys are jars of Stilton. Despite their high price and prestigious look some manufacturers use these jars as a place to dump their crumbling and sub-standard cheese. Only by going to a top retailer can you be sure this isn't what you are buying.

Cheese Storing

At one time hard cheeses were wrapped in a cloth wrung out in vinegar and stored in a larder. It kept the cheese well, but no better than wrapping it in foil or cling film and putting it in the refrigerator. Cheese doesn't like being stored in plastic or left in the warm. Both make it sweat and encourage mould. Wherever it is, a couple of sugar lumps kept with it will discourage mould, though if it does form it is harmless and can just be pared off before the cheese is eaten.

When storing a whole round of cheese, such as a Stilton, turning it top to bottom each week will help to keep it in peak condition. Otherwise the moisture may drain down, creating a soggy base and an over-dry top.

Mozzarella is another cheese which needs to be kept moist, but in this case by being immersed in water.

Soft cheeses really need a larder rather than a fridge, but as this is seldom possible the next best is to keep them in the cool until they are perfectly ripe. Only then put them in the fridge and be sure to bring them out to warm again 2–3 hours before serving.

Sealed pottery pots of cheese will keep for 2 months. In contrast, any 'sell by' date on a packed cheese assumes it will be eaten within 3 days of that date. However, I find the life of cottage cheese in the refrigerator can be extended slightly by treating it like a paint tin and storing it on its lid.

COCONUTS

To pick a good coconut shake it beside your ear. It should be heavy for its size, with three dry eyes and a clear sound of milk moving inside as you shake it.

COD'S ROE

Take a close look at cod's roe in March, April and May and you will often see it isn't looking as it should. These are the months to avoid it in the fishmonger and particularly at the fish and chip shop, for a lot of the 'cod's roe' isn't cod at all. In the other months the best roe to look out for is Icelandic.

COOKED FOOD

How fast cooked food goes off depends very much on what is in it, as well as on the temperature you are storing it at. Any food with alcohol in will keep longer than the same dish would without it. Herbs such as sage and thyme also extend the life of a dish.

CRAB

The best time to buy crabs is between June and September, when they are at their peak. If a crab has just been cooked it should have white rubbery-looking froth clinging to it in places. This falls off after the first day. Unfortunately some fishmongers wipe it off, perhaps to confuse the customers, perhaps because they feel people will dislike it. Try to get close enough to the crab to smell it. When perfectly fresh it has almost no smell. As it ages it first smells slightly fishy then develops a hint of ammonia as it starts to go off.

As crabs change their shells it's the weight of a crab that counts, not its size. If you pick a big one that has just changed shells and is loose inside it you won't get value for money.

A fresh crab will keep for two days in its shell in a refrigerator. But once dressed it must be eaten the same day.

CRAYFISH

A fresh crayfish is a lovely sight. It has a clear orange tone to the shell with a fine sheen on it almost like silk. Crayfish keep better than any other shellfish and will last a week in a refrigerator. As it ages the sheen gradually goes.

CUCUMBER

When I was a child one of the familiar sights of summer was a cucumber standing stalk end down in a jug with an inch or two of water. Kept like this, in a cool place, with the water changed daily and a piece of charcoal in the bottom a cucumber keeps almost as well as in a refrigerator.

DRIED FOODS

The basic keeping time for dried foods such as flour and beans is 6 months. Though pasta, rice, instant coffee, custard powder and packet soups last a year.

Nuts are a special problem. Being oily they can go rancid quite soon in a warm atmosphere. If you have kept nuts for several months always taste them before putting them in a dish — the taste of rancid nuts can overpower anything. Think twice before buying them in bulk.

It is all too easy for biscuit beetles to be introduced into your house in a packet of food and spread like wildfire to all the dry foods in a cupboard. These are also the foods rodents will go for. Even if you think neither will ever visit your house it's a good idea to keep these foods in jars. Bulk buys go nicely into sweet jars — free from sweet shops.

EGGS

Egg Buying

The idea that brown eggs are tastier or better for you is purely an old wives' tale. The only difference is in the type of hen they come from, and all you get for the extra money is the prettiness of a brown egg. Free range eggs are a different matter. Free-ranging hens are likely to have had a better and more varied diet than caged birds and this will make their eggs tastier and more nutritious. Though if their diet has been worse — and it can be — the eggs will be poorer.

Egg Storing

Egg shells are not only one of the most elegant bits of packaging ever created, they even carry an egg preservative in the form of an oily coating. Bacteria can only enter the pores of the egg if this coating is broken down by water. This is why it's a bad idea to wet the fingers — especially with spit — so as to make the eggs easier to hold: a trick some people actually recommend.

Eggs should only be wiped with a damp cloth if they simply cannot be stored as they are. Small flecks of dirt should be wiped off with a dry one, or left on.

Eggs look lovely in baskets and used to be kept that way — in larders. Rustic basketsful in modern kitchens will simply go off faster, however picturesque they look in glossy magazines. In a refrigerator or a larder below 50°F (10°C), they will keep for several weeks, although they need to be away from strong smells which they might absorb. They should rest with the pointed end down because the yolk gradually rises to the top. If the round end is uppermost the yolk sits safely against the air sac instead of sticking to the shell.

As a child I used to help my mother store cheap spring eggs in water-glass for the winter. Now that prices vary little and space is short this is scarcely practical. But it can sometimes be useful to put eggs in store for a few weeks. The simplest method is the old farmhouse one of rubbing lard all over the shell. This preserves them by keeping moisture and carbon dioxide sealed inside the shell. A variation of this method is used commercially in America to extend the shelf life of eggs in the shops during hot summer months. Like this they will last 2–4 weeks in the warm, or 4–6 months in the cold.

Keeping Opened Eggs

If you have cracked more eggs than you intended to, beat a $\frac{1}{4}$ teaspoon of salt or sugar into each egg, and put it in a bowl covered with a lid or cling film. The salt or sugar will stop it coagulating when cold and the egg will keep up to a week in the refrigerator, or can be deep frozen.

A whole egg yolk should be covered with a little water to prevent a hard skin forming. A broken one should have a pinch of salt or sugar beaten in. Either will last 2 days in the refrigerator, closely covered.

Egg whites will last a week closely covered in a refrigerator, but I always find it a delusion to imagine that I will find a use for an odd egg white within that time. Far better to pop it in an ice cube maker and deep freeze it until it's really needed. Once frozen, whites can be turned out and stored in a bag. They will keep 6 months in a deep freeze and still whip if thawed slowly in the refrigerator — though not as well as before.

FISH

Fish Buying
Go to a mediterranean fish market and watch peasant women buying fish and you'll see how it ought to be done. They pull open the gills, turn the fish over and draw a deep breath of its smell. Freshness is everything with fish and the signs to look for are bright eyes, a clear sheen to both sides of a fish, and on round fish a rich red inside the gills. Within 2 days a fish looses its sheen, then the eyes begin to be dull and concave, and the inside of the gills goes a dingy brown. Smell also tells you a lot. A really fresh fish has only a faint hint of it, which grows steadily with age.

Plaice and lemon soles are special exceptions to the rules. They have to be 3 days out of the water before they are eaten. Some people say it's the brightness of their spots which shows their freshness — it isn't. The brightness varies between individual fish of the same age. The tell-tale signs are any hint of sliminess on the underside or a green tinge just below the gills.

Keeping Fish
Lemon soles, from a fishmonger, should be eaten the day they are bought — they will have had their 3 days out of the sea. Other fish will keep 2–3 days in a refrigerator, if you can stand it, because the drawback is that they must be on an open plate, not wrapped up. So the rest of the refrigerator will be fishy. Fresh salmon will keep 4–5 days.

If fish is to be deep-frozen it should be wrapped in foil, not plastic. Foil will prevent the fish becoming dry in the freezer, and unlike plastic, it won't make it sweat and smell as it thaws.

Smoked Fish
A friend of mine was given vacuum-packed smoked salmon and,

imagining the vacuum pack would keep it fresh, put it in her office drawer against a special occasion. When she opened it some weeks later the only 'special' thing about it was the smell. Vacuum packs only keep food for 36 hours, out of a refrigerator.

It is also wrong to imagine that because a fish has been smoked it will keep, like smoked meat, longer than normal fish. It is probably no coincidence that the fish which are smoked are usually oily fish, which on the whole keep less well than others. Originally they were probably smoked to at least give them an equal keeping time. They should be eaten within 3 days if kept in a refrigerator.

FLAPJACKS

How well biscuits store is often a matter of how damp the atmosphere is, as very few tins are really airtight. Some people find that if their flapjacks (the rolled oats type) go soggy in a tin they keep excellently in an earthenware jar.

FRUIT

Storing apples well is partly a matter of knowing your apples. Some will store, some won't, and the length of time they can be kept varies with each variety. Among the popular ones Beauty of Bath and Worcesters won't store: specialist nurserymen will tell you which ones will.

If you plan to store apples, handle them carefully and pad any basket you're gathering them in. They bruise easily, especially on a hot day, and bruised apples will rot.

Opinions vary on whether they should or should not be wrapped in paper for storage. But papered or not, they should never be touching one another. Lay them out with small spaces between them in boxes or on shelves. The store room has to be cool, dark and well ventilated, without being damp. There should also be no strong smells around or the apples will absorb them.

Pears should be stored in exactly the same way as apples, but lying on their sides.

GAME

The season for game runs from August to March, although different forms of game have their own months. Straight from a shoot game birds should be hung by the neck in a cool place just as they are. Those who like a gamey taste usually consider a bird well hung when the feathers just above the tail come out easily. Just how long this will take depends on the weather and the time of year. Early in the season it could be as little as 5 days, but in December it could be 2 weeks. In thundery weather game should be watched very carefully as it can suddenly ripen.

A hare should hang for 5–10 days before it's skinned or gutted.

When buying game the usual sign of a young bird — a pliable breast bone — holds good. On hares look at the ears, they should look thin and young.

Once plucked and gutted a ripe pheasant will only keep for 2 days in the refrigerator, so will a hare. Whereas venison will keep up to 4 days and guinea fowl as long as 5 days.

GRAPES

If a vine flourishes it's easy to have a glut of grapes, but fortunately they store well in a cool place. Cut them with a good piece of stalk and push the stalk into a bottle or jar containing cold water and a little charcoal. Then keep them in the cool until you need them. They should keep several months, and with a little luck give you home-grown grapes for Christmas.

LEMONS

The less air circulates round a lemon the longer it seems to keep. Once cut, put it face down on a saucer and cover it with an inverted glass in a cool place.

LOBSTER

A fresh lobster has a certain spring to its tail. Try pulling down the part which is curled under. If it snaps smartly back it is freshly cooked. After 24 hours the tail starts to become slacker.

A freshly cooked lobster will keep 3 days in a refrigerator.

MACAROONS

Stored by themselves, macaroons soon lose their luscious squishy centre and become dry and biscuity. Prevent this by putting a piece of bread in the tin with them.

MARROW

The popularity of prize marrow competitions seems to have spawned the idea that the bigger the better. In fact marrows are at their best when 8–10 inches long, with skin soft enough to scratch through with a finger nail. At that size they need no white sauce to camouflage them. They are perfect cooked till they have only just lost their crispness and served with no more than butter and a grind of black pepper and parmesan.

MAYONNAISE

Home-made mayonnaise is almost impossible to make in exactly the right amounts. To prevent the part which will be left over going oily, make the mayonnaise in the usual way, then for every 3 yolks in the recipe beat in 2 tablespoons of very hot water.

Mayonnaise should be stored covered in a cool place, not in a refrigerator. But if the choice is between a hot kitchen and a cool refrigerator the refrigerator wins.

MEAT

Buying

Butchers vary greatly in the quality of animal they buy and the care they take in storing and cutting meat. There is no way anyone can buy good meat from a bad butcher. When new in an area, buy something very basic like a lamb chop from each butcher in the district. Cook them all at the same time and see which tastes the best. But don't even bother to buy from one where any of the meat has dry, dark patches or where there is a strong smell of meat as you walk in.

Keeping

It is wise to eat pork within 24 hours of buying. It goes off faster than any other meat and must not be eaten on the turn. Veal also has a short life. Beef and lamb will keep for 2–3 days in the refrigerator. Both will keep best if wiped with vinegar and covered with chopped onion. An even simpler way to keep a slab of meat, such as steak, is to pepper it very liberally on both sides. The onions or pepper can simply be wiped off when you want to cook it. Mince is an exception and must be cooked the day it's bought.

When it's going off raw meat will become slimy on the surface and smell unpleasant. Cooked meat will become dry, smelly and have spots of mould.

MELONS

When a melon is ripe the end opposite the stalk ought to be slightly soft and on some types there will be the beginnings of small cracks round the stem. A good melon will also have a fairly strong smell.

Watermelons are an exception. They have no real smell, no cracks round the stalk and the other end softens very little.

Once ripe, melons go over the hill fast. Even in a refrigerator they seldom keep more than 2 days, and they need to be completely enclosed in plastic or the smell will linger in the refrigerator for days.

MILK

When I was a child, and most homes lacked a refrigerator, milk was stood in a dish of water and a thin cloth, weighted round the edge with beads, was put over it to trail in the water. The cloth soaked up the moisture which evaporated in the breeze and, as evaporation mysteriously uses up heat, this kept the milk cold. It is still an excellent way of keeping anything cool when camping. If the milkman will co-operate the method is equally good for keeping the milk on the doorstep cool till you return from work.

Milk and cream absorb smells so easily that a saucer of milk on one of the shelves is an old cure (not very effective) for a smelly refrigerator. Milk products should be kept covered all the time, and, though it's a small point, opening a foil-topped bottle by pressing the lid with a thumb makes closing easy. Tearing it up from the edges doesn't.

MUSSELS, SCALLOPS, OYSTERS AND FRIENDS

No self respecting mollusc stays open when attacked. So to check if they are fresh, tap them before you cook them. If one fails to close it is dead, dangerous and must be thrown away. (Scallops, however, are sold open.)

Nowadays the old adage about an R in the month no longer holds good. Oysters and most other shellfish can be had all the year round, imported from some part of the globe. However, if you want native British oysters buy between September and February. Native mussels are in the shops from September to November. Eat all shellfish the day you buy them.

MUSTARD

A pinch of salt added to the powder type of mustard when it's made up will help it stay moist and keep its aroma.

OLIVES

The cheapest way to buy olives, and the way to get the best selection, is to buy them loose. Fortunately they store well in a jar of olive oil. Date the jar when you start it and only top it up for the next 9 months, as olive oil only keeps well for a year. After that another jar can be started and the old oil used up in cooking.

ONIONS

Making a plait of one's own home-grown onions is marvellously satisfying, and not too difficult — but it takes time. While an old stocking, well laddered to let in the air, can be filled in no time at all. Hung in a cool place it makes a very good onion store. (This is also a good way to store bulbs.)

PARSLEY AND WATERCRESS

For reasons which escape me, both parsley and watercress are usually sold in quantities which would garnish a banquet, not a meal. So one is left with a rapidly wilting or yellowing remainder. I dread to think of the amount I wasted before I discovered that if you wash them well, shake them dry and put them in a glass jar, with a tight lid, either will keep for more than a week in a refrigerator.

PASTA

If you are able to get freshly made pasta it should be eaten within 24 hours as it moulds very fast.

PATÉ

Shop-bought paté, and prepared meat such as frankfurters, will keep for 3 days in a refrigerator. If it has been out of the fridge, on a picnic, eat it the same day.

PINEAPPLE

The ripeness of a pineapple can be tested by just pulling at one of the outer leaves in the tuft. If it comes out easily the pineapple is ripe. Brown patches show a pineapple is over-ripe.

In a refrigerator it should be kept in a tightly closed bag or there may be pineapple-flavoured milk.

POTATOES

Some varieties of potato are much better for certain dishes than others. Fortunately, waxy potatoes such as Pentland Javelin, Maris Piper and Ulster Sceptre appear in summer and are just right for salads. Floury varieties which suit mashed and jacket potatoes are in the shops from September. For flavour the outstanding new potatoes are those from Jersey, and later in the year Epicure is the kind to look for. If a greengrocer doesn't know what he is selling ask to see the sack — the name will be written on it.

Potatoes need cool dark storage but even then they may try to sprout in spring. This is the time to buy smaller quantities than usual so they can be eaten before they begin to grow.

POULTRY

Buying
Wiggling a bird's breast bone is not something one can do much in these days of deep-frozen supermarket fowls. If a bird isn't frozen it's the sure way to tell if it's young. On young birds the end of the breastbone should be as bendable as the end of your nose. As a bird ages this slowly hardens and turns to bone. Any bird with a firm breastbone is certainly no chicken, though it may be a tasty boiling fowl.

In some parts breastbones are broken to make them seem young. So feel carefully.

Keeping
Poultry goes off easily and should really be eaten the day it's bought even if it is in a refrigerator. It will keep better with a raw onion in the body cavity and a sprinkling of pepper, and with chopped onion over the outside.

In thundery weather poultry can become thunderstruck and turn bad in as little as 2 hours. The first place that a bird shows that it's off is under the wing where it turns greenish.

PRAWNS

Prawns are usually frozen at sea, so they should not be bought and re-frozen. Most fishmongers will sell you the prawns deep-frozen if you ask for them. Once thawed, prawns keep 2 days in a refrigerator.

PRUNES

Old-fashioned dried prunes kept much better than today's juicy ones. The freezer is the best place for juicy prunes if you are keeping them more than a few months.

RABBIT

The young rabbit, like the young hare, will have thin young-looking ears and should not have very horny claws.

Rabbit is a bad keeper. Even in the refrigerator it will only last a couple of days.

SALAMI

The whiter the fat in a salami the fresher it is. It should keep a few months in a refrigerator, but the flavour will be best when it has been out of the fridge for a couple of hours.

SALT

In areas where damp makes the salt clump together, and fail to run, put a few grains of rice with it. The rice will absorb the moisture and keep the salt running freely.

SOFT FRUIT

Left in their punnets soft fruits will often go mouldy within a day. Put carefully into a colander or sieve so the air can get to them, and kept in the fridge, unwashed, they will keep much better. How long that will be depends on how long ago they were picked.

A better way to store currants is to strip them from their stalks and put them in a bowl, well sprinkled with castor sugar. Left like this, in the fridge, they will make their own juice but lose none of their firmness. In fact the perfect way to eat red currants is just like that with thick cream.

Blackberries, on the other hand, lose some firmness after 12 hours if sugared; and raspberries and strawberries soften considerably and are only fit for mousses and fools.

In Italy they use icing sugar when they keep soft fruits like this. It makes a sweeter, more syrupy, juice which some people may prefer, although I find it too cloying.

TEA

Tea tends to pick up moisture and the smell of food around it and needs to be kept in an airtight container away from strong smells. Like this it will last 3–6 months.

Tea's ability to absorb smells can be used to advantage. A few pieces of zest of lemon or orange can be put with China tea to enhance its flavour.

TINNED FOODS

Buying
Baskets of cut-price dented cans may offer a bargain, but you must pick the tin carefully. If the dent is on the seam it may have caused a small air leak which will rot the food inside. If either the top or bottom is domed the contents have gone off already. Tins with rust on them are an equally bad buy. They may already have overrun their shelf life.

Storing
Our forebears knew just how old the food on their shelves was because they had bottled and dated it themselves. The best we can do is to date each can, packet or frozen item as we get it home. That won't mean that it didn't stay too long in the shop but it does make it possible to routinely use the older tin on a shelf, even if a new one has been put in front of it.

Stored in a cool dry place, most tinned foods last 2 years. Prunes, rhubarb, fruit juice, and milky foods only keep a year, and other fruit and potatoes 18 months. The long-lasting foods, to lay by for a siege, are fish in oil and solid packs of meat. Both keep as long as 5 years. Though packs of meat weighing over 2 lb (1 kg) are an exception, for they need refrigeration and last only 9 months.

Once opened, a tin must be emptied out. If food is kept in it there is a slight risk of the coating on the inside of the tin deteriorating and allowing the lead which seals the seam to enter the food.

TOMATOES

Visitors to Italy often marvel at the great trusses of tiny tomatoes they see hanging up in winter. Few seem to realise that an ordinary British tomato, like Moneymaker, will ripen indoors in the winter in just the same way, and keep for months.

Before the frosts pick every green tomato to the very last tiddler, leaving the stalks attached. Those which are bruised or without a stalk won't keep and must go for chutney. The rest can simply be laid out on any broad window ledge and left. Use them as they ripen. I have had tomatoes right through to March this way, and the cherry-sized ones make a lovely garnish for winter salads.

WALNUTS

The traditional way to store walnuts from the tree is to put them in a barrel of sand or salt.

WINE

Buying

There are two approaches to getting good value for money in wine. One is to buy the relatively cheap wine, which some of the discriminating chain stores are offering, designed to be drunk at once. The other is to buy a quality wine and store it. Good wine improves for a number of years, stays at a peak and then declines, so the name of the game is to buy it on the way up, and store it till it reaches its peak, rather than buy it at its best when the price is highest.

Storing

Storing wine is not as difficult as might be imagined. Experts differ, but the fundamental aim is to keep it in conditions which won't trigger sudden changes in it. For this it needs darkness and an even draught-free temperature of about 55°F, but it will tolerate anything between 50°F and 65°F. So a cupboard under the stairs, or the space under the ground floor floor-boards may be fine.

If it cannot be stored correctly good wine should generally be drunk within 4 weeks, though a robust wine might run to 6, depending on the conditions.

Given the right conditions the length of time a wine should keep varies with its type and its year. The weather affects the acidity and tannin content of grapes, and these in turn affect the way it keeps. An ordinary wine from a good year may keep as long as a good wine from a poor year. So anyone who isn't going to become a wine expert needs to cultivate a good wine merchant and take his advice on what to buy and how to store it.

If you lack a good wine merchant the rough rules are these. Not all wine improves with keeping. Plonk stays plonk till Doomsday (or rather, it gets worse). A new Beaujolais is designed for a short life and needs to be drunk within 6 months. After a year you could have pricy vinegar.

Among good wines the typical pattern of a good red Burgundy is 6 years maturing, 6 peak years, and 6 gently declining. Bordeaux takes longer than the same quality from Burgundy. Probably 8 years for a good one, and some may take as long as 15 years.

White wines mature faster and fade faster. A good white Burgundy could be ready in 3 years, half the time of its red counterpart — and only sweet ones, like the famous Château Yquem, develop with real age.

Champagne

How long you keep champagne is a matter of nationality. The French drink it at about 4–5 years old. The British keep it a little longer.

Port

In some families there used to be a tradition of putting down vintage port when a boy was born, ready for him to start drinking when he came of age at twenty-one. For, by a happy chance, port takes 20 years to reach its peak and will last another 30.

Once opened and decanted a vintage port should be finished in 3–4 days. An ordinary port, with the bottle well stoppered, will keep 2–3 weeks after it has been opened.

Yourself

CLOTHES AND SHOES

One of the nicer luxuries in life must be to have a lady's maid or a gentleman's gentleman on hand to press, hang and generally keep one's clothes impeccable. This chapter is for those few millions who, like me, have to rub along without such help. It lets you into some of the secrets of buying, storing and caring for clothes and gives the solutions to those familiar sartorial crises when a zip sticks, dresses refuse to stay on hangers and trouser knees bag unwearably.

BELTS

If you lose the little band which holds the end of a belt down there's no need to be left with it flapping. It can be held flat by tucking a small piece of chewing gum under the end. Even better is that rubbery substance sold to hold posters to a wall.

When a colourless polish is needed for a belt or a handbag you needn't rush out and buy one. Use a pure colourless beeswax furniture polish instead, or apply the mixture given for cleaning leather books (*see* Book Bindings). Rub excess polish off very thoroughly.

BOOTS

Down the years people have used all sorts of mixtures to waterproof tough walking boots. One much used on farms in the past is the following: In a very low oven, or over a pan of boiling water, melt together 2 parts of beeswax to 1 part mutton fat. Mix this well and brush it onto the boots while it is still hot, making sure it gets well into the crack round the welt. Next day wipe off any excess and rub up.

A quicker method is to oil the boots, including the soles, with castor or linseed oil and rub mutton fat into the welt. Oiling the leather soles of heavy boots and shoes in this way is meant both to waterproof them and to extend their life. On the uppers oil also breaks down the hardness of leather which has been in store for some time. These methods are for tough walking boots, of course, not fashion boots.

COLLARS — VELVET

I learnt the hard way that the pile on velvet can mysteriously disappear through being in contact with the metal hook of a coathanger, leaving a line completely bare. To prevent this, sew a rectangle of fabric, preferably the same as the lining material, at the centre back of the neck. This hangs inside the coat when it is worn but can be flipped back over the velvet collar when it is on a hanger. I should add that not all velvet loses its pile, but it isn't something I would want to chance again.

DRY CLEANING SUBSTITUTES

In the days before ubiquitous dry-cleaners housewives had all sorts of ways to get clothes clean. A very popular cleaner was vinegar. A dessert-spoonful in $\frac{1}{2}$ pint (250 ml.) of water will sponge the grease off the collar of a suit or coat and go some way to removing the shine on knees and elbows. Though for shininess a much used remedy in the past was sponging with the water from boiled-up ivy leaves: a treatment which an elderly Welsh woman I know remembers working well on her school clothes. (Ivy water was also used to wash black silk and was said to keep it a better black than any other.) On some clothes water and ammonia was used in the same way as water and vinegar, but the danger here is that the ammonia will shift the dye. These treatments were for old-style heavy pure wool cloth and don't necessarily work so well or so safely on modern cloths.

One treatment that is safe is the one for cleaning a dirty silk blouse or shirt. Sprinkle the dirty areas well with Fullers' Earth, leave the blouse in a plastic bag for several days, then shake thoroughly, getting rid of all the Fullers' Earth. This won't make the blouse as clean as a good dry-clean will, but it will be a good deal cleaner than it was — certainly clean enough to wear if you can't get to a dry-cleaner.

FUR

Buying
Sex is the most important thing with mink — but not for the reasons you might suppose. A peculiarity of the mink is that male pelts are very different from female ones, so a coat is always made of one or the other, never of a mixture of both.

If you can afford it the female pelts are the ones to go for. The fur is silkier, lies flatter, and feels lighter than the male. So a female coat is more comfortable to wear and much more flattering to the figure. Not that it necessarily looks better at first sight. In fact the bushy male fur can look richer off the body. It's when you put it on that the female fur comes into its own. Both sexes will last equally well, but you will pay a premium of some 18–20 per cent for female flattery. If you don't want to look like a dumpy dowager it will be worth every penny.

Though know-alls sometimes ask the sex of other furs, this sex difference is unique to mink. On all other furs the only qualities to look for are the depth and thickness of the fur, and a wise buyer will bend a fur back and see how thick it is near the pelt. Bear in mind that soft furs, from rabbit to millionaires' chinchilla, last far less well than a hard fur like mink. And though white furs may look most glamorous when new, nothing can be done to stop them yellowing with age.

Care
It sounds ridiculous but the counsel of perfection is never to sit on a fur coat and always to wear a silk scarf round the neck to prevent make-up getting on the fur.

Modern furriers use new processes which pare the skin to a bare minimum. Though the furs are lighter and pleasanter to wear they are also more vulnerable than those worn by previous generations. Wet is the greatest enemy. Water should be shaken off as soon as possible and the coat hung in an airy place indoors as soon as possible. Drying a fur near heat could cause skins to distort and crack, so don't be tempted to take a hair dryer to it.

Cleaning
The old method of cleaning light fur by working damp starch into it, leaving it to dry and brushing it out, is not a safe method for today's thinner skins. Working warm bran into dark furs is another old method which is more suited to the old-style furs. Today's furs really need professional cleaning, but even then over-cleaning is bad for them. Once every 2–3 years is enough.

Stains on Fur
Make-up stains are the most common stains on fur. The way to remove them is very gently to work magnesium carbonate, French chalk, or Fullers' Earth into the fur with the fingers. Leave it in for about 30 minutes and gently shake it out. Other stains can be removed by sponging the fur with a clean damp, *not wet*, cloth, working with the lie of the fur.

Storage
The major hazards are moths and woolly bears, so a plastic bag seems

ideal. *It isn't*. Polythene causes fur to gradually dry out, change colour, and split. Instead a fur should be stored in a tightly closed dark-coloured cotton, silk, or linen bag in the busiest cupboard in the house — pests like to be undisturbed. Take it out and inspect it every month. A sign to look for is a tight twist of fur. This means a moth has made a nest for its offspring who will soon emerge onto their dinner. Furriers say putting sachets of lavender in the bag, in the pockets of the coat, and at the neck is as good a moth prevention as moth balls without making the coat unwearably smelly. So the lavender bags of yesterday have obviously been underestimated.

GLOVES

My grandmother taught me that before first wearing a new pair of leather gloves they should be put in a warm place for a while. It's a good idea because the warmth makes the leather more supple so it stretches to the hand without any strain on the stitching.

Of course, this isn't much help if the gloves themselves are a size too small. So her other tip was not to wear gloves for a while when shopping for a new pair. Wearing gloves compresses the hand, making it seem smaller than it really is, so you may be tempted to buy the wrong size.

Cleaning Gloves
There is probably no really safe way of thoroughly cleaning gloves at home, because so much depends on how the leather was dressed, but there are a few ways to make them look better. A careful rub with a very clean India rubber will take some of the dirt off smooth leather, and rubbing white suede gloves through warm flour, with the gloves on your hands, will take some of the greyness off them. If the suede is dark a suede brush can be used, with infinite caution, to restore patches which have become smooth.

That still leaves the problem of gloves which have become unwearably dirty. If you have to wash them one of the safer mixtures is pure soap dissolved in hot milk. If equal parts of milk and water are used to rinse them and they are dried very carefully, away from heat, they may come out well. While they are drying wriggle the leather a little from time to time to stop it drying flat and stiff.

HANGING DIFFICULT NECKLINES

Wide-necked dresses which are likely to have their necks stretched by the weight of the fabric, or to fall off the hanger in a crumpled heap, need extra tape loops. The best support is provided by the method museums use for period costumes. Sew a piece of straight hem binding firmly to the point where the bust dart meets the waist. Put the dress on a padded hanger and pass the tapes over the hanger and down to the waist at the same point at the back, and pin and sew the tapes so they are just short enough to take the weight off the shoulders.

If the neckline is very wide, fix a loop inside each shoulder. It should be just long enough to loop over the hook at the centre and keep the shoulders of the dress on the ends of the hanger. Unfortunately this is only practical if the dress has sleeves, otherwise the loops are likely to show.

HANGING SKIRTS

The loops inside most skirts are better than nothing but they hitch up the side seams and distort the hang of the skirt. This is particularly bad for pleated skirts, as it opens the pleats. If the skirt opens at the back a far better place for the tapes is where some couturiers put them. They attach one end of each tape at a point about a third of the way round the front waistband, the other end a third of the way round the back. The tapes must be long enough to lie neatly along the inside of the waistline at each side when the skirt is on. If there is a central pleat a single loop which will slip over the hook of the hanger and hold the centre, so the pleat hangs perfectly, is a good idea as well. Or you can attach four loops of tape, two of them at the front to take the weight of the pleats, and two at the back in positions to match the front loops. Then you thread the front loops through the back ones (which can be quite small) before slipping them onto a hanger.

HATS

In the days of panama hats and boaters they would be cleaned with lemon juice applied on a soft nailbrush. Sometimes the hat would be left in the sun with the lemon juice on it to bleach, before being wiped with a damp cloth. If you need to get a very dirty hat clean add a drop of washing-up liquid to the lemon juice, but no more than a drop. When a straw hat gets damp it's inclined to shrink so, if you don't have a hat block, it's as well to wear the hat until it dries. I wouldn't recommend cleaning a precious hat like this but it will improve a school hat or an old boater.

If the fabric hat-band inside a hat has become greasy, try rubbing it with warm water containing a good dash of vinegar. This usually removes the grease. If it doesn't, try a drop of hair shampoo on a damp cloth. This

If the worst has happened and someone has sat on a felt hat it may be possible to restore it by gently steaming it on the inside with the steam from a kettle, and then putting it back into shape. Use crumpled tissue paper to keep it in place until it cools. Then brush it with a soft brush, working with the nap of the felt.

LEATHER

Grease is the worst stain you can have on leather handbags and so on, and speed is the first essential. Cover the mark immediately with Fullers' Earth or Talcum powder and leave it on the mark for a day or two. This should absorb some, if not all, of the grease.

I've seen it suggested that the glue for repairing cycle punctures will remove grease from leather. I have tried it. Maybe I used the wrong glue but all it did for me was produce a sticky stain on top of a greasy one.

Clean leather, other than suede, with saddle soap.

MAKING CLOTHES LAST

An old lady I once knew used to say 'One keep clean is better than ten make cleans'. This is horribly true. All forms of cleaning take the life out of clothes, whereas brushing a garment and hanging it carefully after wearing, and leaving it to air overnight, then putting it away for a couple of days to rest before wearing it again, will extend its life considerably. This prevents the dirt from working its way into a garment and gives the fabric time to spring back into its correct shape in places where it was stretched. It is especially true of men's suits.

MARKING CLOTHES

When marking ink has to be used to name clothes or linen it is inclined to spread and blur. This can be prevented by first marking the garment with a soft pencil and then going over this with the ink. On most fabrics this will give a clean line.

A name-tape isn't much help if a child is too young to read. The way round this is to put on the name-tape plus a distinctive button. A small child will recognise the button and put on the right garment. Which saves a lot of bother.

PLASTIC

Belts and other plastic accessories are easily cleaned with soap and water. But when a mark, such as a biro stain, won't come off use methylated spirits. Meths removes biro and some other marks from plastic like magic — but try a test patch first, somewhere inconspicuous, to make sure it won't harm the plastic. Use only a very little on a soft cloth and rinse the place carefully afterwards.

PRESSING

I once had two French students staying with me. With only a handful of clothes apiece they exuded chic in a way I have seldom seen. I am sure one reason was that, to my daily exasperation as I tried to make breakfast, they would never don anything without pressing it first. So every garment looked like new. Careful pressing always pays dividends.

First-class army batmen have the best pressing technique of all. They first press the garment with a damp cloth over it and then they iron it through brown paper. The paper absorbs the moisture which the damp cloth put in, and by drying out the fabric it makes it hold the pressing far better.

Even if you don't want to go to that much trouble it's still more effective to use a cloth than a steam iron. It also avoids the risk of scorching the fabric or putting an unwanted shine on it by rubbing with the iron.

Pressing Bagginess
Ideally, of course, bagginess would never occur in the seats of skirts or the knees of trousers because the wearers would always remember to hitch the garments up before sitting down, and would never wear them long enough to cause a real problem. But life is not like that.

On trousers the most effective way to remove looseness of the knee is to put the inside of the front of a leg uppermost, lay a well damped cloth over it and press it with a fairly hot iron until the cloth is flat. Then re-iron with brown paper under the iron. When both legs are done they can be turned to the right side and the same procedure followed to put in the creases. For a knife-edge crease place a piece of natural pine over the crease just where it has been ironed and let it cool before moving to the next bit. The method for skirts is basically the same.

Pressing Lapels
The fold of a lapel, on tailor-made suits for both sexes, is designed to be a

gentle roll, not a sharp crease. So lapels of such suits should be opened out for pressing, not pressed down flat against the jacket. The reason why so many suits are sold with flat lapels is simply that mass manufacturers use pressing machines and so find it cheaper and quicker to make them that way. No good tailor ever does so.

Pressing Pleats

I have often seen pleats pressed so the underfold leaves an unsightly line on the surface, which seems rather a waste of all the work that went into the pressing. The way to avoid this indentation, on pleats of all sorts, is to slip a piece of thin cardboard into the underside of the pleat, covering the underfold. The material is then pressed onto the flat cardboard, and the straight edge of the cardboard can be used to ensure a perfectly straight pleat.

If a pleated skirt or shirt is to be packed for travelling, or stored for any length of time, two *loose* tacking stitches in a big X at the bottom of each pleat will hold it in place perfectly. The X should be sewn the moment the pleat is pressed. There's no need to finish it off, just leave a long end for easy removal. This may sound a lot of bother but when filming abroad I found it much less trouble than finding a good presser in a strange hotel — and then wondering if the garment would be returned in time for the deadline.

PULLOVERS

If you don't have the nice little gadget which removes the balls of rubbed-up wool from pullovers, a wire suede brush used very, very gently works. So does an electric razor, provided you hold the surface of the jumper absolutely flat.

When a pullover is destined for heavy wear it's far quicker and easier to put a leather patch on each elbow when it's new than when it is thin and stretched out of shape.

SCHOOL TROUSERS

It is wild optimism to suppose that any small boy will wear trousers for any length of time without going through the knees. The one way to lengthen the life of the knees is to glue a patch inside the front of each knee before any wear takes place.

SHOES

Smelly Shoes

Bicarbonate of soda has an amazing ability to remove smells. Sprinkle a teaspoon of bicarbonate of soda into each shoe and shake it all over the inside and by morning even the foulest shoes will smell almost like new.

Shoe Shopping

It is a curious fact that few people ever leave a shop with the pair of shoes they went in to try on. This may be due to the fickleness of human nature, but it is more likely to be a failure to follow the golden rule of shoe shopping. This is — always try on the first pair of shoes once more after trying on the others. The reason for this is that coming in from the street the first pair which is tried on almost always seems tight. The longer you sit in the shop and the more shoes you try on the more rested your feet are, and the more used to the tightness of new shoes.

Canvas Shoes

Canvas shoes seem to be dust magnets and get tatty faster than any others. Brushing them after each wearing stops the dirt working into the cloth. This is worthwhile because they don't always respond well to deep cleaning. If they have to be thoroughly cleaned a light scrub with mild washing-up liquid in tepid water is best. They need to be wetted as little as possible and dried quickly away from strong heat — for example, not too close to a fan heater or hair dryer set on low. If they get too wet or dry too slowly they are liable to shrink and yellow.

Driving Shoes

Like everyone, I always knew driving in high heeled shoes was bad for them. However, I thought it was because it rubbed the leather. What I didn't know till my shoe-mender took me to task, was that the main damage was in straining the shank, which could cause the heel to come off.

Patent Leather

The trouble with patent leather shoes is that they are very prone to drying and cracking. Cleaning them often with creamy milk or with vaseline is the way to prevent this — and far better than branded cleaners. If the shoes are already dry, leave the vaseline on for a while before rubbing it off. As they easily develop lines they need to be kept in shape with shoe trees, or with balls of paper in the toe and a springy stick from toe to heel.

Shoe Polishing

There are two types of shoe polish now on the market — wax and silicone. Wax is the better of the two. It gives a deeper shine and is better at keeping out the wet. Top shoe repairers say the commonest fault they see is putting on too much polish and taking off too little. The easiest way to prevent this is to use the same brush for putting on and taking off. I know it sounds odd, but it is a great incentive to use only a little polish — and a lot of Britain's top shoes are done this way. Some polishes come up most easily when polished immediately, others when left to dry overnight. It is a question of experimenting. What I wouldn't recommend to anyone is the exhausting army method of literally boning the shine up.

If the polish in a tin has become hard and cracked all you need do is put the opened tin over boiling water and it will return to normal.

Salt-stained Shoes

The white salt stains which appear on shoes when the roads have been salted in winter are extremely hard to remove —and the treatment is risky. But salt stains are so unsightly it can sometimes be worth trying. Mix a mild washing-up liquid with an equal amount of white spirit and enough water to make a creamy emulsion (say 1:1:4) Work this over the entire shoe, giving extra attention to the salt line, before rinsing and drying gently. This will remove the polish and, with luck, the stain.

The shoe can be repolished when it is totally dry. Unfortunately the salt may come through again if it has burnt into the entire thickness of the leather, as it often has. No treatment can do more than remove the surface salt.

Squeaky Shoes

In a man's shoes the commonest cause of squeaking is friction between the two layers of a leather sole. Oiling the soles well with linseed oil several times should cure the squeak when the oil reaches the point of friction. The oil will also extend the life of the soles — but carpets should be avoided for a while.

When a woman's shoe squeaks it usually means the metal arch support that forms part of the sole has worked loose. Fixing it is a job for a skilled shoe mender.

Shoe Storing

When I was a child we used to ask people the riddle: 'What flies high, flies low, has no feet and wears shoes?' To our delight nobody ever solved it. The bit that always foxed people was 'wears shoes', because the answer was 'Dust'. It does wear them too, in the sense of wearing them out. In fact nothing could be worse for shoes than their usual home loose at the bottom of a cupboard. Far better to take advantage of the fact that shoe shops give away the best container for the clothes they sell. If shoes are cleaned after use, and put away with shoe trees in the box they came in, they will stay in perfect condition for years. Stored in a plastic bag they may develop mould marks which are virtually impossible to remove.

Suede Shoes
It's very important to brush suede in only one direction, and lightly, or it will feather and look shaggy. Once suede is shaggy there's little that can be done to improve it. Shiny matted suede is different: rubbing it gently in one direction with a fairly coarse sandpaper will often bring it up.

Tight Shoes
New shoes which are slightly tight can be made very much easier by warming them before putting them on, to give the leather more stretch.

If there isn't time for that, try putting them on, taking them off and putting them on again. It sounds silly, but for some reason they always feel easier the second time.

Shoes which have a place that really pinches need other treatment. Hold the shoe so the inside of the part that needs stretching is over the jet of steam from a kettle. When it is just warm rub it into shape with the round end of a broom handle or the bowl of a spoon. Then either wear the shoes or pack them very tightly with newspaper to hold the stretch. Don't boil your shoes. Warm-foot heat is all you need.

STOCKINGS

A lot of people tell me that freezing nylons beside the ice cubes, then thawing them and dripping them dry makes them last twice as long. Not so for me — but if you don't have a cat, freezing could work for you.

At one time women soaked their silk stockings in water in which bran had been steeped to prolong their life. Though if they wanted a good fit they used a soaking in vinegar and water instead.

ZIPS

If the problem is the zip itself, and not a piece of cloth caught in the underside, all you have to do is rub the teeth of the zip very thoroughly with the graphite of a soft lead pencil. On dark fabric it is even easier to puff a little powdered graphite on the jammed part.

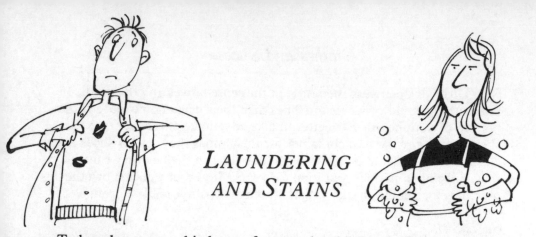

LAUNDERING
AND STAINS

Today the steamy kitchens of my early childhood, filled with the pervasive smell of boiling sheets and the creaking of the mangle, seem like another world. A world I, for one, am glad to be free from. But the freedom is less complete than one supposes. Modern detergents and stain removers are not always the panaceas they are cracked up to be and, for all the blessings of man-made fabrics and washing machines, special items still need to be hand washed, difficult stains treated, and tricky fabrics ironed. Of course in an ideal world one would simply hand such problems to an expert laundry or dry cleaner and leave it to them. Unfortunately there are more laundries and dry cleaners than there are experts to staff them, so using any but the most reliable can be more an act of faith than of wisdom.

When such expertise isn't to hand the best solution, like it or not, is to tackle the problem oneself. In this chapter I have brought together some of the most useful bits of know-how which were second nature to the women who toiled over those steaming coppers of my childhood, and added some of the techniques which are used by top launderers and dry cleaners. For cleaning, being a craft, has resisted the adoption of new methods for their own sake and many professional methods would hardly have surprised a Victorian, and can easily be used in the home.

LAUNDERING

ANTI-FREEZE

The trouble with hanging washing out in frosty weather is that if the wind whips it when it's frozen the threads may be so brittle they snap. A couple of tablespoons of salt in a basin of water for the last rinse will stop it freezing and prevent this.

BOILING

The smell of boiling linen has to be one of the nastiest smells ever to pervade a home. If whites *have* to be boiled, putting a few left-over halves of squeezed lemon in the water will reduce the smell and help to bleach the whites at the same time.

CORDUROY

Put corduroy into a washing or dry-cleaning machine, and the chances are it will pick up every bit of fluff which is loose in them. The way to avoid this is simply to turn corduroy inside out before putting it in the machine — as a clothes-conscious Frenchman taught me. Iron it on the wrong side, too.

DAMASK

Double damask dinner napkins figure more in tongue twisters than in everyday life. But if they *are* needed the secret of immaculate damask is to iron it very damp indeed with a rather hot iron. It then comes out marvellously crisp and smooth and a far cry from the flabby stuff which ironing it too dry produces. White damask can take a hot wash.

DAMPING

Steam irons are an asset, but on most fabrics a thoroughly dried-in crease needs more moisture than even the best can produce. There is really nothing to beat the old system of damping and rolling up each item and leaving it for a few hours. It halves the work of ironing and gives far better results. If you're in a rush hot water spreads faster than cold and using a houseplant sprayer makes the clothes evenly damp but not so wet you can't, at a pinch, wear them straight after ironing.

DYE RUNNING

There's no telling which dyes will run and which won't, so it's a good plan to wash a new garment by itself. Test its fastness by using water as hot as the fabric will stand. The worst culprits are red, blue and purple. Indian fabrics run more easily than European ones, and silk of any sort can spell trouble. Clothes stained by others should be re-washed at once.

There is no way of making a loose dye so fast it can safely be washed in a machine with other clothes. What can be done is to soak it in salt water, using a tablespoon of salt to each pint (500 ml). This will at least make the dye fast enough to prevent serious fading.

EMBROIDERY

Old embroidery may be very fragile, and certain old dyes are very unstable. It is worth getting advice from a museum before attempting to clean it. Given the right support for the fabric a solitary dry clean in a coin-operated machine might be better than a careful wash.

Modern embroidery just needs pure soap and gentle handling. If marks show from the transfer ink, methylated spirits will remove them, but check that it won't also remove the dyes from the yarn. The less embroidery is handled in washing the less the chance of displacing the stitches, so soaking in warm soapy water is the answer. Then press the water through it with a sponge.

Cut the risk of dye running by lying it out flat to dry. Iron it, while still rather damp, face down on a thick towel covered with a sheet. If there is any open work cover it with white tissue paper or, no matter how careful you are, the iron will catch in it.

EXTRA DIRTY WASHING

Shirts and sheets teenagers have forgotten to change, overalls, and greasy washing of all kinds come clean more easily the old fashioned way. Before washing just soak them overnight in hot water containing half a cup of ammonia to each gallon (4 l). Unfortunately this is less help with muddy dirt, and ammonia has a tendency to fade coloureds, so it's a method best kept for the white wash.

The way to deal with extra dirty patches and the grime on collars and cuffs is to rub a moistened cake of soap on the place a short time before putting the garment in the wash.

FADED COLOURS

Some fading isn't fading at all. What has happened is that at each wash a little of the soap has been left in and this has gradually clouded the colour. Try rinsing 'faded' clothes in water with a good dash of vinegar in. This can sometimes get rid of the soap and bring the colour back.

The same treatment can be used on black clothes which have developed a whitish bloom and on nylon which has gone that nasty greyish yellow. A build-up of soap is often the cause in both cases.

FRINGED SHAWLS

Water puts the devil into the threads of fringes. Even the most careful wash can produce an appalling tangle to tease out and press — and even then it may never look the same again. The way professional finishers avoid this is to tie the tassels together in small groups. Either bind them with thread or use small strips cut from old nylons.

When washing the shawl, carefully squeeze the soap through each bundle in turn or they will stay dirtier than the rest of it. Lay it out flat to dry with the bundles undone and carefully smoothed in place. All this may seem very laborious, but having washed a fringe the seemingly lazy way I can assure you it makes far more work in the end than this does.

GLAZED CHINTZ

At one time housewives would stir the starch water with the end of a candle to give a slight waxy gloss to the fabric. The following recipe for treating glazed chintz takes that one stage further. It is said to work very well. Having washed the curtains or covers add 4 oz (125 g) of white wax to 2 pints (1 l) of very soapy clean water. Add an equal amount of starch water and immerse the chintz in the mixture. Press the water through the fabric very well before wringing or spin drying it. Iron it while it is still very damp, ironing on the right side, to bring up the shine.

HANDKERCHIEFS

Grandma knew what she was at when she put handkerchiefs to soak overnight in warm salty water. The salt loosens the mucus and allows the wash to make them thoroughly clean. Use a tablespoonful of salt to each pint (500 ml) of water.

IRONING

In the days before irons had thermostats there was a sure way to test the heat — you spat on it. As a child I quickly learnt to tell the heat by the speed at which the spit fizzled up. It is still a useful knack to acquire for when the thermostat breaks or a travelling iron lacks that refinement.

Ironing is faster with the heat reflected back into the fabric. Putting a sheet of aluminium foil under the ironing cover and its pad achieves this cheaply.

LACE

Lace varies so much in age and fragility there is really no easy rule of thumb on how to treat it, except that it should never be rubbed or wrung.

Lace in good condition can have the suds gently pressed through it by hand. More fragile lace, which won't entangle, can be put in a closed container of soapy water and gently shaken. Very fragile lace, or lengths liable to tangle, should be spread out on a board covered with a sheet of polythene, covered with a layer of net and cleaned with suds on a soft brush.

Whatever the method, let lace soak for ten minutes before washing it and use pure soap, not detergents. For fine old lace distilled water should be used at every stage.

After rinsing pat out the excess water with a towel and very gently pull it into shape and dry it flat. If it needs to be pinned into shape lay it on softboard covered with polythene and slip stainless steel pins into the spaces between the threads, never into the threads themselves.

Lace Stiffening

Lace always used to be stiffened with gum arabic rather than starch, and it gives better results. A typical solution is $\frac{1}{2}$ a pint (250 ml) of boiling water poured on 1 oz (30 g) of gum arabic. Stir this until the gum arabic dissolves and allow it to cool before putting in the lace. The strength can be varied to suit the lace you are stiffening. Iron under tissue paper.

Tinting Lace

A friend of mine has a beautiful blouse in soft pinkish cream silk trimmed with deep cream lace. It looks exquisitely expensive but is in fact an old white silk blouse she bought at an Oxfam shop. The secret of its marvellous colour is that she used the old way of tinting lace and steeped the blouse in tea. Coffee can be used in the same way and both tend to tint the fabric an attractively different shade to the lace. Of course, neither tint is fast — but then re-tinting is so easy this is no great problem.

LACE OR NET CURTAINS

If the curtains are large or the sunlight has weakened them the great danger is that washing will reduce them to shreds. The best way to guard against this is to use the technique which museums employ on fragile fabrics. This is to fold the curtain very carefully into a manageable square or rectangle and use long tacking stitches to sew all the layers together before washing.

Soak the curtains overnight in warm soapy water to loosen the dirt and keep the bundle as flat as possible when washing it. Just press the water through without rubbing or twisting it, and add a tablespoon or so of salt to the final rinse to give the net back some of its original crispness.

Nylon curtains often dry best if they are rehung while very damp and gently pulled into shape in the window. Lace, on the other hand, dries best laid flat on clean grass in the shade. If you've no grass to lay it on, place it evenly over a line with the line running down its length. Iron the curtain with a cool iron, placing tissue paper over to stop the lace catching on the iron.

LINEN

Linen has an undeservedly bad name for being hard to iron, because once it is too dry no amount of steaming or spraying will bring out the creases. The secret is to iron it so damp it's almost wet. It will then come up perfectly with a very hot iron, with no trouble at all.

Unless the dye is loose, linen can take a hot wash and is actually stronger when wet than when dry.

LOOSE COVERS

Ideally the material for loose covers should be shrunk before being made up, but life isn't always like that. If it hasn't been, soak and wash the covers in warm water, rather than hot, half dry them and put them on the chairs while still quite damp, then iron. That way they may become tight covers but at least they won't end up smaller than the chairs.

RINSING

Granny knew a thing or two when she used to put a good dash of vinegar in the last rinsing water. The acid in the vinegar helps to rid the clothes of the alkaline soap. So much so that it can even be put in the washing machine instead of fabric softener. At the same time it gives a slight crispness to silk and similar fabrics. I remember when I was a child a little vinegar was always used to rinse hair ribbons so they would stand up nicely in bows.

SHIRT IRONING

In the days when families were large, and drip dry shirts weren't even a gleam in the eye of the inventor, knowing the fastest way to iron a shirt was a necessity. It is still a very useful skill and the art is in the order of the ironing.

With the shirt unbuttoned this is: the collar, ironing from the points towards the centre to avoid corner creases; the shoulder yoke, if there is one; the cuffs and each side of the flattened sleeves, taking the underarm to the cuff as an edge whether the seam is there or not; the back; then each front.

To fold it, button it up, lie it on its front and fold the edges inwards in the usual way. Turn it over and touch up the upper part of the front and the folded down collar, if they need it — though they won't if you've handled it carefully.

A blouse follows the same order but the sleeves shouldn't be ironed flat.

For packing, lay tissue paper on the back before folding, to avoid sharp creases.

SILK

Washing
The washability of silk varies enormously. The first thing to listen for is a rustle. It is likely to mean the silk is 'weighted' with a dressing and must be dry-cleaned. Texture is also a clue. Most flat silks wash well but those with any special texture should usually be dry-cleaned. Crêpe de chine falls somewhere in the middle. With the right expertise it can be washed but it will wrinkle and shrivel at the drop of a hat. At the same time white crêpe de chine may be yellowed by repeated dry-cleaning. It can be a Hobson's choice.

The other pitfall is that the dye may not be fast even if the fabric is washable. Test the dye by damping an inconspicuous part of the garment then ironing it on a piece of white material. If no dye comes out on the white material the dye is fast enough to wash.

If you go ahead with washing, use pure soap in warm water and be careful not to wring or rub. High temperatures and strong chemicals — such as bleach — can do great damage to silk and must never be used.

On the last rinse put $\frac{1}{2}$ cup of white vinegar in for each gallon (4 l) of water. It will give the silk what the cleaning trade delightfully calls 'scroop' — a certain crispness. This is one of the age-old methods which professionals still swear by when the rest of us have forgotten it was ever used.

Ironing
Silk is impossible to iron well unless it is evenly damp all over. The trouble is it never dries evenly. The way round this catch 22 is to let it dry completely then put it in a plastic bag with 2–3 tablespoons of water, to an average shirt. Leave the bag closed overnight and in the morning it will

be evenly damp all over and iron like a dream. If you can't iron it the next morning don't leave it more than 24 hours in the bag or it will probably get mildew and the stains may be impossible to remove. Even so, for unpatterned or colour-fast silk this is a far less risky form of damping than spraying or steam ironing because either will leave water marks on some silks.

Shantung is the exception to this. It needs to be ironed when bone dry as damp ironing can mark it.

SMELLY CLOTHES

Second-hand clothes may look good but smell alien, and neither cleaning nor stain-removal totally remove this smell. However, deodorant does. Rub a roll-on deodorant directly onto the area and leave it to soak for a while before rinsing it off. A heavy smell may need several applications but it should gradually come out unless it is in a lined and interlined garment, such as a man's jacket, which will be impossible to clear. The only problem with this treatment is that manufacturers can change the composition of their deodorants so what works safely today may create a stain tomorrow. My tests suggest Mum is *currently* both safe and effective — but do a test patch whatever the fabric or deodorant.

SOAKING

Some washing powders make great claims for their powers and emphasise that after an overnight soak with them dirt and stains will come out like magic. The truth is that an overnight soak in any reasonable soap powder will do the same — it's not the powder but the soaking that does it.

STARCH

It's a pity old fashioned powdered starch is so little used. It gives a far better and more versatile finish than spray starch, and for a fraction of the cost. And, unlike the spray variety it doesn't give a lethal sheen to the floor under the ironing board. Just use as directed on the packet.

If some salt is added to the starch or it is stirred with a wax candle the garment will have a glossier finish, and adding a little glycerine stops the starch sticking to the iron.

SUN BLEACHING

At old houses one can sometimes find lawns surrounded by box or yew hedges which are called 'the bleaches'. In the old days the household linen was boiled and laid out on these lawns to bleach in the sun. Sun is still a good bleach — when there is any. Put the wash out with the soap still in it and let it dry well in the sun before rinsing and putting it out in the sun to dry again.

TIES

Ties should be regarded as a minefield. The colours are often loose, the fabric is usually bias-cut and liable to twist irreversibly when wet, and the interlining is prone to shrinking, twisting and wrinkling. Which should be enough to convince anyone that ties are best left to professional cleaners. But if a tie has to be cleaned at home there are a few basic precautions. Run a line of tacking stitches right round the edge to hold the layers together. Try any spot treatment on the centre back of the tie to check the dye reaction, and when pressing into shape slip a piece of cardboard up the inside to stop the imprint of the underseam coming out on the front.

VELVET

Velvet cannot be ironed on an ordinary ironing board if you lack a special pressing pad. The only way to smooth it is to improvise. A classic improvisation is to hold the creased part stretched tight in front of the steam from a kettle, with the wrong side to the steam. Another is to damp the back and draw it across an iron. Now that we have hair dryers and fan heaters they can also be played on the damped and stretched back of this difficult fabric.

WASHING MACHINE OVERFLOW

The quickest way to kill the suds from an overflowing machine is to put a large dollop of fabric softener, or vinegar, into the machine. Either will neutralise the chemicals which create the suds.

WOOL WASHING

Although the three enemies of wool are heat, rubbing, and wet, careful washing is actually better for pullovers than dry-cleaning. For the best results dissolve pure soap in hot water then add enough cold to make it cooler than the hands. Soak the pullover in this for 10 minutes and then press it against the bottom of the basin until it's clean and rinse it in equally cool water. Putting a teaspoonful or so of glycerine to each quart (1 l) of water in the last rinse will leave the wool wonderfully soft, and will even improve acrylics.

It's important to get the wet out of wool immediately and a machine spin is undoubtedly the best way to do this. Putting it through an old fashioned mangle, between two towels, is the next best — but I haven't seen a mangle in years. So failing a machine, towel wringing may be the only answer. It's a method I learnt on a farm long before washing machines were common. Lay the garment flat on a large towel. Turn one of the long edges of the towel in and roll it to make a long swiss roll. If two people each hold opposite ends of the towel and twist in contrary directions until no amount of effort will twist the towel any tighter the water will be well wrung out. You might think this method would twist the jumper out of shape. It doesn't because the towel holds it in place.

If a jumper is too wide and too short, hang it up to dry — it should stretch nicely. If it isn't, don't hang it but lie it flat on a towel until the worst of the damp has dried out.

When the time comes to hang it up an inflatable hanger is best. Failing that, thread a stocking through the jumper from the end of one sleeve to the other. Peg the stocking to the line at each end and where it comes up through the neck. This avoids the marks from hard hangers or from pegs, either of which would stay till the next wash.

Men, whose girl friends have failed to leave their stockings behind, can slip a thin shirt in the jumper just as if it were being worn under it, and pin the shirt to the line.

The less wool is pressed the better. If it has to be, then put a cloth between the iron and the sweater, and keep the iron temperature low.

STAINS

SOME GENERAL POINTS

Most stains come out if you act fast enough, many don't if you don't.

There are not many occasions on which I would recommend people to abandon good manners and even modesty, but the moment when a friend spills tea on your carpet, or a waiter knocks red wine down your front, is not the time to smile politely, sit tight, and say it doesn't matter. I tried that once and my furniture has the stain to prove it. Immediate action is what is needed. Of course, people may feel uncomfortable at the sight of someone taking instant action, but in the long run it is a lot less embarrassing for them than knowing they have ruined something.

The first thing to do is get rid of any excess. Press up under the stain with a clean white cloth while scooping solids up with a spoon or dabbing liquids with a second white cloth. I emphasise white because it is easy to grab the first thing to hand, as I once did a red napkin, only to find that it ran. As my luck goes the dress was cream.

Stains must never be rubbed, only dabbed. Movement across the surface of the fabric can damage the structure of the threads, leaving a permanent mark even after the stain itself has been removed. So dodge companions who want to rub away helpfully.

The best course is to get the garment to a first class dry-cleaner while the stain is still damp, and tell him what the stain is. If this means taking a dress off and crossing town to a dry-cleaner in only a coat, it can be worth it if the dress is a favourite — though this could be tricky in summer. Failing that, keep the stain damp and isolate it carefully from the rest of the garment until you can get it to a cleaner. If you can't get it to a cleaner, or the stain is on furnishing, it is often possible to remove the stain at home. Treat carpets like wool or acrylic fabrics.

How to remove a stain

Stain removing is as much a matter of patience as of know-how. Most substances which rapidly shift stains shift dyes equally fast, so it is always worth trying a gentle, slow-working remover first and gradually escalating the treatment. But some gentle treatments can take a day to work.

Whatever is being applied, put a clean white pad under the stain and keep renewing it as the stain loosens. If the stain is right through the material, work with the wrong side uppermost. Then dab the stain-remover onto the mark with the fingertips or clean cotton wool or a rag, and gently tap it through it *again and again*. This is what the trade calls tamping, and explains why impeccable dry-cleaning can be expensive.

Either hot or cold water can set stains permanently, so whenever water is used it should be lukewarm, though there are special exceptions.

Treatments cannot be neatly divided into those for washable fabrics and those for 'dry-clean only'. Sometimes the only possible treatment is water-based and fortunately most dry-clean fabrics are fairly tolerant of limited amounts of cool water. If they weren't rain would cause more trouble than it does, but *see* Be Warned. After spot-removing, any wet must completely dry out before dry-cleaning or the fabric may felt, but stain removal is normally only the first stage in cleaning the whole garment as it will usually leave a cleaner patch.

BE WARNED

Proprietory Cleaners
Using proprietory cleaners can leave what cleaners picturesquely call a 'sweal' — a round mark which can be difficult or impossible to remove. Always feather the edges as you work.

Methylated Spirits and Friends
Methylated spirits, lighter fuel and other spirits can shift some dyes and cause sweals. They should only be used with great care after testing them on an inconspicuous place. Besides affecting dyes, they may harm the fabric itself if it contains cellulose acetate, as many fabrics such as Tricel do.

Acetone
Acetone will remove certain stains but the price could be high. It melts cellulose acetate fibres, and these aren't just found in the obvious fabrics such as Dicel, Tricel and Tricelon. Dab acetone on some pin-striped suiting and you could have a stripe without the pin. The fine line in what seems like pure wool suiting is often cellulose acetate. Amyl acetate, from most chemists, will remove the same stains without this hazard.

Bleach and Friends
Bleach, hydrogen peroxide and ammonia are all able to fade fabrics, and need careful testing somewhere where a mark won't show. Bleach is the worst offender, and is also very bad for wool and cellulose acetate fibres.

Problem Fabrics
There are some fabrics on which home-cleaning should never be attempted. Among the commonest are lurex, taffeta, silk chiffon, silk jersey, watered silk, brocade and velvet (except acrylic velvet and cotton velveteen). Plus any silk which has a rustle, as it may be tin-weighted and thus need professional care.

BALLPOINT

The oxides in ballpoint pens vary with the manufacturer. Some makes are far harder to remove than others. The choice of treatments is soap, milk, hair lacquer or methylated spirits. Soap is by far the safest. Simply rub a block of moistened white toilet soap over the mark and press the soap through the stain with the fingertips till it starts to shift, and rinse with lukewarm water. Hair lacquer can work miraculously, especially on man-made fabrics, but may create its own stain. Milk, the hotter and sourer the better, works well but slowly. Methylated spirits is faster but can shift some dyes. (For red ballpoint see Ink.)

BEETROOT

Wipe the stain with a damp cake of soap, moisten it with a few drops of ammonia, and tamp this through the stain till it loosens. Rinse with lukewarm water. If this fails some people swear by gin or vodka.

BLOOD

Blood is one of the few stains which breaks the luke-warm water rule. The albumen in blood is most easily broken down by cold salty water. Used while the blood is wet it will come out without a murmur, but dry stains are more resistant. Fabrics which cannot be soaked can be tamped with the same solution plus, if necessary, a drop of household ammonia. Wash in cold water until the stain has completely gone.

CHEWING GUM

The best way to remove chewing gum is to hold the back of the fabric over the steam from a kettle until the gum is soft enough to be pulled off. Pick off the tiny remnants with tweezers. Alternatively make the gum hard and brittle by holding a lump of ice over it, or if the fabric is tough enough, put the garment in a freezer. On velvet or corduroy the pile is very likely to come off with the gum, so only the steam method can be used, and used with great care. A perfect result may be impossible.

CHOCOLATE

If tamping with lukewarm water and soap fails to shift chocolate stains, soaking them in glycerine should do the job.

EGG

If the dye is fast the best treatment for this is old-fashioned household ammonia, but if there is any risk of the dye running use $1\frac{1}{2}$ teaspoonfuls of borax in $\frac{1}{2}$ pint of water (250 ml).

FATS AND OILS

To suggest cleaning oil with oil sounds odd but it works. The best way to remove heavy motor oil is to use Oil of Eucalyptus or, failing that, dripping. Either will break down the heavy oil to a point where other cleaners can remove it. Just tamp either well into the stain and leave it for an hour, or until it's thoroughly softened. Then tamp it out with soap and water. If there is a choice of drippings use a thin one, such as chicken fat.

Ordinary grease and fat can be largely drawn out by covering the stain with Fullers Earth, light magnesium carbonate, or at a pinch, talcum powder, and leaving it for a day. On washable fabrics the mark can be finished off by tamping it with moist toilet soap, leaving it overnight and then washing it. Which is, incidentally, the best way to deal with greasy collars and cuffs. On 'dry-clean only' fabrics the stain can be tamped with methylated spirits or lighter fuel (*see* Be Warned, page 153).

FRUIT

Although the dark fruits are the ones which seem harmful, even lemon juice can stain, so it is worth treating any fruit stain immediately. Don't believe those who say it should be covered with salt or damp bread: neither will do much good. The possible treatments are tamping with white vinegar — especially on non-washable fabrics — with hot milk, or with $1\frac{1}{2}$ teaspoonsful borax in $\frac{1}{2}$ pint (250 ml) water. Turpentine is especially good for blackcurrant stains.

What cleaners often use is alternate tamping with a drop of household ammonia then with a drop of hydrogen peroxide (use 20 vols diluted with 70 parts water), over and over again. But this is the method most likely to affect the dye, so it's wise to try the other ways first.

Another blockbuster method, to try when others fail or a stain has set in through incorrect washing, is to stretch the cloth very tightly across a heat proof vessel and pour boiling water through the stain from a great height.

GLUE

The temptation with glue is just to say 'don't get it on anything', because the enormous range of chemicals used make it a cleaning nightmare. Nothing which can be bought over the counter will remove the hard permanent glues safely, and even the products dry-cleaners use can only be used on absolutely pure cotton, silk or wool. Some of the softer glues respond to amyl acetate or lighter fuel or methylated spirits, which carry risks on certain fabrics. Failing those, and with even greater risk, a paint stripper like Nitromores may work.

Many glue manufacturers make special solvents for their own glues and should be able to advise on the effect they will have on fabrics.

GRASS STAINS

Grass stains should come out with a bit of patience if they are rubbed between the finger and thumb with moist toilet soap. Tamping glycerine through the stain is also safe and effective, and so is methylated spirits on some dry-clean only, fabrics. If there is a shortage of time or patience, a soak in a mild bleach solution should cure white cottons.

HAIR LACQUER

It is safer to spray on hair lacquer before dressing as it can stain some fabrics. Anything washable can be tamped with $1\frac{1}{2}$ teaspoonfuls of borax in $\frac{1}{2}$ pint of water (250 ml).

INK

Ink isn't a problem, it is at least two problems. Red ink usually contains an eosin dye which is a devil to get out, whereas blue ink is comparatively easy, unless it is indelible.

Blue Ink et, almost, al
Milk may sound an unlikely solvent for such a heavy stain as ink but it works miraculously on all colours except red. It should be either hot or sour — the hotter or more sour, the better. An inky handkerchief can simply be boiled in it for the quickest results; more fragile items should be soaked or tamped in the hottest milk they can stand. Salt and lemon juice will also shift some brands, while others vanish before ammonia.

Red Ink and Indian Ink
Red ink is very prone to spreading, so great care needs to be taken. The first weapon should be ammonia, tamped on and sponged out, or alternate tamping with ammonia and moist toilet soap. If that fails, and the dye will stand it, tamp with methylated spirits, or *in extremis* with hot methylated spirits, *heated over a flameless heat*.

156

Ink on Carpets

Ink on carpets or thick piles should be *immediately* sprinkled with salt to absorb the excess. When the salt has taken up the ink, brush it off carefully and treat the carpet with one of the above treatments, remembering that carpet dyes are very easily shifted. Milk must be well shampooed off afterwards or it will turn sour and smelly.

Felt Pen Ink

The ink from felt pens should come off if the stain is treated as if it were ordinary blue ink. Permanent felt pen is the exception. This is very hard to remove and the only home treatment which will touch it is petrol, which is very liable to affect dyes and needs to be used with great caution.

LIPSTICK

Lipsticks vary in their composition but Oil of Eucalyptus removes most lipstick stains quite easily. Dab it on, being very careful not to smear the lipstick any farther, and leave it to soak into it. Then tamp it carefully out with more Oil of Eucalyptus or wash it out with soap and lukewarm water. If the stain isn't cleared by Eucalyptus try glycerine or alcohol. Lipstick-stained handkerchiefs will boil or bleach clean.

MILDEW

Mildew is one of the trickiest stains. It will sometimes respond to tamping with moist soap and white chalk, but if that fails hydrogen peroxide in a 10% solution can be used for tamping or soaking.

MUD

Mud is very easy to get off if you wait till it's dry, dabbing at it while wet only pushes the dirt into the fabric. Brush off when dry and tamp the remainder with soap and lukewarm water, or plain water on dry-clean fabrics.

NAIL VARNISH

The point to remember is never to use normal nail varnish removers, instead use amyl acetate which is safe provided the dye is fast. (*see* Be Warned)

PAINT

Paint is the classic case of a stain which should be treated immediately. Wet paint comes off very easily with white spirit, turpentine or paraffin, but once it's dry none of these work well. Hot vinegar will sometimes remove newly dried paint, and amyl acetate will soften cellulose paints, while other paint may respond to tamping with equal amounts of ammonia and turpentine mixed together.

When all else fails it is a matter of resorting to proprietory paint-brush softeners and strippers — with the obvious risks to the fabric, though they can be less harsh than one might expect. Start with the gentlest and work up, testing each time on a patch which won't show.

PERFUME

If perfume causes a stain it will be because the alcohol in it has affected the dye. There is no cure for this.

PERSPIRATION

Perspiration may be acid or alkaline according to a body's state of health. Acid stains will come out when tamped with an alkali such as ammonia, and alkali stains respond to an acid like lemon juice. Don't worry about which stain you have. Whether the stain is on a sock or under a sleeve it does no harm to try one and, if it doesn't work, switch to the other. The trouble is, perspiration can both stain and bleach, and nothing will reverse the bleaching.

PUPPY PUDDLES

When a puppy puddles on the carpet, slosh soda water over it immediately — the carpet, of course, not the dog. Mop up the lot with a clean cloth, re-damp it with soda and wipe it clean. If the puddle is caught before it dries this will completely prevent a stain.

Cat puddles need the same treatment, and though I haven't tried it on toddler puddles I suspect it would work. It's a good idea to mask the smell a cat leaves by giving a final wipe with water containing a few drops of ammonia. This will discourage the cat from returning to the same spot. But try it out on a test patch somewhere it won't show, because ammonia disagrees with some carpet dyes.

If no soda water is handy a mineral water, such as Perrier, can be used instead and works almost as well.

RED WINE

Don't panic when the waiter knocks the red wine over you. Simply call for a bottle of very good white wine on the house — insist on its excellence. While that is coming, mop up the excess red with a white napkin, and turn away the people who want to throw salt on you. Then, with a clean napkin underneath, pour enough white wine over the stain to saturate it. Sit back while it soaks in and cheer yourself up with a glass of the excellent white, before rinsing the stain out with lukewarm water.

The white wine usually rinses out with no trouble, taking with it the red wine, but if any traces remain keep them damp with white wine until you can get the garment to a good dry-cleaner, or wash it. If the accident is not in a restaurant any cheap white wine will do, and it is just as good on carpets and furniture as on clothes, even when the stain has dried.

Some believe in spreading salt on red wine. The trouble is you can't predict whether this will work or not. I have seen carpets it sucked the wine out of, leaving no trace; and equally those which were left with a deep stain. And it seldom helps on clothes.

In France they treat fresh red wine stains with mineral water by simply soaking the garment in it immediately, and on some fabrics and wine plain cold tap water does the trick if you act fast. For old red wine stains the treatment is to damp them with white wine or soak them for several hours in glycerine before washing them out. If that fails, tamping with equal parts hydrogen peroxide and water may be the only answer.

RUST

I first discovered the treatment for rust when a beautiful cream silk dress from the 1920s developed dark stains from an iron chain. As the stains made it unwearable I felt I had nothing to lose by trying the old-fashioned salt, lemon juice and sunlight treatment. Very very gradually the stains lightened until they vanished entirely, leaving the fragile silk looking as if they had never existed.

To use this treatment wet the stain with lemon juice, sprinkle it with salt and put in in the sunlight. Keep re applying both as soon as it begins to dry, until the stain goes. This may well take all day. As the stain should not be left half treated overnight, start early in the morning.

There is a snag however, on some fabrics the lemon juice may act as a bleach, on others as a stain. Treat the stain as for fruit stains. In most cases it will be far less noticeable than rust.

SCORCH MARKS

People swear by decidedly odd recipes for curing scorch marks: rubbing with a silver coin is one and a mixture which includes Brown Windsor soup is another. The method professional cleaners use is to repeatedly dab the mark with hydrogen peroxide (20 vols diluted with 70 parts water) until it vanishes. This can, however, cause bleaching so it could be worth trying some of the traditional remedies first. Linen can be rubbed with a slice of lemon and left in the sun, and on delicate fabrics a paste of magnesium carbonate and water can be applied, left to dry and brushed off. There are also a lot of advocates for the following mixture — 2 oz (60 g) of Fullers Earth, ½ pint (250 ml) of vinegar, and 2–3 chopped onions boiled together and left to get cold before being applied, left to dry and brushed off.

TAR

Now that most European beaches are tarry, a vital piece of holiday equipment is Oil of Eucalyptus. It is far and away the best tar-remover for skin, clothes and anything else. It is also one of the few which can be used on a tarry dog without hurting its skin.

On fabric carefully scrape off the surface tar, tamp it well with the oil and leave it to work. When it is loose wipe a moist cake of soap over and tamp with fairly hot water. Repeat if necessary. If the Eucalyptus has been forgotten, dripping or diesel fuel are good, and better than petrol, but tend to spread the stain. Lard well worked in and left a good while is quite good, and oil has some effect. But butter, which is often recommended, is just a waste of time and butter.

TEA

Tea will come out remarkably easily if glycerine is worked into it while the stain is still wet, and washed out with lukewarm water. If the stain has dried, leave glycerine to soak in and tamp it well with it before rinsing and washing. Or tamp with lemon juice or acetic acid. On cotton or linen the stain can be stretched taut and boiling water poured through it from a height. This works best if the stain is soaked in glycerine first.

Coffee stains need the same treatment apart from the lemon juice or acetic acid.

TIPP-EX

It was an emergency call from a friend, who had tipped a bottle of

Tipp-Ex down a navy blue dress, which first alerted me to the difficulty of removing it. The solution is white spirit, which will remove it entirely, but it works best if the major part of the fluid has been carefully scraped off the instant it spilt, *before it had time to dry*.

UNKNOWN STAINS

All too often one doesn't realise a stain is there till days after it was made. When that happens, and there's no way of telling what caused it, start by tamping with soap. Then if that fails move to the treatment for whatever stain its colour suggests it might be, using the gentler options first.

VASELINE

Vaseline sets for ever if it encounters heat. So vaseline needs to be tamped with turpentine and completely removed *before* being washed or ironed.

WAX

Wax melts off easily when it's ironed. All you need do is put clean blotting paper or kitchen roll over, and if possible under, the stain and iron it with a hot iron. Keep moving the paper so the wax is always in contact with a fresh area.

WHEN ALL ELSE FAILS

When a stain resists all treatment or has been mishandled and set firmly, give nature a chance with it. An old French method of removing difficult stains is to rub damp block soap on the stain and lay it on grass in the sunlight. Stains which would shift by no other method have vanished completely this way, though it may take a day or so to work.

The treatment of last resort is to stretch the stained area tightly over a heat-proof vessel, such as a pyrex jug, and pour boiling water through the stain from a very great height. This will blast out stains which nothing else will shift but I need hardly say that it's a treatment some fabrics would be ruined by.

GLOSS AND GLAMOUR

It is only forty years since beauty care was mainly the province of the family recipe book and back-room products from the chemist on the corner. It would be crazy to try to return to those days, but a lot of good babies were thrown out with the bathwater when we gave our unquestioning allegiance to the big cosmetic companies. Some old-fashioned treatments are so cheap and good it is a shame not to use them, and there is also a marvellous confidence in knowing that you can look after your skin or hair, if you need to, with only a few basic ingredients which you can find anywhere in the world.

For safety's sake just bear in mind that people who are allergic to certain foods are likely to be just as allergic to them on the skin. And it is as bad as to put stale ingredients *on* the body as *in* it, so perishable ingredients must be stored in a refrigerator and used when absolutely fresh, or they may do more harm than good.

BAD BREATH

When I was a student a Singalese friend noticed my horror at the quantity of garlic she was putting in our curry — I was convinced none of my boyfriends would come near me for days after. She assured me that if I chewed cardamom seeds after the meal the smell would vanish. I did, and it did. I have since discovered that it is known in France as the only true antidote to the smell of garlic. Just chew the cardamoms in their husks and when they are soft swallow the seeds and throw away the husks.

If no cardamom is available, chewing and swallowing half a lemon, pith, rind and all is — if you can stand it — next most effective. Chewing coffee beans, or parsley and vinegar, are ways of masking the smell but the effect is very temporary. Of course they will also briefly mask bad breath from teeth needing dental treatment, or from constipation. But both these need to be treated, not masked.

If you want to take it a stage further and have fragrant breath you could always try this old recipe. 'Take of sherry one gill (¼ pint, 125 ml). Add to it a good pinch of ground cloves and of nutmeg, and ¼ oz (8 g) of cinnamon and of bruised caraway seeds. Let this stand for a week shaking it twice a day before straining if off and adding 10 drops of lavender and five of otto of roses.' It is said that 2–3 drops of this on a lump of sugar 'will secure a breath of flowers'.

BLEACHING

Camomile Blond

Camomile has been used for centuries as a lightener for fair hair. Take a handful of camomile flowers — fresh or dried — boil them in ½ pint (250 ml) of water for 5–10 minutes. Strain them and squeeze all the juice from the flowers, adding the juice of ½ a lemon to the liquid. This mixture, used as the final rinse every time the hair is washed will show no effect at first but will gradually lighten the hair over the weeks. One of the great advantages of camomile is that it is impossible to get a harsh result, and it leaves the hair feeling and smelling wonderful.

Chemical Blond

If you can't be bothered to boil up camomile and don't mind the drying effect of chemicals, using a little hydrogen peroxide in the final rinse will slightly lighten the hair — say a tablespoon or so of 30 vols hydrogen peroxide in a pint of water, on fair hair. On brown hair it can sometimes bring up a reddish tint which may, or may not, look good.

Lemon Blond

It seems crazy to pay a fortune at the hairdresser to get hair sun-streaked when the sun can do it so much more easily. The ancient secret of getting the maximum blonding out of the sun is to put lemon juice on the hair before sunbathing. Either squeeze the juice over the whole head or fold a slice of lemon round a chosen strand and run it down the length. It is a slow, gentle bleach, but used on fair hair every day during a holiday it should make a marked difference by the end. It certainly did to the model who first showed me this method. Like all bleaches it dries the hair, which will need conditioning.

BODY BEAUTIFUL

An elderly Austrian who had marvellously youthful skin on her body told me her secret was to rub liquid paraffin all over before bathing. I can vouch that though it may not be up to asses' milk is makes an enormous difference to a dry skin. If, like me, you don't have time to maintain that degree of care every day, a few drops of the oil in the bath are better than nothing. But it really is worth returning to the all-over routine when sunbathing and swimming.

CLEANSING CREAM

The simplest instant cleanser for the face if you've forgotten to pack yours is an egg beaten up with olive oil. Just spread it on the face and wipe it off with warm water and cotton wool. The trouble is it goes off rapidly and is not suitable for skins which aren't dry.

Unfortunately all the very best old recipes for cleansing creams call for spermaceti. As this comes from whales it is beauty at a price I'm not prepared to pay — or recommend.

This recipe from an old formulary is for a very large quantity but could be cut down to any size. 'Take 1 lb almond oil (500 g), 1 lb rosewater (500 g), 1 oz (30 g) white wax, 1 oz (30 g) spermaceti (substitute wheat-germ oil) and a few drops otto of roses. Melt the wax and warm the oils and rosewater and beat well together.'

A cream with a slightly different balance of ingredients is a cold cream made by warming 1 oz (30 g) of white wax and beating into it first 4 oz (125 g) of almond oil and then 4 oz (125 g) of rosewater.

COMPLEXION

Today we seem to give most attention to the outside of the complexion. Our grandmothers did the reverse — and some of them looked rather good on it. A magazine a century ago instructed: 'If you want a face that looks like leather, then become a confirmed tea and coffee drinker. If you want blotches and pimples revel in a bill of fare that includes hot bread, pastry and late suppers.' Today beauticians would be warning you against bread at any temperature (unless it was wholemeal) and would be more concerned with the greasiness or spiciness of the food than with the hour at which you ate it. But the basic principle is that no amount of cosmetics will compensate for the effects of a bad diet.

The ideal diet for the skin is low on fat and spices, high on raw fruit, vegetables, roughage and water. Though if you switch to a diet like this the body may so enthusiastically clean itself out that spots appear for a while.

Spoil-sport though it sounds to say it, two major destroyers of the complexion are smoking and alcohol. Alcohol dilates the blood vessels, opens the pores and reduces the muscle tone. Smoking creates wrinkles. Research has shown smokers have more, and deeper, wrinkles than non-smokers. It also brings on the menopause slightly earlier, which suggests it may be affecting the hormonal balance and therefore be having other subtler ill effects on the skin.

French Complexion Secrets

A Frenchwoman famed in the last century for her beautiful skin is said to have guarded her secret to her death. Upon which her maid told the world — presumably for a price. It was only to wash in rainwater and rosewater and to massage into her skin, after each wash, a tablespoon of fresh cream mixed with a teaspoonful of lemon juice. With today's polluted skies the rainwater could be a mistake, but the rest certainly does make the skin feel good — though I suspect the cream would be too much for a greasy skin.

Another French beauty is said to have kept a perfect complexion by using an ointment which included pounded houseleek. This fleshy rosette of a plant is said to contain substances which help the skin to make new cells. It may well do so, it certainly feels good on the skin and can be used in any home-made skin cream or face pack.

CONDITIONERS

For Greasy Hair

A conditioner which the Edwardians swore by, and I find excellent, is a good dash of cider vinegar in the last rinse. Its great advantage is that it counteracts the alkali of the shampoo and keeps the right acid-alkali balance in the hair. This makes the hair beautifully shiny and manageable.

For Normal Hair

Rosemary has been used on hair for centuries, and is cropping up more and more in commercial shampoos — though I doubt if they really contain much of it. For the real thing put 3–4 sprigs of rosemary, as long as your finger, in a jug, pour on boiling water and leave them to steep for an hour. The strained liquid used as a final rinse works as well as any commercial conditioner and leaves the hair smelling deliciously of the herb.

Lacking the cosmetics of other centuries the Victorians set great store by lovely hair, and one of their favourite ways to give shine and body to it was to use an egg. Simply beat it with a little water or cider vinegar and massage it into the newly washed hair. Leave it for 5–10 minutes before rinsing it off with cool water. Beware of using hot water, it will convert the mixture into scrambled egg and then it is a devil to get off.

This is an excellent conditioner for hair badly dried-out by too much sun or bleach.

Conditioner to Give Body to Hair

A mixture of lemon, oil and honey both conditions the hair and gives it body. The way to make it is to mix 1 dessertspoon of honey with 2 tablespoons of corn oil and 1 teaspoon of lemon juice. Leave this on the hair for 10 minutes before shampooing.

Deep Conditioner for Dry or Lifeless Hair

The West Indians know more than most people about the way sun, wind, and salt can dry the hair. They also have one of the best remedies. Put a couple of spoonfuls of coconut oil on the hair, work it well in and wrap a hot towel round the head for half an hour. Then wash the hair as usual. It makes the hair wonderfully soft and manageable though I'm told it dulls the colour of blond hair. Incidentally, if you are using this on holiday don't leave the coconut oil in the sun. It rapidly goes rancid and the smell is terrible.

A West Indian with grown-up children but not a grey hair to her head told me that using coconut oil plus a West Indian product called soft candle meant you would never go grey. She may be right, but though coconut oil is now sold in most chemists I have never been able to find soft candle to try it.

In Mediterranean countries they have always used olive rather than coconut oil to condition the hair. Although I don't find it quite as good it is certainly worth using when in that area.

CUTICLES

There is no need to buy cuticle cream for a home manicure. Ordinary petroleum jelly is just as good for the cuticles — and very much cheaper.

DRY SKIN

With so many seemingly complex cosmetics on the market it is hard to believe a simple mixture can do any real good. Yet I find there is nothing to touch a simple mixture of glycerine and rosewater when skin looks dry. Flakiness and fine lines seem to vanish almost overnight — which is why it has been used for generations. The proportions can be adjusted to suit your skin and it can be mixed and kept without refrigeration. I use a large spoonful of rosewater to 2 of glycerine and smooth it on at night, or wear it around the house during the day, rinsing off what remains several hours later.

It has a slightly sticky feel which some may find annoying, but the results are worth the slight discomfort. And, of course, it should really be used to prevent dryness rather than to cure it.

EYE MAKE-UP REMOVAL

A little baby oil on cotton wool removes eye make-up just as well as the special eye make-up removal pads. Though some people find both irritate the eyes and should use cleansing cream instead.

EYELASH LENGTHENING

There are three schools of thought on eyelash lengthening. In the old days women used animal fat, especially bear's grease, to increase their flutter. More recently castor oil was advocated, while some even say the lashes should be trimmed to make them grow — with blunt-ended scissors, I hope. It is a matter of taste and hard to prove either way. For myself I'm betting on animal fat and using lanoline.

FACE MASKS

Face masks have been used for thousands of years and are very much a matter of using what is to hand. For example crocodile dung was used in ancient Egypt — fortunately we have little to hand. It is just a matter of deciding what condition your skin is in, and picking the right ingredients to help it. There are no rules. And one of the delightful things about a face mask is that it acts as a very strong signal to the household that you don't want to be disturbed: which makes it almost as good for the temper as for the face.

Masks must always be freshly made and none of them should be applied to the skin around the eyes. Also bear in mind that if you are allergic to something when you eat it, your skin is likely to be allergic too.

Strawberry Face Mask

The celebrated French beauty Mme Tallien is said to have preserved her much-envied complexion by strawberry masks. It is the easiest of all masks to make and an excellent way to use up squishy strawberries at the bottom of the punnet. Mash 2–3 strawberries and spread them on the face. If you have dry skin include a teaspoon or so of top of the milk. Leave the mask on for 15 minutes, while lying down (otherwise it tends to slide off). Rinse off with tepid water. Strawberries are astringent and this tightens the skin, closing the pores and smoothing out fine lines. It is also said to slightly bleach freckles. It should not be used by those allergic to strawberries.

Yoghurt Mask
This is an updated version of the old mud pack, and is good for oily skins. Mix plain yoghurt to a cream with Fullers Earth and spread it on. Leave it for 20–30 minutes and rinse off with tepid water.

Pears and Cream
Pears moisturise and nourish the skin, so if a pear has gone sad and inedible mash it with a little cream and spread it on the face. Give it 20 minutes and then rinse it off with tepid water.

Oat Pack
The most basic face pack of all is oats stirred to a rough paste with hot milk and a touch of honey. Honey can in fact be added to any face mask. It attracts and holds moisture in the skin and seems to be mildly anti-septic — it has been used on wounds for centuries. Older skins benefit from it particularly. Half an hour is not too long to leave this pack on before rinsing with cool water.

Herbal Masks
All sorts of herbs have been used in masks at various times, but the most popular is the houseleek which can be pounded to a mush with almond oil and rosewater. Used often enough this is meant to keep the skin youthful — though to use it often enough you would have to have walls and roof smothered in houseleeks. So perhaps houseleeks should be planted against a girl's growing-up as port once used to be laid down for a boy — though I'd like houseleeks *and* port.

FACIAL WASH

A few years ago cosmetic companies suddenly discovered what derma-tologists, and women, had known for years: that many women can't use soap on their faces without making their skin feel like a parchment lampshade. In response to this belated discovery they launched a lot of high-priced facial washes. Just as good is a low-priced creamy wash which dermatologists have been recommending for years. It is called 'emulsifying ointment' and is scent-free and non-allergic. All it lacks is glamorous packaging. Most chemists have it if you ask them, it just isn't on display.

FEET

If feet are swollen from a day of standing or shopping the cure is to wash them in tepid water and lie down with them sloping up a wall, so they are a good deal higher than your head.

One of the most soothing footbaths is a handful of salt in warm water. Leave the feet in the water, and wiggle the toes about from time to time, until the water is cool. Take time to relax the rest of the body as you sit there because tired feet almost always make the body tense. Dry the feet and massage them with cream if they have dry skin, or with powder if they sweat easily.

Rough skin can be kept down by using a pumice stone at every bath, and dry skin should be rubbed nightly with a few drops of glycerine. Horny nails can be rubbed to normal thickness with a pumice stone while in the bath. Cut the nails straight across, never on a curve.

HAIR RESTORERS

Hair restorers have been a favourite part of patent medicines for well over a thousand years and almost everything has been tried. A manuscript in the Middle Ages favoured prevention rather than cure. It instructed its reader 'powder your hair with parsley seed three nights a year and the hair will never fall off '. A Victorian treatise took a more dictatorial tone saying 'the growth will very soon sensibly increase' if the head is rubbed nightly with equal parts of olive oil and spirit of rosemary, plus a few drops of oil of nutmeg. Sensibly or not, I rather doubt if it did. Even more unlikely is the commonest recommendation of all—to rub the head with a raw onion. Though this crops up so regularly down the ages that one begins to wonder if there is something in it. However, a ladies magazine of 1852 remarks that the treatment 'is not infallible'.

The only hair restorer for which I have contemporary evidence is coconut oil. My own hair grows much faster when I use it and I know of a man who used it to restore at least a semblance of hair to a previously bald pate, though I suppose that might have been coincidence. Anyone who wants to try it for themselves should use it as given in conditioners.

HAND CREAM

The simplest way of keeping dry or hard-working hands smooth was taught me by a farmer's wife in the North of England. It is simply to rub in a drop or two of neat glycerine every night. It works far better than one would think possible. In fact I find it the best hand treatment of all.

Some people may find glycerine alone too sticky to bear and prefer the recipe used by an East Anglian family. They mix equal amounts of glycerine, water and Eau de Cologne together in a bottle and shake it well before using it.

In farmhouses in the old days jars of lard, goose grease, or lanoline used to stand ready for the hands to be dipped into before going out in the wind. The same fats were also rubbed on the paws and ears of sheep dogs when the winter was bitter. On both man and beast they make a good, if slightly messy, protection against chapping. Lanoline especially is good for children at that age when they always remove their gloves no matter how cold the wind.

If the hands are already chapped an old farmhouse recipe for treating them is to soften $\frac{1}{4}$ lb (125 g) of lard. Then mix a little rosewater, 2 yolks of eggs, a large spoon of honey and a little oatmeal. Work this to a fine paste, spread it on the hands and wear cotton gloves to hold it on overnight.

A recipe for a more conventional hand cream than any of these is to mix together $\frac{1}{4}$ lb (125g) of white wax, 2 oz (60 g) almond oil, and $\frac{1}{2}$ oz (15 g) spermaceti. Instead of spermaceti use glycerine or more oil.

HANDS

Extra Dirty Hands
If your hands are so filthy soap won't get them clean just rub vaseline on them for 5 minutes. After that the dirt should come off with soap and hot water.

Rough Hands
Even the best hand creams have no immediate impact on hands roughened by gardening or carpentry, because they still leave all the rough bits of skin sticking up to catch on everything. What does work is a smoother I learnt from a friend who was always roughing up his hands working on his car. Pour vegetable oil into a cupped palm and add the same amount of granulated sugar. Then rub the hands together *hard* for 5 minutes, making sure that the mixture is rubbed well over every bit of skin. Then the sugar will rub off all the rough ends of skin. Rinse the hands and leave them as they are unless intending to sew or knit. In which case wash them to get rid of any oil and apply hand cream. I find this is the only treatment which allows me to sew silk after a day's gardening.

Smelly Hands
Smelly hands are a perennial problem to anyone who cooks. Luckily the

remedies are there on the kitchen shelf. The classic cures are vinegar, lemon juice, or salt. Each cures a different range of smells. I always start by rubbing lemon juice on my hands, because that copes with most things (which is why a slice of lemon was always put in finger bowls), and move to the others if it fails. It is also important to use cold water to wash the hands, not hot. Hot water opens the pores and lets the smell penetrate, after which it's far harder to remove.

Stained Hands
Stained hands usually come clean with lemon juice, but some stains, such as cigarettes, need hydrogen peroxide. Dab it on until the stain vanishes and rinse the hands very well afterwards. *For safety use 20 vols rather than 30 vols of peroxide.*

HEATED ROLLERS

One of London's top hairdressers will only use heated rollers if they have a thin layer of foam rubber over them. He says that put straight against the hair they cause it to dry and split. If there is no time to sew on foam rubber, wrapping a piece of soft tissue round also does the trick. There is the bonus that long hair no longer entangles in the spikes of the rollers as you take them out.

HENNA

If henna takes all too well and brings the hair up a flaming orange the fire can be subdued by repeatedly washing it in gin, methylated spirits or surgical spirit. Of the three gin is much the most effective and the least rough on the scalp.

HERBAL BATHS

Herbal baths have a long tradition and almost any herb or spice which takes your fancy can be added to the bath — rosemary or thyme, cloves or cinnamon. Strictly speaking the herbs should be put in a muslin bag suspended in the bath. But if you grow your own and have enough to spare it looks far prettier to put them in loose. Incurable romantics can throw in a floating flower or two as well. Bags of bran or oats used also to be suspended in the water to soften it and were used over and over again, till they stopped releasing their creamy liquid.

LIPSTICK

A slight gloss on the lips, presumably to simulate moist receptiveness, is one of the oldest tricks in the beauty book. Vaseline works as well as anything, but glycerine tastes better. Those who have the time can mix the two for putting on bare lips or over lipstick.

MAYONNAISE CONDITIONER

Mayonnaise can reach a stage where it isn't quite rank and rancid, but neither is it fit to improve the taste of other food. At this stage don't throw it away, use it as a hair conditioner for dry hair. Massage it well into the hair, wrap a hot towel round and leave it for half an hour before shampooing. If your hair isn't dry and your face is, use it as a face pack. Eggs and oil are equally good for hair or skin.

NAILS

All the old saws about not filing nails to and fro, not using scissors on them, and cutting toenails straight across are quite true. Rather boringly nails do prefer to be filed with an emery board, not a metal file, and will split more easily if cut or rubbed back and forth.

Immersion in water makes the nails grow faster and a diet rich in gelatine strengthens them, though I've always wondered how anyone could bear to eat enough gelatine to make a difference.

The old remedy for nails which have become thickened and opaque is to dip them daily in a slice of lemon.

Nail Varnish
If the lid on your nail varnish habitually sticks, try putting a layer of vaseline on the screw threads of the next new bottle. That ought to stop it happening.

Nails look longer if varnish isn't taken to the outer edges of the nail. And the varnish stays on longer if you run your thumb round the end of the nail while it's still wet. This removes any minute overhang that might catch and chip.

Nail Varnish Removing
If the nail varnish remover runs out, acetone, surgical spirit, or even that dreadful perfume Aunt Edna gave you, will do instead. The only drawback is that acetone dries the nails and the smell of perfume can cling for hours. Either way, wash the nails well afterwards, and put a little oil or vaseline on them.

Nail Polishing
The old fashioned way of giving a shine to nails was to buff them up with nail powder and a chamois buffer. It's still a good way to give a finish to hands which aren't attractive enough to make conspicuous with nail varnish. A little whiting makes an excellent nail powder and the nails should be buffed in one direction only. If they are rubbed to and fro they will overheat, dry, and split.

Keeping Nails Clean
The way to make nails easy to clean after doing even the grimiest job is to fill the space under them before you start. A thick wedge of lanoline under each nail will effectively stop dirt getting in. Don't fill the gap under the nails with soap. Unless you have very sweaty hands the soap will dry and simply drop out.

OPEN PORES

An old Algerian treatment for open pores works extremely well. Steam the face over a bowl of boiling water for 10 minutes with a towel over the head to keep the steam in. Then, while the face is still very hot, rub a slice of lemon thoroughly all over the greasy or open pores. Leave the lemon juice to dry on the skin before rinsing with cold water.

Open pores are very often combined with blackheads. If this is the case steam the face, then with very clean hands remove the blackheads, re-steam and apply the lemon juice. Blackheads should always be removed when the skin is hot and the pores open to avoid bruising the surrounding skin.

Another way to tighten and refine pores which need attention is to spread lightly whipped egg white on the skin. Leave it for 20 minutes before rinsing it off with tepid water.

Those who have this problem should avoid alcohol and spicy foods as both encourage the pores to open.

PAINTY HANDS

If you've been painting and need your hands to look respectable again the best cleaner to use is equal amounts of turpentine and paraffin, or turpentine and linseed oil. Help the mixture along with a pumice stone if the paint is hard. Afterwards wash the hands very well and rub a slice of lemon all over them to kill the smell.

PERFUME

Oil has the ability to hold perfume. So a little touch of oil wherever you are about to put perfume will make the smell linger. Warmth brings out the smell of any scent, so it will make a greater impact if you put it on pulse points — the side of the neck (not, as I've often seen, the bone behind the ear), the inner wrist, and for more intimate moments the inside of the elbows and thighs.

Not even the warmest skin will bring out a perfume which has been left for long exposed to heat and light. It may look glamorous on a dressing table but it will keep its strength better in a cool drawer or cupboard.

Perfume Changing

Scent sprays don't have to be pensioned off when you switch from one perfume to another. Ammonia will get rid of the smell of the old scent which lingers in them. Put a teaspoonful of ammonia in $\frac{1}{4}$ pint (125 ml) of water. Fill the spray with this and spray it through until it's empty. To completely clear the scent of a heavy perfume it may be necessary to repeat this a number of times. Then rinse well.

ROUGH SKIN

The best value in beauty aids must surely be the old fashioned pumice stone, so beloved of nannies. Nothing matches a rub with soap and a pumice stone for smoothing the skin all over the body, from goose flesh on the upper arms to the roughest feet — and pumice lasts a lifetime.

SCAR PREVENTION

Vitamin E seems to have an extraordinary ability to help healing. Scabs are much less likely to form scars if they are dabbed with Vitamin E oil. The same oil put on newly scarred skin will also help clear the scar. Though how much it will do depends very much on the scar. It is certainly worth using on something like a nasty scratch on the face, but it is unlikely to help a burn.

SETTING LOTION

At one time beer was all the rage as the setting lotion in smart hairdressers all over London. It was the start of the back-to-natural-products trend which has now put a flower or fruit on almost every shampoo, no matter how tenuous the connection. Beer may no longer be in fashion but it still makes an effective setting lotion.

SETTING — EMERGENCY

In the days before heated rollers made emergency hair setting easy there were two popular methods of reviving sagging hair. One was to damp the hair with Eau de Cologne and set it and dry it in the usual way, which was far faster than using water because Cologne evaporates so easily. The other method was to set the hair then wrap round it a towel wrung out in very hot water. After the steam had penetrated for a few minutes the hair was dried as usual.

SHAMPOO

Nettles are meant to stop the hair falling out, and cure dandruff. Whether they do or not, they certainly make the hair shiny. An old Irish recipe for nettle shampoo instructs you to 'cook a big lot of nettles' in water for an hour and strain the liquid onto soft soap. Then mix the two well together and bottle them. Chemists seldom stock soft soap nowadays but a good pure soap grated finely and thoroughly dissolved in a little boiling water will do instead. Shake the bottle each time you use it, as the mixture will separate.

SHAVING

Maybe it's the rose-tinted spectacles of childhood, but I swear that I remember a day when men had marvellous complexions. That was before electric razors, and I'm sure it was due to the daily massage with a shaving brush. Whether this is so or not, there is certainly no nicer way to wash a face of either sex than with a real old-style brush. It goes into every pore and leaves the face feeling twice as clean.

STATIC ELECTRICITY

My hair is not manageable at the best of times but once, just before I had to present a live television programme, static electricity set it flying in all directions like demented candy floss. I was busy calling upon my fate and cursing my lot, as each stroke of the brush made it worse not better, when the make-up girl started on it with a metal comb. Suddenly the static vanished and it returned to only its normal level of unmanageability. A metal comb, she explained to me, was the only sure way to rid hair of static. I have never been without one since and it works every time.

STRETCH MARKS IN PREGNANCY

When contemplating a smoothly bulging navel it is all too easy to forget that the smooth skin could end up looking like a rather badly hammered copper bowl if you don't look after it. Whether or not you get stretch marks depends on three things — your skin type, the size of the bulge, and how you take care of it. For two out of three the ball is in your court.

Keeping to a low starch, low fat diet with lots of fresh fruit and raw or lightly cooked vegetables will keep the weight down and put the skin in peak condition (as well as being excellent for the baby). I'm told that in China they have, for centuries, avoided eating extra salt when pregnant. This is a wise move because salt helps the body to store liquid and extra liquid is just what you don't want to store in pregnancy, or you will be even larger than nature intends. There is the bonus that a low salt diet is good for the high blood pressure which can be a problem in pregnancy.

The skin needs feeding as much as the body. Vitamin E oil seems to have the special ability to help the skin make new cells and it should be rubbed on the bulge and breasts each day. It may also be worth taking Vitamin E capsules. A few drops of oil of comfrey and some glycerine used with the oil on the stomach will make it even more effective.

There are those who say that taken in sufficient quantities Vitamin E can even cure old stretch marks — though I personally doubt it.

SUN SCREEN

For noses that turn scarlet after a brief encounter with the sun a very good sun block is a thick layer of zinc and castor oil ointment — the sort that is put on babies' bottoms. It's a measure designed only for those self-confident enough to accept that looking silly with their nose a brilliant white on holiday is less awful than looking silly with a flaking scarlet one afterwards. Nude sun worshippers will find it just as useful on shoulder points, bosoms and other parts that stick out.

SUNTANNING

In the old days there used to be only one rule for not getting sunburnt: don't sit in the sun. So there are no old recipes for suncreams. Since a suntan became desirable a lot of home recipes for speeding up the process have sprung up. For years the beaches of France have been full of people smelling like salads as they smother themselves with a mixture of olive oil and wine vinegar. Those who want to cheat add a few drops of iodine to give a tint to the skin even before the sun does its job. While those bent on preserving the tan afterwards bathe the skin with tea (at the risk of tanning it in more than one sense), or apply grated carrots.

In hotter countries ointments based on coconut oil are popular and I'm told that sesame oil mixed in with it makes the skin tan even faster.

None of these provide a sun screen. So now that so many commercial preparations have been shown to cause severe skin reactions in some people there is really a choice between the risk of a reaction to a sunscreen and the risk of burning without it. For though oil certainly works for some, on a fair skin or in very strong sun it will cause rather than cure sunburn. My own favourite mixtures for dry, easily bronzed skin are 1 part rosewater to 2 parts each of glycerine and almond oil, or equal parts liquid paraffin and glycerine.

SWOLLEN EYES

I have always thought nature made a bad mistake when she ordained that crying makes the eyes swell — it is bad enough feeling miserable without looking ugly as well. Fortunately she also gave us cucumbers. Place thin slices of cucumber over each eyelid, renewing them as soon as they get warm, and lie down for as long as possible. It won't quite work miracles, but almost.

If cucumbers are out of season use cold tea bags or witch hazel on pads of cotton wool. Or, for a really romantic recovery, gather fresh rose petals — assuming they haven't been sprayed with chemicals — crush them to a pulp and lay them on the eyelids. While you are at it maybe you should lie about in silk underwear and wait for him to kiss you better.

TONING LOTION

One of the oldest and nicest toning lotions is made with 3 spoonfuls of rosewater to 1 spoonful of witch hazel. Rosewater softens the skin, while witch hazel tightens it and is antiseptic. These proportions should suit a normal skin, but greasy skins will be better with equal amounts of each. Whatever the proportions, the mixture will keep well in a bottle.

An excellent toning lotion, but one which won't keep, can be made from elderflowers, which have a long-standing reputation for making the skin smooth and supple. Pound a handful of elderflowers to bruise them, then pour over 1 pint (500 ml) of boiling water. Leave this to steep for 2–3 days and then strain off the liquid and squeeze the last drops from the flowers. As this lotion goes off rather easily the wisest course is to keep a little for daily use in the refrigerator and freeze the rest.

For those who have spots a good antiseptic tonic lotion is an infusion of thyme. While older skins may benefit from infusion of houseleek.

Any of these herbal toners can be mixed with some witch hazel to make them more astringent and antiseptic. Alternatively a little cider vinegar could be added. If you use soap on your skin this will help to restore the acid-alkali balance after the alkali of the soap. In fact one of the great advantages of making such lotions yourself is that you can make them to suit the needs of your particular skin.

POSSETS AND POTIONS

In my grandmother's handwritten recipe book, recipes for curing indigestion and treating coughs jostle those for hunter's beef and apricot cheese. As late as 1945 the reverse was also true and a large section of the official pharmacopœia read more like a recipe book with its use of glycerine and orange flower water, saffron and gelatine. There were also mysterious ingredients such as 'Essence of Jockey Club' and remedies with homely names like 'Chelsea Pensioner'. Many people can also remember the days when someone in their village knew the even older tradition of healing with plants and acted as the unofficial doctor to everyone who lived nearby.

The advent of modern drugs destroyed all this and a great deal of ancient wisdom was either lost or misunderstood. Nowadays, for example, people tend to think herbs are either much safer or much less effective than modern drugs — depending on whether they are in the pro or anti-herb lobby. Neither is necessarily correct. The chemicals in plants can be therapeutic like digitalis and quinine; can be deadly, like the arrow-poison curare; they can work powerfully on the brain, like opium or cannabis; or they can be mildly antiseptic, like thyme or soothing, like dock leaves. So the real difference between a home-made plant remedy and medicine from a laboratory is not the power but the lack of standardisation.

The balance of chemicals in a plant changes with the weather, the time of year and the ground it grows on. So the coltsfoot from valley X may be a better medicine than the coltsfoot from hill Y. And, of course, any infusion must be absolutely fresh. All of which means there is rather

178

more to making some of the old remedies work than meets the eye. Even so, many of them — both herbal and non-herbal — are a valuable supplement to conventional medicine, though not an alternative to it.

In first aid some of the old ways must be firmly rejected in favour of the best modern methods — and these I have given. In both areas it may be worth regaining a little more of the self-reliance our grandparents took so much for granted. But it is always wise to check with a doctor before using any treatment, conventional or unconventional.

ACHES

At one time most housewives had their favourite recipe for an embrocation to rub on deep seated aches. This one comes from the notebook of a nineteenth-century housewife in Yorkshire 'Pour 1 pint of malt vinegar over 2 eggs in their shells. Leave until the eggs have dissolved completely before beating in ¼ pint of turpentine.' (The metric eqivalents are 500 ml vinegar and 125 ml turpentine.) The housewife's note in the margin said simply, 'Good'.

Interestingly doctors are beginning to use vibrators to relieve certain types of intractable pain. So it may be that the counter stimulation of the nerves by rubbing, when applying the embrocation, accounts for part of its success. Simply rubbing or massaging aches and pains can certainly help considerably.

ARTHRITIS

Cider vinegar has long been held in some country districts to bring ease to arthritis. It can certainly do no harm to substitute cider vinegar for any other vinegar in the diet, but, as few people use vinegar every day, those who want to try cider vinegar as a remedy should take a teaspoonful of cider vinegar and a teaspoonful of honey in hot water every day. Certainly when my mother tried this she found her hands became far less painful and the stiffness lessened, and many other people say the same.

Honey and cider vinegar, even in such a small dose, must certainly affect the body's chemistry, for my mother discovered that a perfume which had previously suited her very well suddenly changed and became rank and unpleasant on the skin. So it is probably best not to use perfume when taking this mixture, though it produces no body smell at all if perfume is avoided.

Cider vinegar is by no means the only old remedy for arthritis. A handful of Epsom Salts in a hot bath each day is another popular one.

BEE AND WASP STINGS

The best treatments for bee and wasp stings come straight from the store cupboard, but they are different because basically bee stings are acid and wasp stings are alkaline. Bees leave their stings in but wasps don't. With a bee sting the first move must be to remove the sting. Then soothe the skin with a solution of bicarbonate of soda and water to counteract the acidity. Wasp stings should simply be bathed with vinegar.

The only trouble is that if you confuse these treatments the sting will hurt more, not less. Fortunately it's not difficult to remember which goes with which, as B stands for both Bee and Bicarbonate, and W and V are enough alike for easy remembering.

If either sting is in the mouth, sucking an ice-cube will help.

Young children, and a few adults, can become very allergic to bee stings. The first signs are excessive swelling and difficulty in breathing. THIS NEEDS RAPID MEDICAL ATTENTION.

BITES

Most insect bites are acid, so if you are being driven mad by itching you could use a popular country remedy — a dab or two of your own urine. It sounds odd but it works.

For those who dislike that idea the best antidote is a mild alkali such as bicarbonate of soda or washing soda, with a little water, dabbed on the place. Soap can also reduce itching: moisten a finger, rub a cake of soap to collect a good film of soapiness, and dab it on the spot.

BURNS AND SCALDS

MAJOR BURNS NEED RAPID MEDICAL ATTENTION, and *on a child a relatively small area of burnt skin can be serious.*

The treatment of burns has changed radically in the last hundred years. At one time it was to apply fat and cover them up. That is now considered very much the *wrong* treatment. NO fat or ointment of any sort should be put on a burn or scald.

It was the experience of pilots in the last war which led to the modern treatment for burns — treatment which men have instinctively used for centuries. It was found that pilots who bailed out into the sea were less damaged by their burns than those who bailed out over land. For a brief, and painful, period credit went to the salt. Then it was realised that the body holds the heat and goes on burning after the source of heat has been removed, so it was the cooling effect of the water which was helping.

Any scald or burn should be immersed in cool water or held under a cool running tap for at least ten minutes, provided it can be put under water fast. If you have to run a bath to put the patient in it will take too long to do any good. Milk will do, if it happens to be nearer to hand than water.

The greatest risk with large burns is infection. Don't wrap them tightly but cover them very lightly with the cleanest available cloth — a freshly laundered sheet or pillow case, for example.

Applying honey to small burns, such as one gets from a hot pan, rapidly takes away the burning sensation and helps the burn to heal.

CATARRH

Inhalations have always been popular for easing catarrh in the head. For a heavy cold one of the best is Oil of Eucalyptus. Fill a small bowl with boiling water and put in a few drops of Oil of Eucalyptus. The sufferer should then bend over the basin and drape a large towel over both head and basin to keep the steam in, and breathe deeply. Eucalyptus is not only healing and antiseptic but has powerful decongestant properties, so this brings very rapid relief when the head feels intolerably bunged up.

Eucalyptus can also be used in ointment form, by mixing 2 tablespoons of vaseline with 1 tablespoon of Oil of Eucalyptus. A dab of this is put in each nostril, preferably after an inhalation, or it can be rubbed on the neck and chest before going to bed, so the vapour rises in the night.

Another old remedy for nasal catarrh, which comes from Ireland, is rather more spartan — but some people find it works. Put a teaspoon of pure sea salt and a teaspoon of bicarbonate of soda in a pint of boiling water. Leave this to cool and bottle it. When the head is congested the mixture is poured into the palm of the hand and sniffed right up each nostril. Which it is said to loosen the catarrh and allow it to be blown out. (*See also* COLDS and COUGHS, overleaf.)

CHILBLAINS

Anyone driven mad by chilblains could try a traditional remedy warmly recommended to me by a young woman in Cambridgeshire. It was given to her by her mother-in-law after every remedy in the chemist's had failed to help. Simply bathe the chilblains in your own urine. Well, no one could claim it is an expensive treatment, and she insists she is not a crank and that her chilblains responded after very few applications and gradually ceased to occur.

I can't vouch for that remedy because mine were cured by another home treatment years ago. It was a course under ultra violet lamps. It made my chilblains vanish, never to return, no matter what the provocation.

CHILDBIRTH

For centuries old wives have told young ones to drink raspberry leaf tea to make labour easier. Unfortunately no one can run a labour through twice, once with and once without the tea, so proving that it helps is difficult. However, having drunk it assiduously myself before three labours of amazing ease and speed I am prepared to believe the old wives knew what they were talking about. It tastes quite pleasant and is made with fresh or dried leaves, just like ordinary tea. Drink a cupful, or more, twice a day from at least the fourth month until the end of pregnancy. It's no good leaving it till the last minute and expecting miracles. If the contractions stop for no good reason, a pot of the tea may help to get them going again.

Drinking raspberry leaf tea also seems to help period pains. It is important to drink it for a couple of days before the period as well as during it. Most good health food shops sell it.

COLDS

The following medicine 'for a newly taken and violent cold' comes from the notebooks of a Welsh farmer who, in the 1850s was the unofficial apothecary in a remote part of Carmarthenshire.

'Take about 4 oz spring water and in a convenient vessel put to it 3 leaves of good tussilago [coltsfoot] and a finger of maiden hair and a stick of liquorish. Make the water warm and when it is ready to boil put in the aforementioned ingredients, the liquorish being first sliced and minced. Cover the pot well, let it boil and then having presently strained it let the patient drink it like hot tea, being already in bed. Do this 3–4 times successively or until there be no more need of medicine.'

The 'maiden hair' was probably the plant better known as Maid's Hair or Lady's Bedstraw, a mild kidney stimulant. The use of both coltsfoot and liquorice is interesting. Both have now been found to contain substances which reduce inflammation and soothe the moist membranes of the nose and throat. Coltsfoot also suppresses spasmodic coughing, while liquorice helps the body to produce and expel phlegm. It was probably a wise mixture.

CORNS

One of the most popular treatments for corns was to soak bread in vinegar for a couple of days and apply the bread nightly to the corn, like a corn pad. This does gradually soften the corn, layer by layer, so it can be removed. Some people also say that cutting a dip in a turnip and filling it with salt produces a juice which is excellent for softening corns.

COUGHS

There are plenty of elderly people who can recall the dreadful smell of goose grease going rancid under the brown paper which kept it on their chests when they were ill as children. There is no evidence that the goose grease did any good, though the rubbing and the warmth may have helped, but other old remedies for coughs and catarrh really do work.

My favourite is a treatment I was given by an elderly Indian friend, and have used every since. She learnt it from her mother who was the unofficial 'doctor' to her area. Heat a teaspoonful of powdered turmeric with a mug of milk. When it is almost boiling strain it into a cup and sweeten it. In India they sweeten it with jagri, an almost fudge-like form of pure sugar cane, but a teaspoon of honey does very well instead. Drink it hot three times a day. Turmeric in milk has a soft, almost scented, flavour which even children enjoy, so this is no hardship. Some relief will be felt immediately but its full effects are not usually felt till the third day. I have found it far more effective than anything on the chemist's shelves and it is almost as good for bronchitis as for chesty colds.

Another remedy for a cough comes from Ireland. It uses a vegetable which, unlikely as it may seem, has been used for chest complaints in many parts of Europe. Scrub a turnip till it is free of all dirt, then slice it thinly. Discard the final slice so that the reconstituted turnip will have a flattened side to stand on, then stack the slices of turnip together, sprinkling moist brown sugar between each slice. Leave it in a cool place for 2–3 days for the juice to run out. The liquid should be taken a teaspoonful at a time several times a day. There is just one problem: it tastes so delicious children will guzzle the lot immediately unless it is kept out of reach.

Thyme is thought to contain elements which supress a spasmodic cough and a traditional Swiss medicine for whooping cough is an infusion of thyme. Bring a tablespoon of chopped thyme leaves to the boil in a pint (500 ml) of water. Allow it to stand for a while, then drink it like milkless tea. (*See also* CATARRH, page 181.)

CRAMP

There are all sorts of remedies for cramp and which of them works seems to depend very much on the user. Rolling a bottle to and fro with the foot works quite well for cramp in the instep, while a hard rubbing movement up the back of the leg seems to help cramp in the leg. Equally there are those who swear by a nutmeg kept in the pocket or a sockful of corks inside the bottom of the bed. However, by far the most widely acclaimed remedy is grasping a magnet — the bigger the better — the moment the cramp comes on.

CUTS AND GRAZES

In the old days the automatic treatment for a cut or graze was to suck it. Even gritty grazes were sucked after washing. That was before mass advertising convinced everyone that only branded antiseptics could defeat germs. Now the pendulum has swung. Strong antiseptics are frowned on by experts as doing more harm than good, and sucking one's own cut or graze is approved of once more. If a graze needs cleaning, ordinary toilet soap and water are best. Disinfectants must never be used.

One rather dubious old treatment was the cobweb bandage. Taken fresh from the hedgerow cobwebs might seem acceptable, but it is difficult to believe that a dusty old house cobweb could do anything but harm. However, I have heard of more than one person having severe cuts bound with cobwebs, only to have them heal perfectly.

A more acceptable old remedy is an infusion of thyme or witch hazel. Both are natural antiseptics and help skin heal. Witch hazel is most easily bought from a chemist. To use thyme, pound a few thyme leaves and pour on a little boiling water. Leave it to infuse a while and then wash a cut or graze with the liquid. New research has also restored honey to favour. Cuts dressed with it, or even with sugar, have proved less likely to go septic.

IF THE CUT HAS SOMETHING DEEPLY EMBEDDED IN IT THIS SHOULD NOT BE REMOVED. It may have severed a major blood vessel and be holding back the bleeding. A football fan was stabbed with a nail file not long ago and his life was saved because a first aider got him to hospital without removing the file.

DEEP BRUISING AND HOUSEMAID'S KNEE

A Welsh professional boxer recently used flower power to win a major fight at the Albert Hall.

Being a powerful puncher, Colin Jones had so bruised his hands that he couldn't use them. Normal medical treatment had helped, but not enough to let him fight. So his trainer resorted to an old Welsh miners' remedy: he boiled a large bundle of leaves and stalks of marshmallow till they became a pulp, let them cool till the heat was just bearable, then laid the mush on the hands and bandaged it on as a poultice overnight. With this treatment the hands returned to normal in time for the big fight.

It seems miners in Wales have successfully used this plant for generations to treat miner's knee — a condition akin to housemaid's knee. How many applications are needed, depends very much on the severity of the condition, though no one knows whether the healing is caused by chemicals in the plant or simply by the warmth held by the poultice.

DENTURES

I don't know what people do with their dentures but the breakage rate is apparently extraordinary. It even caused problems of morale in the war — especially with parachutists.

Unfortunately dentures cannot be glued, as glue would soften the plastic and make professional repairs almost impossible. So if they break just before a special occasion the only recourse is to apply well chewed chewing gum to both sides of a clean dry break. It won't let you eat, but it can help you smile.

When the denture cleaner runs out, soapy water and a nail brush are almost as good.

DIARRHŒA

My grandmother had a sovereign remedy for this, learnt from a Maltese doctor at the turn of the century: a measure of port and a measure of brandy mixed together and drunk three times a day while fasting. It was well tried and tested by her family and friends when stationed at Port Said and assailed by the dreaded 'gypie tummy'. In fact, in my experience, the only bug it has failed to vanquish is Russia's secret weapon known to many as 'the Leningrad Express'.

I suspect it is the port which does the job, not the brandy, as I have found that port works very well on its own. Karen Blixen, in one of her books tells how an African labourer, stranded miles from any safe water, was in danger of dying from dysentry and she gave him some port she had with her — and he recovered. I wouldn't suggest using it for dysentry but its power is certainly remarkable.

Not eating is a vital part of the treatment, but it's hard to stick to it.

Those who weaken should eat plain boiled rice with lemon juice squeezed over it. This fills the stomach without giving the microbes too encouraging a diet.

In Britain a tea of blackberry leaves is an old country treatment for diarrhœa, while eating guava shoots is favoured in some hot countries.

DIURETIC PLANTS

It is always interesting when a plant's name indicates its medicinal value. The French name for dandelion is *pissenlit*, which means 'pee-in-the-bed', after its diuretic properties. These must also have been well known in Britain: at one time children in country areas would warn each other not to pick dandelions lest they wet their bed that night. In fact the dandelion is not so potent as to make even a child wet its bed, but it does help the body rid itself of excess fluid. So dandelion leaves are a useful addition to salads at times when water retention may be a problem, such as during pregnancy or menstruation, and when slimming.

Lovage (*Levisticum officinale*) is a less well known but better diuretic than dandelion, as it contains derivatives of coumarin. A tablespoon of finely chopped leaves brought to the boil in a pint (500 ml) of water makes a tisane which can be drunk hot or cold. Chopped up, this herb gives a slight celery taste to salads and soups.

EARACHE

In the old days a few drops of warm oil were always put into an aching ear to soothe it. It was then plugged with cotton wool. But beware, it is easy to overheat a small quantity of oil. Test it cautiously with the tip of a finger and double check on the inside of an elbow before putting it in an ear.

Earache is also soothed by a pad of cotton wool soaked in warm castor oil put on the bones behind and in front of the ear.

EYES

Grandma's way of removing an eyelash or a piece of dust from the eye with the corner of a clean handkerchief is still the best method. If it's hard to get at, try blowing the nose: this sometimes moves the speck to the inner corner of the eye. Or hold your head under a cool tap so the water runs over the eye.

There are just two hazards. It's dangerous to use an eye bath if there is something in the eye and a speck embedded in the black area of the eye should be left in until a doctor can remove it. There is a risk of scratching the cornea.

GRIPE

I was in an Indian grocery when a panic-stricken young man rushed in asking for fennel seeds. As lack of fennel seeds doesn't usually strike panic in anyone I asked him why he needed them so desperately. It turned out that fennel water was the only thing which kept his baby happy. It was a baby so tormented by gripe that it had to be on sedatives until his wife learned about fennel water from a Polish friend. It seems that in Poland it is as traditional to give fennel water to babies as it is for Italians to eat fennel after dinner, or the French to drink fennel-based liqueurs — because it stimulates the intestines and relieves wind.

The Polish recipe is a small teaspoon of fennel seeds infused in a mug of boiling water until cool enough for a baby to drink, then strained and sweetened to taste. It is given before, after or with meals and can be used from when the child is a few weeks old. The father who gave me the recipe swore it worked better than anything the doctor could provide. The Indian shopkeeper agreed. It was, she said, a well known remedy in India. Which is not surprising because old fashioned gripe water, sold by chemists, is made from dill — a plant in the same family as fennel.

HANGOVER PREVENTION

Enjoyable though it is, alcohol is a poison, so to prevent a hangover (i.e. alcohol poisoning) one needs an antidote, and not a hair of the dog. A science journalist once told me Vitamin C had been found to be the answer, because it broke down the chemical structure of alcohol. I have never managed to trace the research. However, several years of totally unscientific trials among my acquaintance suggest that about 1 gr of Vitamin C taken with as much water as possible before going to bed does prevent a hangover.

Drinking plenty of water, preferably with a little salt in, counteracts the dehydrating effects of alcohol which concentrate it in the blood. But by itself water will only reduce, not prevent a hangover.

If the worst has happened and a hangover has struck, take the Vitamin C and water, and add a soluble aspirin or two, plus a pinch or so of bicarbonate of soda. Aspirin and bicarbonate of soda put together kill the pain and neutralise the acid in the stomach. Which is just what those effervescent hangover tablets do — at a higher price.

HEADACHE

A good cottage remedy for a headache is a pot of tea made with 2–3 cloves in it. This may not sound as if it would work but in my experience it does. A gentle massage of the top of the neck, forehead and temples can also cure headaches, especially in children.

HICCOUGH CURES

I have always thought most hiccough cures scored higher as spectator sports than as help for the sufferer. It's not easy to drink from the wrong side of a glass, for example, without pouring half the contents down one's front. So I suspect the reason why no one ever suggests the one infallible cure, is that it isn't much fun for the spectators. It is simply to drink a teaspoonful of neat vinegar.

INDIGESTION

A doctor's family I know has a curious way of curing wind. They eat burnt toast. Not as silly as it sounds because the burnt bread ought to be adsorbent like charcoal and draw into itself the surplus gasses. It certainly seemed to work when I tried it, but the taste was awful.

Anyone who regularly suffers from indigestion should try one of the herb teas. Peppermint tea is very good and is sold in most health food shops. Made just like ordinary tea and served without milk, it's an extremely pleasant drink. The menthol in it calms the digestive tract and helps digestion. Infusions of fennel or dill are as helpful as peppermint but less pleasant to take. All these herbs will grow in most gardens, but unfortunately peppermint is not one of the rampant mints and it would take a sizeable planting to provide tea for the whole year.

Of course the English always have a strong suspicion that the French only claim so many of their liqueurs are digestive as an excuse to drink a little more. Nonetheless the herbs which go into them are often the very ones which do aid digestion. So the affluent or self-indulgent have a good excuse for trying a little glass of Crème de Menthe, Benedictine, or Chartreuse after meals to see if it works for them. Though I expect few would care to indulge in Cynar, the drink made from artichokes, which the French drink for the liver, and which certainly tastes like medicine.

INSOMNIA

A New Zealander told me he had great trouble sleeping until he learned that a couple of comfrey leaves in a bath before bed produced irresistible drowsiness. He found it so effective he warned me strongly against trying it in the morning and then driving.

Unfortunately I haven't been able to try comfrey, but a number of herbs are reputed to induce sleep. The most commonly used is probably camomile tea and it seems to work as well today as it did for the herbalists who wrote about it hundreds of years ago. Either make an infusion with half a dozen flower heads dropped in boiling water, or use one of the sachets which are now sold. Camomile is meant to be especially good after a heavy meal as it contains antispasmodic substances which help the digestion.

A more potent herb is Valerian — but it tastes terrible and smells worse. For those who can face it a teaspoonful of finely chopped root put in a cup of cold water, brought to the boil, strained and drunk is a sure aid to sleep.

At the other end of the scale of pleasantness are hop pillows, honey, or, best of all, honey and whisky in hot milk. All of which probably predispose people to sleep rather than having a real effect on the body.

JET LAG

When travelling by air there are usually two things working hand in glove to make one feel awful. I'm not referring to the architects who design terminals for our inconvenience and the authorities who mismanage them, but to alcohol and altitude.

Flying is a dehydrator, so is alcohol. Put them together and you have a recipe for giving the body a tough time. And, of course, as the body runs low on fluid the alcohol becomes more concentrated. In fact an awful lot of jet lag has far less to do with time than with Martinis. It may seem rather puritanical, especially to those with free booze in First Class, but the recipe for arriving in good shape is to avoid alcohol completely and drink the occasional glass of slightly salted water.

Incidentally, babies, having a very large surface area in relation to their volume, are especially prone to dehydration in the air, and in babies dehydration can be a serious matter. They need more liquid than usual on long journeys although, if they have been sedated for the journey, they won't necessarily be crying for it.

MIGRAINE

A man I know used to suffer from migraines so crippling he was sometimes unable to find his way from a taxi to his own front door. Then a friend suggested he should try feverfew. Having unsuccessfully tried everything conventional medicine could offer, he felt there was nothing to lose. That was two years ago. After he began taking feverfew his migraines gradually became weaker and finally stopped entirely. He now eats one leaf of feverfew a day (it tastes foul but he says it is more than worth it) and in winter takes a feverfew tablet a day. As an extra precaution he also avoids certain trigger foods, though he says avoiding these never did the trick alone.

It seems that although no one knows precisely why feverfew should work when conventional drugs fail it is very similar to ergotomine tartrate which is used to treat migraine. Of course, migraine is known to have more than one cause so that it responds (or doesn't) to more than one cure, but anyone who wants to try feverfew should have no problem acquiring it, though some people are allergic to it. It is one of the camomile family and grows wild in many areas, going by the names Featherfoil, Maydes Head, or Bachelor's Buttons because of its boss of yellow stamens. Nurseries sell it as *Chrysanthemum parthenium* or *Tanacetum parthenium* and it will grow happily even in a windowbox.

In the old days feverfew was, as its name suggests, used against fevers, pains and inflammations of all kinds and there is some evidence to suggest it may well be a help to sufferers from rheumatism and arthritis.

NETTLE STINGS

In country districts children once used to chant:

> *'Nettle go in, dockin come out*
> *Dockin go in, nettle come out.'*

For all I know they may still do so, as a reminder that rubbing dock leaves on a nettle sting brings swift relief. For, by a happy chance, where nettles grow so does the dock. In gardens where, being less tenacious than nettles, the dock has been killed off, sage or mint leaves are the best substitute, but they lack the power of dock.

NOSEBLEEDS

It is extraordinary how a whole mythology of nose-bleeding cures has built up with no foundation on effectiveness or commonsense whatever — keys on the back, ice on the forehead and so on will do no good at all. What does work is firm pressure to the nostril immediately above the point of bleeding for 20 minutes, or until the bleeding has stopped.

PAIN KILLING

Probably no one has ever mastered the control of pain better than the sages of India, and at times when pain is unavoidable it's not difficult to use a technique based on their practices. Breathe deeply, focusing all the attention on the inflow and outflow of the breath. On each outflow concentrate on totally relaxing the body, checking off points of tension one by one. Do this constantly while the pain lasts. The secret is in the concentration on relaxation, which works in two ways. It reduces the awareness of pain by focusing the attention elsewhere, and it also breaks the cycle whereby pain creates tension which then creates greater sensitivity to pain.

Skin-deep pain, say from an injection or pulling out a hair, is very much less if the area of skin is pulled as taut as possible.

PICK-YOU-UP

The most traditional remedy of all is to make a fuss of the patient in one way or another. There is now quite a lot of research to show that people do get ill when they are lonely or unhappy, so making an ill person feel cherished and cosseted makes a lot of sense. This may have been one of the great benefits of old herbal remedies. One must have felt a lot more cherished when people scoured the hillsides for the right herbs than one does when they just pop down to the chemist.

Special foods are a good substitute for that demonstration of caring, especially for children. For example there is something wonderfully comforting about an old fashioned egg pick-you-up. To make it, heat a mug of milk and stir in enough honey or syrup to sweeten. Beat up an egg and add it to the milk, beating well until thoroughly mixed, and stir in 1–2 teaspoonfuls of rosewater. Serve it while still hot with a sprinkle of nutmeg or cinnamon on top.

This is as nourishing as a meal, and I have found even egg- and milk-hating children will enjoy it if a few drops of food colouring are added to turn it a vivid pink or green. Adults, on the other hand, may prefer sherry, whisky, or rum, to rosewater.

PILL POPPING

Topsy-turvey though it may seem, it is very much easier to swallow a pill which is placed under the tongue rather than on it. The tongue seems to want to disloge the intruder and send it straight down the throat.

POISONING

POISONING NEEDS IMMEDIATE MEDICAL ATTENTION. Films and television shows have been very misleading here: someone may be seriously poisoned and show no symptoms at first. So this is no field for amateur diagnosis and the following treatments are the stop gaps recommended by Britain's major poison unit for use while the doctor is being reached.

If someone has swallowed household or garden chemicals, or any other potentially corrosive substance, give them milk or neat lemon barley water to drink, or failing that water. These soothe, and dilute the poison. The only exception to this is if the substance was oily, for example paraffin, in which case milk must not be given as it would help the poison to be absorbed.

With such poisons it is extremely dangerous to encourage, or even allow the patient to vomit. As it comes up some of the vomit could be inhaled and burn the lungs. This is even more serious than the effects of these chemicals on the stomach.

If the poisoning has been caused by tablets the best immediate treatment is a laxative dose of Milk of Magnesia and plenty of milk, barley water, or water. With tablets it is also a good idea for the patient to be sick. Your finger or their own tickling the uvula — the little finger of the soft palate which hangs down above the tongue — should do the trick. *But a child should NEVER be given salt and water to make it sick*. This is one old fashioned treatment which is extremely dangerous. Large doses of salt can be more harmful to a child than the tablets which have been swallowed, and children have died of salt poisoning.

RHEUMATISM

Flax seed (*Linium usitatissimum*), also called linseed, is a very old rheumatism herb, and sufferers from rheumatism tell me it does really help. Soak 2 dessert-spoons of the seeds in half a cup of water for a few hours and take a dessert-spoon daily. Or make a poultice of hot water and the pounded seeds on gauze and apply it to the aching joint. It may be that the benefits come from the way the poultice holds the heat rather than from any special chemicals in the plant.

Taken internally flax is mildly laxative and as a poultice it can also be used on boils. The poultice should be applied 2–3 times a day.

SHOCK

The treatment of shock is one which has completely changed in the last few years. Giving hot sweet tea was once the remedy. Today this is very much frowned on. Shock usually goes with injuries and if the patient has had anything at all to eat or drink it will be impossible to give an anaesthetic for some hours. *Anyone in shock needs medical attention.* Meanwhile keep them lying down, lightly covered, and if the legs are uninjured raise them slightly.

SHORTS v. LONGS

Thanks to a quirk of biochemistry, you are more likely to get drunk on whisky and ginger ale, or gin and tonic than on either spirit by itself. It is all to do with the way sugary additives react with alcohol to produce changes in the body. So, if you must have a drink and drive, taking spirits neat or with a low calorie top-up is safest. Alcohol with a sugary additive, on an empy stomach, could make you unfit to be behind the wheel, while still below the breathyliser limit.

SNORING

Snoring is something which clearly drives listeners to desperate measures because a number of people have written to tell me of a cure which is rather less than kind. It is to sew a large cotton reel to the centre back of the snorer's pyjamas (it is always wives who do this) so the poor man is prevented from ever lying on his back. One woman went a step further and stuck the reel to the man's back with adhesive tape.

SORE NOSE

A sore nose from repeated nose blowing can easily be avoided by using only silk handkerchiefs. Not as extravagant as it sounds. A metre of soft silk lining material, converted into handkerchiefs, lasts far longer than nose-roughening tissues to the same value.

The other preventive measure is to keep the cold wind off the damp nose end. If you can't stay indoors put a little pure lanoline or vaseline round the nostrils. Even more effective for babies and young children, who don't notice they are looking odd, is zinc and castor oil ointment.

SORE THROATS

Whisky has long been held to be a remedy for colds, though I suspect it does little more than make the sufferer feel less miserable about being ill. However, where it really is good is on sore throats. Gargling (then swallowing) neat or only slightly diluted whisky will anaesthetise a sore throat for long enough to let you get to sleep. Gargling with whisky or rum just before speaking will give a relaxed throat enough timbre to be audible. Gargling with soluble aspirin while the grains are still floating in the water is also very good.

For children a tablespoon of sage or thyme leaves well chopped and steeped in a pint (500 ml) of boiling water makes a good gargle, which is soothing and antiseptic. Adding a dessert-spoon or two of glycerine makes it even better.

SPLINTERS AND THORNS

It is a pity that the best treatment for splinters, sea urchin spines, and anything else embedded in the skin, is hard to find in Europe — it is paw paw. This fruit contains an enzyme which breaks down protein so it softens the skin tissue around the splinter. This doesn't mean that it does any harm to the skin, in fact it encourages healing. The way it's used is to apply a little of the mashed pulp and keep it under a bandage until the thorn will come out easily.

When no paw-paw is to hand heat is the best aid. Small splinters will come out more easily after a soak in a hot bath. Large ones may need a poultice. Mix castor oil, as hot as the skin can comfortably stand, with flour to make a thick paste and apply this under a bandage for 12 hours. The thorn should then come out more easily. Sometimes a small thorn can be drawn out by pressing the place over the neck of a bottle filled with steaming hot water.

SPRAINS

A rather nice old country 'cure' for a sprained wrist is to tie the second and third fingers of the hand together. It is not, of course, the tying together that cures but the rest which this inconvenient reminder enforces.

Among the herbs comfrey is one which has long been known as a 'knit bone' and some people find it soothing for sprains and aches. Make an ointment by melting a jar of vaseline over hot water and stirring into it a good bunch of very finely chopped and pounded comfrey leaves. Rub the ointment onto the sprain or any area of deep ache. In Switzerland compresses of comfrey are also used for bruises, gout and varicose veins, so it's possible this ointment could have wider uses. I have also heard of a poultice of comfrey completely relieving the pain in a thumb which had been shut in a door.

The most simple aid of all was given me by an elderly chemist who had practised in the days when those who could not afford doctor's bills turned to the chemist for help. He says that plunging a sprain alternately into hot and cold water for ten minutes stimulates the circulation and helps the body to heal itself. There are also those who swear by binding a sprain in brown paper. Not, perhaps, as silly as it sounds. It is warm, light and just stiff enough to immobilise the joint and make it rest.

STITCHES

A stitch in the side is rapidly cured by bending over and kissing the knee. If one kiss doesn't work, and it usually does, keep straightening up and bending to kiss the knee till the stitch goes.

STYES

The houseleek, or *sempervivum* — that fleshy rosette-shaped plant which grows on cottage rooves and stone walls — has definite healing properties. Its juice is particularly good for curing styes. Which is more than can be said for the other traditional 'cure' for styes — rubbing them with a gold wedding ring. Lacking the houseleek, try bathing the stye with diluted witch hazel, from a chemist. It is very soothing and healing for any irritation around the eyes.

SUNBURN

If you have forgotten the sunburn lotion don't panic. With sunburn there are three problems — the skin has become painfully overheated, and both the moisture and the oils have been dried out. So anything which cools and puts back oils and moisture will help. Cucumber grated and chilled is a marvellous relief to hot skin, especially if mixed with an equal amount of fresh cream. Alternatively it can be mixed with rosewater and glycerine. A chilled mixture of thin honey, cream and glycerine is also very good because it both heals and helps the skin to hold moisture. So is plain yoghurt. Failing all else plain milk is a great deal better than nothing.

TEETHING

Nothing has yet been found which is more soothing to a baby's gums than a steady rub with a clean finger, especially if it is dipped in a tiny drop of oil of cloves.

TIRED EYES

A few herbs bear witness to their medicinal properties in their names. Eyebright is one of them. At one time this herb was thought to be so potent that herbalists claimed that if only it were used more often, spectacle makers would go out of business: a grossly exaggerated claim, for it has a very mild action. Though a teaspoonful of the herb brought to the boil in a cup of water is still a soothing eyebath. It should be used well strained and very fresh, just after it has cooled thoroughly.

Weak tea, without milk, is another soothing eyebath, and lying down with the eyes covered with cold tea bags reduces tiredness. So does cupping the eyes in the heels of the hands for a few minutes while thinking black — a useful trick I was taught by a physiotherapist and often used when studying or taking exams.

TOOTHACHE

Dentists use oil of cloves as part of temporary fillings, but the special ability of cloves to ease toothache was known centuries ago. Despite this long usage, and modern respectability, no one knows exactly why cloves work. Chewing them with the teeth which are hurting, or tucking a minute ball of cotton wool soaked in oil of cloves into the cavity of a tooth, can often relieve pain faster than modern analgesics. What cloves cannot help is the pain from a problem such as a deep abscess. If no cloves are available I am told the next best aid is a drop of rum on the tip of the tongue, and then tucking the tongue into the cavity.

If the cause of the pain is an abscess or an erupting tooth, holding mouthfuls of very hot salty water over the place will sooth it for a while. I have also known of mouth abscesses being cured by taking regular doses of Epsom Salts and bathing the mouth repeatedly in a hot water solution of Epsom Salts. Though I have been told by dentists that this could not possibly help!

TOOTH EXTRACTION

When a socket bleeds after a tooth has been removed the oldest mouth rinse is still the one dentists recommend — a dessert-spoonful of salt in a tumbler of warm water. This cleanses and removes the taste of blood without interfering with the body's own healing.

If the jaw is aching, as it often does after an extraction, press ice cubes wrapped in a cloth against the cheek. The cold both numbs the pain and reduces the bruising which the extraction may have caused.

TOOTH KNOCKED OUT

If a child's tooth is knocked out that isn't necessarily the end of the story — it can be put back. The secret is to get it to a dentist within 1–2 hours, and to keep the tooth warm and moist meanwhile. It can be kept in the child's cheek, if he or she is old enough not to swallow it, or in yours — teeth don't mind alien saliva.

This will only work if the root is not fully adult. But as there is no fixed time at which teeth come of age it is worth trying this with any teenager.

TOOTHPASTE

In some parts of England there are people with fine teeth who have cleaned them for years with coal dust, salt, or bicarbonate of soda. The fact is it isn't what you put on the brush that counts but how well you brush. Toothpaste, dentists tell me, is only a lubricant mouthwash and vehicle for fluoride — whatever the advertisements say. When the toothpaste has run out, or been forgotten, a dab of salt or bicarbonate of soda will do as good a job and leave the mouth feeling just as clean. Though in the long run it lacks the benefits of fluoride.

TRANQUILLISERS

The very word *balm* suggests something calming and soothing and this herb does seem to have the ability to help people who are feeling tense. In fact I was told by one doctor — who was not a herbalist — that she felt it was as good as valium. Lemon balm, with its soft scent of lemons, makes a very pleasant drink. Take a teaspoonful of finely chopped leaves and pour over it a cup of boiling water. Leave this to infuse a little before drinking it like tea, sweetened with honey if you wish.

ULCERS

A drug derived from liquorice is used in the treatment of stomach ulcers and some people believe that an infusion of liquorice root, or even eating liquorice sweets, may be some help to sufferers. It is, after all, a remedy which it is no hardship to try.

WARTS

The wart must surely take the prize for the complaint with the greatest number of home remedies: rub on dandelion juice, broad bean fur, common soda, bread and vinegar, meat which you then bury — the list is endless, and bizarre.

Why such a mythology should have grown up round something so unimportant is a mystery. It is possible any of them may have worked, provided the user was sufficiently convinced. But three plants do seem to have a special reputation as cures — the sun spurge, the houseleek, and the greater celandine. In all cases it is just a matter of rubbing the juice of the plant on the wart nightly till it vanishes. The sun spurge (*Euphorbia helioscopia*) is probably the easiest to find as it grows as a weed in so many gardens. *Unfortunately it is the only one of the three which should never be used, because the repeated application of its juice could cause a severe skin reaction in the long run.*

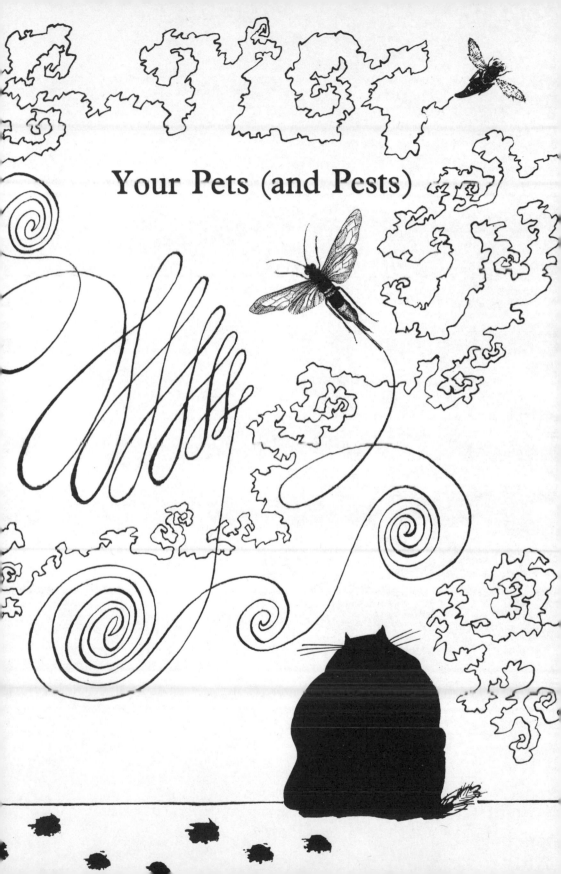

Your Pets (and Pests)

PETS AND PESTS

The potting sheds of yesterday must have been a murderer's paradise, stocked as they were with arsenic and strychnine, red lead and quick lime. It was very far from being the time of gentle methods and safe chemicals which some imagine and many of the old methods of pest control are either inadvisable or unobtainable today. Fortunately there are others which are safer, and usually older, and still have much to contribute. It has to be admitted, though, that few old techniques are as powerful as today's blockbusting chemicals and a serious infestation of any major pest is best dealt with by pest control experts, such as those on a local authority.

ANTS

At one time cottagers used to plant peppermint beside the door to keep ants out. Unfortunately modern ants are less house-trained and never seem to consider using the door. Though if they are found in the house they will certainly have come in from the garden. As they do seem to have a great dislike of peppermint some essence of peppermint on cotton wool stuffed into their entry hole should deter them. They will also avoid turpentine and cloves. If you need to kill them, rather than deter them, a mixture of sugar and borax sprinkled where they run is an old and tried method — but not one to use near small children or pets.

If sugar and borax can't be used, or the ants are breeding faster than you can kill them in the house, the answer is get at the nest. Tradition has it that a branch of wormwood laid over the nest will make black ants vacate it, which is certainly pleasanter than a modern insecticide and less violent than the other old method which is to open the nest and pour in boiling water.

AQUARIUM CLEANING

Water snails are very underestimated creatures. A few ramshorn snails put in an aquarium will do an excellent job of scavenging and cut out a great deal of cleaning.

BATS IN THE ATTIC

I have been told that if you have bats in the attic the way to get rid of them is to place a stuffed bird of prey, such as a barn owl, where they will see it as they fly in. It probably would scare them away but it would be a pity to do so. These beautiful timid creatures don't entangle themselves in anyone's hair and they do an excellent job in the garden, keeping down midges and swooping on night-flying garden pests. To drive them away would be to turn out a friend.

BED BUGS

Bed bugs are more common than one might suppose. They are odd disc-shaped creatures which earn themselves the name 'Mahogany Flats' from the deep red-brown colour they turn when gorged with blood. They breed with appalling speed and there is no home treatment to kill them — though I did hear of a writer in an earlier century suggesting the cracks in the bed should be filled with gunpowder and lit, which should have done the trick! Short of such Draconian measures this is a job for professional pest control, and local authorities will help.

BUDGERIGARS

Budgerigars can make very disappointing pets. Half the fun is teaching them to talk, but this they won't do if you buy too old a bird. If it doesn't start learning before it's three months old there's no chance of success, and it should start at six weeks. The way to pick out a bird under three months old is that there shouldn't be a white ring round the eye or conspicuous black throat spots.

Incidentally, if it hasn't talked within nine months it never will.

CAGED ANIMALS

The biggest pitfall in keeping guinea pigs, mice and so on is that two males in the same cage will fight, probably to the death. Despite their bad reputation in other respects rats are the exception to this rule and will generally live together peacably.

Females together are seldom a problem. The trouble with them is that if they are disturbed just after the birth of their young they may eat them.

Gerbils are the arch offenders in this respect and should be left undisturbed till the young are three weeks old.

CATS

Milk for Cats
The expression about looking like a cat that has swallowed the cream is misleading. Far from looking satisfied the cat might well be looking agonised. Cream is really too rich for cats, especially kittens, and can cause them indigestion. Even milk is better diluted with warm water.

New Homes
The nearer a new house is to an old one the more likely it is that a cat will try to return to its old haunts. Tradition has it that the way to stop this is to butter a cat's paws as soon as it gets to the new house. This certainly makes a cat sit down and clean up but it won't stop it roaming for long. What will help is to let it arrive hungry and feed it at the new place. Cats are cupboard lovers and it's not so much which side their paws are buttered that counts, as which side their bread is buttered. Even so it's advisable to keep a cat in for a few days.

Open Doors
Cats are curious creatures. If a door is opened wide they often have no desire to go out or come in. But open it a crack, so they can't see right through and, convinced they are missing something, they will go through.

Spaying
Only if you spay a male kitten before he is mature can you be sure that he won't mark out his territory in your home by spraying it with a scent which defies all aerosols. The normal age for spaying is 4–5 months, but cats vary, so consult your vet.

CEDAR AS INSECT REPELLER
Tradition has it that the crusaders noticed the clothes in Arab chests were not being attacked by moths and insects while those in their oak coffers were. They traced this to the fact that their enemies used Cedar of Lebanon to make their chests and brought this knowledge of the insect repellent properties of cedar back to Europe with them. To this day the bottoms of really well made drawers are of cedar, and it still repels moths. Camphor wood is far less common but it also seems to repel moths and

silver fish. If you can find a timberyard with cedar sawdust it can be hung in cupboards to deter these insects. It looks best hung in bags, but the simplest container is a nylon stocking.

COCKROACHES

In the literature of pest control nothing, I think, has quite the charm of this very old instruction on ridding a kitchen of cockroaches. 'Spread cucumber peel around. The delicacy is so tempting, and the cockroaches self restraint so small, that in the morning they will be found in a state of stupor.' Which just shows what a lack of self restraint can lead to.

Sadly there is no evidence that that method would work, though another old method might be more successful. Mix together equal amounts of flour and plaster of Paris and spread it on the floor. This would, presumably, sieze up their insides quite dreadfully. A more certain method is to use the insecticide borax. This can be put as a powder round the cracks where cockroaches emerge. Or a cup of borax can be put in a gallon (4 litres) of water and the floor regularly washed with this. It's a slow acting poison so the insects won't drop dead the same day, but it has the advantage of keeping its potency for years. So once it is in the cracks it will go on and on working. It is poisonous, although not violently so, to humans and animals and it should not be used near pets or where a small child might crawl on the floor.

DADDY-LONG-LEGS

If you dislike Daddy-long-legs (Crane Flies) and their stumbling flight, as I do, but hate to kill creatures unnecessarily, have a clear conscience. The larvae can do considerable damage to lawns. When the larvae are a problem the solution is to catch and destroy them. They like warmth, moisture and darkness. So on a warm day water the spot where they are causing trouble, cover it with a sack or groundsheet and leave it until they come to the surface and can be picked off and killed.

DOGS

Destructive Puppies

If a puppy decides that it absolutely has to cut its teeth on a certain piece of furniture the simplest way to stop it is to use its sense of smell. Its sensitive nose will find a really strong smell most unpleasant, so wipe the chosen spot with Oil of Eucalyptus or Oil of Cloves. At all costs avoid aniseed which dogs simply adore. So much so that it has been used in the training of dogs to make them follow, much as gypsies once used Rhodium in the training of horses.

Fights

When I was a child in a small village in Buckinghamshire I saw a local farmer stop a fight between two big dogs by shaking pepper liberally over the heads of the assailants. The dogs' sensitive nostrils were so irritated by the pepper they stopped fighting immediately and concentrated on their noses. It is simple and safe.

Grooming

A Yorkshire woman who bred beagles for show once taught me how to bring up a beautiful shine on a short haired dog. Groom it as usual, then take a piece of clean silk and stroke it firmly all over the coat, rubbing down the hairs. The result is well worth the trouble and the dogs love it.

Man's Best Friend

A point to bear in mind when buying a dog is that though small dogs will usually give their affection widely this isn't so with some other dogs. It is said that among the larger breeds of working dogs males tend to become one man dogs, whereas bitches will befriend the whole family.

Medicine

As most dogs love chocolate the easiest way to give them medicine is usually to pop it inside a soft centred chocolate.

EARWIGS

Traps are still the best way to reduce the earwig population, and keep them from damaging the dahlias. Tuck straw or scraps of newspaper into a flowerpot and invert it on the top of a stake beside each vulnerable plant. Empty the traps each morning so as to kill those which have taken up residence during the night, which is when they move around. If you don't, all you will have done is provide the perfect breeding ground for them.

FLEAS

The classic instruction for catching fleas in a bed is to moisten a cake of soap and very rapidly dab it on the flea. The trouble is if you have fleas in a bed the chances are you have bigger problems than you know. It's a myth that animal fleas won't bite people. They don't usually if the right animal is about — but failing that they work on the policy that beggars can't be choosers.

The problem is worst if an animal dies and isn't replaced or you move into a place which had animals and you haven't any. The flea pupa can stay dormant for months until it feels the vibrations which tell it a living thing is passing. If that's you, then look out. So if there is the slightest chance that the place you are moving into has had animals in, even as visitors, any time in the past year it is a smart move to fumigate it against fleas before you put in anything at all. Aerosol insecticides and fumigation are the only real cures and they are both easier to use without the refuges provided by soft furnishings.

FLIES

Flies of different types dislike different plants. In the old days farmers used to tie bunches of elder leaves to the bridles of horses in harness to keep away flies from their eyes.

Houseflies have different tastes. An elderly man I know picked a bunch of nettles and hung them in a café where they were plagued with flies but unable to use a spray because of the food. Next time he went there the flies had gone and his meal was on the house.

Houseflies also dislike rue, basil, tansy, and the mint family, especially pennyroyal. As basil is tender and likes to grow indoors there is a double benefit in growing it on the kitchen window ledge. It also allows the pot to be put on the table when eating outside. Tansy not only does the job but its lacey leaves look lovely strewn on the shelves of a larder. Mixed mints in tubs by the kitchen door, or in hanging baskets by the window, deter invading flies. Tubs also control these quickly spreading herbs, and keep them to hand for cooking.

FLYING INSECTS

The swiftest, safest spray for flying insects, and especially flies and wasps, is hair lacquer, preferably the firm hold variety. It simply gums up their wings making flight impossible, so you can catch them and kill them.

Pets and Pests

GNATS AND MOSQUITOES

Gnats and mosquitoes home in on their prey by scent and the way to keep them off is to cover every bit of skin with a scent masker. One of the best herbs for this is feverfew which grows wild in Britain and can also be cultivated (see Migraine page 190). Make an infusion by covering 4–5 leaves with a pint (500 ml) of boiling water. Let it stand until it cools before wiping it on the skin. Camomile can be used in the same way, so can Oil of Cloves which can also be put on cloths attached to the bed at night. In Sweden they use birch oil in the same way. If, however, you have none of these try vinegar. It is very much better than nothing.

GREENFLY AND WHITE FLY

Odd as it may seem, greenfly and white fly are so disorientated by mirrors laid flat they are quite unable to fly over them. This curious fact can be used to a gardener's advantage. Plants in the home or a greenhouse can be protected by simply placing a mirror under the pot. Provided the mirror is wider than the plant's leaf-span the flies won't come near it. A plant which already has flies can be 'quarantined' by placing it on a mirror. The flies will then stay on it and can be sprayed off at leisure. This is a useful ruse with cineraria, which so often become fly infested.

Work is going on to find out if foil laid on the ground outside has the same effect, and it looks as if it may.

MICE

Mice are not just unpleasant, they are a health hazard. Quite apart from their droppings there's the fact that they have no sphincter on their bladder so everywhere they go will be contaminated with a continuous trickle. A good old fashioned mousetrap, or a good mousing cat are still two of the best ways of dealing with them. The place for the trap is close to the skirting board because, being timid creatures, mice travel established routes which always include the edges of rooms, where they feel safe. The best modern method kills them with kindness. The sachets of mousekiller contain such large doses of vitamins that the mouse can't cope with them.

To keep mice out while you're deciding how to kill them, block up their holes with one of the smells which they abhor such as peppermint or turpentine. But this is very much a temporary solution. One of the odd features of mice and rats is that their front teeth never stop growing, so they have to gnaw whatever's to hand to keep them down. This can easily

be an electric cable, so even if you keep them out of your flat they can still create trouble, and possibly danger.

MOSQUITOES

As a vital couple of weeks in a mosquito's life are spent as larvae in water, any fish pond is an open invitation to mosquitoes. Fortunately the larvae need to pop up to the surface to draw in air through a little tube, and this is their Achilles heel. A drop or so of fine machine oil on the surface of the water every couple of weeks will kill them by blocking this tiny tube. It's the safest method of all as the oil does no harm to other pond life. If mosquitoes are a problem look for water elsewhere too. It only takes a pint of water to breed a quantity of mosquitoes, so even an old can with rainwater in can be enough.

MOTHS

There is more to house moths than most people suppose. Unfortunately there isn't just one clothes moth, there's a whole group of them ranging in colour from pale golden to a dingy brownish grey with speckles. What they have in common is long narrow wings, like furry wasp's wings, which are quite different from the triangular wings of more attractive moths. They are also very small — between $^1/_6$ and $\frac{1}{2}$ an inch long (3 mm.–12 mm.). As it's not the moth but the caterpillar-like larvae which eat the large ragged holes, it's a question of keeping them from laying eggs. Old fashioned napthalene will keep them off, but at the price of an appalling smell. Lavender and rue will also give some protection.

Fortunately the larvae don't normally chew through packing to get to their next meal so moth proof containers don't have to be plastic. If you can get a good enough seal on a paper bag it will be just as good. In fact I have heard of housewives safely storing blankets by making bags by machining together several layers of newspaper, popping the blanket in and machining up the fourth side. Some even believe this is a doubly good deterrent because moths hate the smell of printing ink, but this hasn't been proved.

SILVERFISH

Although silverfish look furtive when they appear in kitchens and bathrooms they do no real harm. To get rid of them borax can be put round the skirting boards, provided no animals or children are around.

TADPOLES

When a child has proudly brought home a prized jar of tadpoles they very often cause great disappointment by dying for lack of the right diet. Tadpoles are, unexpectedly, carnivores. What they really like is an inch cube of lean meat suspended in their tank. Failing this they find chopped earthworms acceptable, or will gobble up insects brought in from the nearest pond, but if they don't get the meat they need they will eat each other. Once they have legs they must be able to climb out of the water. A few rafts of cork or bark are all they need.

TARRY DOGS

Dogs walked on beaches often get tar on them. Petrol should never be used to remove the tar as it can irritate their skin. Oil of Eucalyptus will remove it with no harm to the animal.

TICKS

The only really unpleasant thing about taking a dog for a walk in the country is the ease with which they pick up ticks. These disgusting pests nestle in the fur looking, when bloated with blood, like baked beans without the sauce. Pulling them off only removes the body leaving the hard mouth parts clamped fast in the dog to cause sores.

The simplest way to make a tick release its hold is to hold the end of a buring cigarette against it. But covering its body with methylated spirits also makes it let go and smearing it thickly with vaseline will make it slowly suffocate and drop off.

WAKEFUL COCKS

I recently talked to a vicar's daughter who swore she could stop cocks crowing and waking people up in the morning — in a vicarage, she said, you had to learn to solve almost every problem. Her method was to fix a piece of wood above the cock's perch just an inch and a half (4 cm) above its head. As the cock lifts its head to crow its comb brushes against the wood and it stops. For a cock being unable to stretch your neck means being unable to crow, so it stays silent. Not being very bright birds, it never occurs to them that they could move off their perch and crow somewhere else.

WASPS

For a whole summer I had a wasps' nest in the ceiling above my bed. It made a disturbing noise but it also convinced me that the old saying that wasps never return to the nest next year is right. They never came back, so there is little need to do anything about a wasps' nest, except wait.

If you wish to set a wasp trap, the instructions for it can be found in this old rhyme:

> *He hath found an old bottle, I cannot say where,*
> *He hath bound it with skill to the back of a chair,*
> *Full of mild ale so balmy and sugar so brown,*
> *He will trap them by dozens, I'll bet you a crown.*

The bottle only needs an inch (2.5 cm) or so of beer to drown the wasps and its just as good tied to a tree as to a chair. Alternatively put some jam or sugary water in a jam jar, cover the top with paper, pierce wasp sized holes in the paper and hang it up. The wasps crawl in through the holes but can't crawl out over the rough inner edges of the holes. A pinch of yeast in either the bottle or the jar should make it irresistible.

WOODLICE

Woodlice are extraordinarily partial to boiled potatoes and the way to trap them, if they are being a nuisance, is to put potatoes in flowerpots laid on their sides near their haunts.

WOODWORM

If woodworm is active you will see holes in the wood with whitish dust at the rim and you may see tiny dark brown very oblong beetles. Though a beetle sighting isn't conclusive because there is a biscuit beetle which looks almost identical and it takes magnification to tell them apart.

The old fashioned treatment for woodworm is to inject paraffin into the flight holes and put it on the surface of the wood. This should kill the beetle which causes the problems but it would also make the furniture more inflammable and do no good for some finishes on the wood. This is an example of the old ways not being the best, though they will stand in if nothing else can be found. Use a modern method if you can.

WOOLLY BEARS

If you find $^1/_8$ inch ($\frac{1}{4}$ cm) long slightly hairy sloughed-off insect skins about your home you have probably been visited by one of the most destructive home pests — the carpet beetle. Once they lived on dead animal matter outside the house and made their home in places like birds' nests. They still do live in nests — which means nests should never be brought into the house — but they discovered that houses had richer pickings and moved in some years ago. There are several forms of these beetles, all about the size of a small ladybird, and they live in the cracks around the edges of the carpet. It is their grubs which do the damage and leave behind the sloughed-off slightly hairy skins which give them the name woolly bears.

Woolly bears have an inordinate appetite for protein. They not only eat silk and wool but will munch happily through man-made fibre if there is the slightest spot of food on it. Unlike moth grubs, which will chomp away in one place, these are itinerant feeders. They will whip into the centre of a carpet overnight to munch up an especially tasty morsel and with it your carpet, leaving the characteristic neat round hole.

To get rid of them you need to kill the adult beetles. Borax powder right round the edge of the carpet is a good measure. And if a carpet is being laid it is a wise precaution to put Borax under the carpet before it is laid. It stays active for years against any insects which might decide to live there. Hanging cupboards can be washed out with a cupful of Borax in 1 gallon (4 l) of water and any clothes they may be living in should be cleaned or washed. It is also wise to put woollen clothes which are not in use into tightly closed plastic bags (the clothes should, of course, be cleaned before they are put away).

It is very hard to eliminate woolly bears completely as they often live in the eves of a house on birds' debris and then walk in down the water pipes. So one drives them away one year only to have their relatives arrive the next.

P.S.

ALL SORTS

This chapter is for those who, like Gilbert's Nanki-Poo, rejoice in 'unconsidered trifles'. A collection of bits and pieces of curious and useful information, from an ancient African way to carry water without spilling it to a modern way to start a damp car or save money on photography. All they have in common is that they could neither be left out nor found a suitable home elsewhere.

BATTERIES

When batteries are fading and there is no way of getting a replacement the last life can be squeezed out by warming them.

If the problem is loose batteries, and the spring can't be adjusted, buy a bar of chocolate or a packet of cigarettes. A wedge of foil from either, pushed in at one end will do the trick, and more than one BBC tape recorder has been kept on the road this way. Of course, any paper must come off the foil first.

BIROS

If your household is anything like mine you will have a collection of biros by your phone, 50% of which don't work — and it's always one of these you pick up to take a message in a hurry. Usually the answer is to take all those that don't work out of their casings and hold the tips in boiling water until they *do* write. The problem is normally that the ball has stopped rotating, and the heat expands the metal just enough to get it going again.

BROKEN GLASS

A thick slice of bread is excellent for wiping up broken glass. It takes in the splinters more safely than a tissue and, unlike a sponge, it carries no temptation to try to rinse it and use it again. Which is a quick way to get glass in the hands.

CANDLES

If candles are too large for the holders put the ends in hottish water till they are soft enough to squeeze down to size — far less messy than scraping off the excess. If they are too small cup the end in foil. Unlike paper, this won't catch fire if they burn right down. If, however, the holder is glass a candle should never be allowed to burn that far down, as the heat of the flame will crack the glass.

People have told me that deep-freezing candles or soaking them in salt water prevents them dripping and makes them last longer. My experiments suggest it makes no difference at all, but maybe I was using the wrong candles. However, varnishing the outside of a candle, if you can be bothered, does make it last slightly longer and holds back the drips.

If drips are a worry some antique shops sell glass drip-catchers which rest on the candle stick. A good substitute for these, especially if the candlestick is silver, is a circle of doubled foil with a hole just large enough for the candle to go through.

Incidentally, the best value in candles is usually to be obtained from the companies which supply churches and undertakers — and if there is an electricity strike these are about the only people who don't run out.

CARS

Battery
When a car battery acquires verdigris the simplest way to remove it is to pour boiling water over it.

Cooling System
There is little point in buying a special product to degrease the car's cooling system, on its annual clean out, when washing soda will do just as well — as a former engineer with Rolls Royce showed me.

Get the engine warm and drain off the system. Then fill it with a mixture of 1 tablespoon washing soda to each pint (500 ml.) of water. Go for a drive to warm the car up and ensure the mixture is flushed right through the system. Whatever the weather put the heating on, or that part of the system could be left out. For the best result leave the mixture in overnight, drive the car to warm it once more before draining the soda out and flushing the system through with plain water. Refill, remembering to add anti-freeze or a corrosion-inhibitor to the final water.

Damp Starting
Geriatric cars which are inclined to get damp points can usually be started on winter mornings after a thorough dry with a hairdryer. Even better,

lay a piece of old blanket or carpet over the engine, under the bonnet — but be warned: *if you forget to remove it before you drive off your car can go up in flames*. Leave the bonnet unlocked with blanket sticking out, to remind you.

Fan Belt

The story that a broken fan belt on a car can be replaced by a nylon stocking is, surprisingly, fact not fiction. Simply putting it round the pulleys on the engine and fan, and leaving out the dynamo is easiest; the stocking will take you further, though the battery won't be charging.

Jammed Parts

A friend was once in the pits at Brands Hatch and saw a mechanic try to undo a bolt, fail, then grab a tin of Coke and spray it over the jammed part. He was then able to loosen it immediately. Coke certainly is excellent for that, but beware: if it isn't cleaned off it can cause corrosion.

Lock

If a car lock is frozen solid, repeatedly heat the key in the flame of a match or lighter before pushing it in.

Radiator Leaks

At one time the British army had an excellent way of dealing with a leaking radiator. It was to drop in an unrolled 'French Letter'. The outflow of water drew it towards the hole where it formed a neat valve till the vehicle got back to base. Unfortunately radiators nowadays are not so simple and not even the British army can get home on a wing and a contraceptive. In fact that ingenious trick could land you with an expensive increase of your problems when the French Letter became unsuitably entangled in the works.

Today a piece of chewing gum over the hole on the outside is probably the best instant solution. Or in extreme desperation try breaking an egg gently into the water. With a little luck it will poach in the heat and become solid enough to block up the hole. And if it doesn't it's unlikely to do any harm. If the hole is in a hose, wrapping it in insulating tape, elastoplast or even sellotape will take you farther than you'd think.

Roof Rack

Roof racks are inclined to rub the paint on a car and make it liable to rust. Prevent this by cutting out pieces of inner tube just larger than the clamps and setting them between the clamp and the car. Normally they increase, rather than decrease, the stability of the rack, but this should be checked.

Windscreens

The best and simplest cleaner for a car windscreen is damp newspaper, as the spirit in the printing ink cuts through the greasy film on the glass. In summer, when half the problem may be squashed insects, it is useful to carry one of those pan scourers which look like knitted plastic rolled into a ball. One of these, with plain water, removes the insects faster than anything else and newspaper can be used to give a final rub. If newspapers seem too makeshift, then use a cloth and put some methylated spirits in the washing water.

I have heard potatoes praised as windscreen cleaners, but they aren't a patch on newspaper or meths. What they are able to do, however, is alter the way water travels down glass. If windscreen wipers sieze up, cut a potato in half and rub the cut face up and down the windscreen in front of the driver. Then the water won't form the pattern of drops which is impossible to see through — for a while at least. You would need to keep re-rubbing if you were going any distance.

CARPETS

Carpets aren't difficult to sew, they just require horny hands. If yours aren't, wear a pair of stout gloves or you will have to give up long before the job is done. Use a curved carpet needle and strong linen thread.

There is no way a wool carpet can be stretched really taut without hiring a carpet stretcher. As this needs to be thumped with the knee, put on a pair of skateboarders' knee-pads before starting. Once the knee is bruised it is too late. As I know to my cost.

Stair carpets are more walked on than any other carpet in the house so the edges of the treads wear out quickly. To avoid this lay the carpet with a spare fold top and bottom and shift the carpet up or down a little each year so the wear is evenly distributed.

CASTORS

If they are to run smoothly the castors under furniture should be lightly oiled with a fine machine oil once a year. Baby oil or liquid paraffin can be used equally well.

CHINA PACKING

When china has to travel any distance the safest way to pack it is to wrap it carefully in strips or sheets of very damp paper, covering each part with several layers. The paper will tighten and stiffen as it dries and make a firm protective layer. The same method should be used for glass. If the item is particularly fragile, or a very rough ride is expected, soak the paper in a weak solution of wallpaper paste. It will form a firm papier-mâché coating on the china and give even better protection. At the other end, soak it in water to remove it.

CURTAINS

Rods and wires will slide easily through a curtain if the inside-out finger of a thin rubber glove, well sprinkled with talcum powder, is put over the end of them first.

An elderly carpenter I know has devised a method by which elderly and disabled people can easily take their curtains down or put them up. He has fixed the curtain rod to a separate piece of wood, painted the same as the window frame. The wood can be raised or lowered by cords which pass through rings or pulleys at the top of the window, and attach to cleats at the bottom. So the curtains are held in place just like the sails of a yacht.

DECANTER STOPPERS

A friend of mine can do no wrong in the eyes of a neighbour since she told him how to loosen the stopper of a decanter containing his favourite port. The method, learnt from her grandfather, was to tap very gently round the stopper with a glass bottle till it loosened.

It is the vibration of glass on glass which seems to do the job when nothing else works. But there is a risk that the glass might chip, so it might be worth trying other methods first. Less risky methods include running the neck under warm water, pouring vinegar round the mouth of the decanter and leaving it to stand for 24 hours, or doing the same with a mixture of $\frac{1}{2}$ teaspoon of salt, $\frac{1}{2}$ teaspoon of glycerine and 1 teaspoon of pure alcohol or vodka. When the time comes to remove the stopper, wrap a warm cloth round the neck of the decanter; then, when the glass has warmed up, replace it with a hot cloth.

DISTILLED WATER

Few seem to realise that there's a constant supply of distilled water in most homes — the refrigerator. As distilled water is no more than moisture from the air which has landed on a cold surface and become water again it's precisely what gums up the ice box. When the refrigerator is defrosted the water from it can be strained of debris through a coffee filter, and bottled for use in the iron, or your car battery.

DRIPLESS DRINKS

Putting a slightly damp cloth on a tray prevents glasses sliding about and automatically mops up any drips.

DYEING

If the colour you want doesn't exist on the shade charts it is usually possible to make it by mixing the shades together. Provided the same brands are used there are no problems. Cold water dyes can usually be mixed with hot water ones and used for hot dyeing, but not vice versa.

Black is one dye which is particularly unsatisfactory. A light colour dyed black almost invariably comes out dark grey, but you can at least ensure that it is a black grey rather than a brownish one by mixing about 2 parts navy blue dye to 3 parts black. This mixture effectively blackens black cotton which has become grey with wear.

EIDERDOWNS

As eiderdowns have a chilly habit of sliding off beds, careful housewives used at one time to sew strips of cloth to them. A strip 4 inches (10 cm) wide and six times as long sewn at the top and bottom of each side could be tucked in under the mattress to hold the eiderdown in place. Duvets which slip off children's beds can have the same treatment.

FIRES

Clothing
Burning clothing should be smothered with a thick towel, blanket, or anything else which will shut out the air and/or be drenched in cold water. Drenching in cold water for several minutes should follow, as it reduces the severity of the burns.

Chimneys
If a chimney catches fire the action recommended by the fire brigade is the oldest one of all — just throw water on the fire beneath it. The steam going up the chimney should start to smother the flames, so keep on adding water so long as the fire is hot enough to produce steam. *Meanwhile, someone else in the house should be calling the fire brigade.*

When Cooking

The commonest fire when cooking is a burning chip pan. Fat not only burns in contact with flames, it is self-igniting above a certain temperature.

Water must never be used to put out burning fat — it will only make the fire worse. Smothering is the answer. Turn off the heat. Put the lid on the pan and cover it with a fire blanket, if you have one. Or use a towel or several tea cloths wrung out in water. *On no account try to move the pan.* Oven fires should also be treated by smothering. Turn off the oven and keep the oven door shut. An oven should be able to contain the heat of anything burning it, at least until the firemen come.

Making-up a Fire

An old wives' tale says that potato peelings put on a fire improve it by making it last longer, and give a less sooty smoke. Research recently done by one of the schools competing in the BBC's Young Scientist of the Year competition showed the old wives were quite right. Potato peelings do act as a catalyst, and make a fire burn better, especially if they are put under the fuel.

A heat-saving ruse much praised in the last war was putting a large piece of pumice or chalk on the fire. It heats up without burning down and so provides 'free' heat.

FIREWOOD

To most people today wood is simply wood, and even those who have wood fires just buy and burn what they can get. Not so our ancestors, who were entirely dependent on wood for fuel and cooking. To them each wood had its properties and it was important to know what they were. Fast-burning wood meant too much fire tending, while wood that gave plenty of heat for its weight meant less to cut and carry. It's surprising how much woods can differ in these respects. Poplar, for example, gives out little more than half the heat of the same weight of oak. So by being selective you can get more heat for your money.

Predictably all sorts of rhymes were created to help people remember which woods to choose. Their guidelines still hold true. One from the North of England runs:

> *Beechwood fires are bright and clear*
> *If the logs are kept a year.*
> *Oaken logs burn steadily*
> *If the wood is old and dry.*

Birch and fir logs burn too fast,
Blaze up bright and do not last.
Chestnut's only good, they say,
If for long it's laid away.
But ash new or ash old
Is fit for a Queen with a crown of gold.

It is by the Irish said
Hawthorn bakes the sweetest bread.
Poplar gives a bitter smoke,
Fills your room and makes you choke.
Apple wood will scent your room
With an incense like perfume.
But ash wet or ash dry
For a King to warm his slippers by.

There are different versions of this rhyme up and down the country but the verdicts on the woods always seem the same and forestry experts say they are quite correct. Though, strangely these verses fail to mention woods that spit. Which can be both annoying and dangerous. The worst offenders are poplar and sweet chestnut. Both are a menace in an open fireplace and always seem to spit like angry cats the moment you try to sit near them. So they are to be avoided, even though there are those who say the best wood for the fire is always that nearest the house.

FROZEN FOOD

If you've forgotten to put the ice packs in to freeze, before shopping for frozen food in hot weather, try this. Fill a couple of small plastic bags with ice cubes, add a dessertspoon of salt to each bag and put these in the insulated bag instead. Provided you get the frozen food in with them well before the cubes have thawed they will keep it nicely cold. The reason is, of course, that the thawing of the ice cubes by the salt has to draw heat from somewhere and in an insulated bag it can only come from the food.

GLASS — AVOIDING CRACKS

When pouring very hot liquid into a glass, or cup, the way to avoid cracks is to pour the liquid in over a metal spoon resting in the glass. Even then I wouldn't take the risk with good glasses.

HANDLE ON BROOMS

It was an elderly Irish carpenter who taught me the best way to put a new handle on a broom. As the handle is almost always too large you hammer the end hard until it is just small enough to squeeze into the socket. Once in it will gradually swell back into shape, especially if you wet it, and make a really tight fit.

LILOS

Lilos, camping pillows with rubber linings, hot water bottles, and rubber-lined mackintoshes should all be stored with talcum powder or French chalk shaken inside them to prevent the rubber sticking to itself. Inflate the lilos slightly after shaking in the chalk, then deflate them. This disperses the chalk to every corner.

MEAT HAMMERS AND BUTTER HANDS

Wooden meat hammers and butter hands should be soaked in cold water for several hours to prevent the food sticking to them. Butter hands may seem totally outdated, but making butter balls with the hands is a marvellous occupation for a young child who wants to help with a special meal but would otherwise get in the way. No matter that no one really needs butter balls, the pleasure in the finished bowl of balls is enough. Use chilled cubes of butter or the task will be impossible.

MINCERS

Mincers are notorious for damaging tables and formica tops with their clamps. To prevent this just put a piece of inner tube between the mincer and the surface.

The easy way to get the very last of the meat out of a mincer is to put a slice of bread through after it. There's the bonus that the bread partly cleans the inside as it goes through.

Mincers rust easily. To prevent this oil all the steel parts with an edible mineral oil such as liquid paraffin before putting them away.

MOVING FURNITURE

Faced with an enormous and leaden oak chest to move, and only three toddlers to help me move it, I recalled the stories of the building of Stonehenge and resorted to rollers. I found even a toddler can slide a broom handle, without its broom, under as you lift. Once you have two broom-handles underneath even the heaviest piece can be moved easily, though, of course this only applies to furniture with a flat bottom.

MUSTINESS PREVENTION

Teapots don't go musty when not in use if they are stored with a few lumps of sugar or some unused tea leaves inside. Sugar also works well in suitcases and vacuum flasks. If a vacuum flask or teapot has already gone musty, soaking it in water containing a little bicarbonate of soda will cure it.

NON – SPILL WATER

In parts of Africa where every drop of water is precious the women have a trick for carrying a bucket without a wave building up on the surface and causing it to spill. They drop a large leaf or two on the surface of the water. It is just as useful a ruse when you simply don't want water slopping over your feet. By the same token stirring the tea in a cup, just before carrying it, stops it slopping into the saucer.

PHOTOGRAPHY

There's no need to have contact sheets made of black and white photographs so you can see which are the best to print up. A negative can be changed into a positive in an instant without paying a penny. All you have to do is put the negative over a sheet of black paper. Have it mat side uppermost and hold it at an angle in a good light. The black and white will then reverse themselves and look as they do on a print. This is because the thick emulsion where the negative is black reflects back the light, so it looks pale, but the thin emulsion where the negative is pale doesn't, so it looks dark.

When taking portraits you can easily get the flattering effect of a softer filter without any of the expense. Just crunch up a small piece of ordinary kitchen cling film into a small ball. When it is very creased indeed stretch it across the lens and take the photographs through it.

PICTURES

If a picture has to be hung against a damp wall, gluing a cork to the back of each of the lower corners will hold it away from the wall. This allows a better circulation of air, and keeps it drier.

PINGPONG BALLS — DENTED

Provided a ping pong ball has no hole in it, heating it in boiling water will make the air inside expand and push out the dent.

RING REMOVAL

Soap works like magic for removing a tight ring. Simply work up a good lather on the ring finger and pull the ring off, twisting it round the finger as you go.

RUBBER GLOVES

The fastest way to get the fingers of rubber gloves right way out is to squeeze up the wrist and blow the glove up like a balloon. If a finger doesn't right itself you know it has a hole in it. A holeless pair can be made out of two for the same hand by turning one inside out; and too tight gloves go on more easily if talcum powder is sprinkled inside.

RUGS

Rugs on top of carpets can be held in place if the hooked half of a strip of velcro is sewn to each corner hook side down. It will then hook into the carpet and be less likely to trip anyone up.

Rugs on wood floors are more comfortable to walk on and far less likely to skid if laid over foam-backed underlay. If the trouble is that the corners turn up, the double-sided sticky pads sold to hold mirror tiles on the walls will hold them down nicely.

SAFETY BELLS

If anyone in a household has very poor eyesight, or is unable to read, small catbells attached to all bottles containing poisons provide an instant warning.

SCRATCH AVOIDANCE

Self-adhesive sticky felt pads can be bought for putting on the bottom of anything which has a rough surface which might scratch furniture, but they can be hard to find. The simplest substitutes are self-adhesive corn pads.

If the problem is a chair or table scratching the floor, glueing a piece of felt or carpet to the bottom of each leg will cure it.

SCREW TOPS

There are four ways of undoing a really stiff screw top. Which works best for a particular top is a matter of trial and error. One of the easiest is to put a wide elastic band round the rim of the top. The rubber gives such a good grip it seems to release muscle power for twisting. Another way is to break the airlock, either by tapping the rim sharply all round its edge with the back of a knife of by giving the top of the lid a few hefty thwacks with the heel of a shoe. Running it under a very hot tap is especially good if a gluggy substance is holding the lid; and if all else fails, pierce a hole in the top

SELF-DEFENCE

Self-defence isn't something one normally thinks of in the home but if one does the problem is to strike a balance between being totally helpless, and using a weapon which is too dangerous and could be turned on oneself. Three coins and a cigarette lighter are a good choice. Put the lighter across the palm of the hand and make a fist over it — thumb outside and tucked over. Place the coins so they protrude between each of the fingers with their lower edges resting on the lighter. A modern version of the old knuckle duster which, as a friend from Special Branch taught me, can lend a lot to even a light blow.

SHEET STORING

Sheets become yellow-looking at the folds if stored for any length of time. The old housekeeper's way to prevent this and make sure the sheets got even wear was always to take the bottom sheet in the pile and put away newly laundered ones on top.

Special sheets which are stored away for a long time should be wrapped in pale blue tissue paper to keep them white, then put in a sealed plastic bag to keep the dust off. They must be perfectly dry before going in the bag or mould could appear on them.

SIPHONING PETROL

It was a peasant in South America who showed a friend of mine how to siphon liquid without risking a foul, and possibly dangerous, mouthful. He pushed a long tube into the bottom of a petrol tank, holding the top firmly in his fist. Then he pushed the spare tube at the top end down as far as it would go into the tank and swung it out again in an arc towards the waiting container. As he repeated this action over and over again he always put his thumb over the end of the tube as he pulled it out and released the thumb as he pushed it in. As he repeated the rhythmical swing of the arm the petrol gradually rose up the tube until it flowed out.

It's a very good method, but there's a knack to it which depends on getting the rhythm and choosing exactly the right moment to move the thumb. Of course, like any other siphoning it will only work if the second container is lower than the first.

SPONGES

When a sponge starts to get slimy, soaking it in very salty water will restore it. It is no good waiting till it is a shrunken slimy lump for then it will never fully recover.

Flannels will never become slimy if they are routinely washed with the week's towels. But if they haven't been washed and are already unpleasant, boil them in water with a couple of spoonsful of vinegar and then put them in the normal wash. Very slimy ones may need several boilings.

SMOKING

Burning candles in a room where people are smoking makes it seem less smoky, and dishes of water about the room absorb some of the smell. A more picturesque method is one I saw in a pub in Wales where they hung bags of straw round the ceiling to catch the smoke. Nothing makes the smoke less dangerous for those who have to breathe it — smokers and non-smokers alike.

SOAP

New soap isn't fully dry, so it dissolves very easily in water. It lasts far better if it is stored in a hot cupboard for a few months before being used.

In our grandparents' thrifty times all the odd scraps of soap were saved and melted down together over boiling water and pressed into a block to use in the kitchen.

SPECTACLES

A pensioner who likes reading in the bath wrote to tell me she had solved the problem of steamed-up spectacles. Since the cause was obviously hot air condensing on cold glasses she just put her glasses in the airing cupboard to warm for a while before bathing.

SPOON CLIP

When making jam or chutney in a large pan the spoon can be prevented from falling in if a clothes peg is clipped to the top of it. The peg then rests on the edge of the pan.

STUCK FAST

Labels and Stamps
Stamps or sticky labels which are stuck together can be separated without tearing if you iron them to melt the glue.

Glasses
If two glasses are stuck one inside the other, fill the top one with cold water and stand the bottom one on hot water and they will part easily.

TELEVISION SAFETY

It's difficult to think of a television as something dangerous, but it can be. If it's unplugged too soon it can hold a charge of electricity which could start a fire. When a television is switched off it should also be switched off at the plug. After that it needs several minutes for the charge to drain away before the plug is taken out of the socket.

It also needs professional inspection and cleaning every year or so. A pile up of dust or Christmas tree needles inside could start a fire.

TENT RUBBERS

It's odd the way tent rubbers always seem to break when there's a high wind, it's pouring with rain, and one is far from a camping shop. An instant replacement can be made which will keep everyone snug and dry. Beg an inner tube from a garage, slash it into rings and push one end of a ring through the tape loop which held the old rubber. Then either peg through both ends of the ring or slide one end through the other and peg it down, according to the length you need.

TRAVELLING HANGER

A pocket-sized hanger can sometimes be a better bet than the wire clothes-cutters hotels provide. Tie a piece of strong string in a circle so it is more than long enough to go twice round a rolled up newspaper. When a hanger is needed roll a newspaper, wrap the string round the centre and tuck one 'end' of the circle through the other. Drape a hotel towel on the hanger — to prevent a transfer of newsprint — and hang it on the nearest hook.

DON'T YOU BELIEVE IT

So many old sayings and methods turn out to be true and effective it is easy to fall into the trap of thinking that old is necessarily good. This is far from being the case. The list of false sayings and dangerous methods which people swore by in their time is endless and some are still going strong. As a cautionary tale here are a few of the false beliefs which should have died out long ago but which some people believe to this day.

AN APPLE A NIGHT

It is widely believed that eating an apple last thing at night cleans the teeth — far from it. It leaves the teeth bathed all night long in acid from the apple, and acid eats into teeth. An apple a day may keep the doctor away, but taken this way it will make work for the dentist.

BOILING MILK

There is a fable that a teaspoon put in the pan prevents milk boiling over — it doesn't. Neither does brushing the pan round the top with glycerine.

BREAD

'Old wives' used to tell children freshly made bread would give them indigestion. I think they knew it wouldn't, and were simply trying to keep the bread for the next day. For the first rule of breadmaking is to make it the day before you really need it. Only with time in hand can you placidly allow the dough to prove in its own time, according to the temperature, and so produce a really good loaf.

FLEAS

A remedy for fleas recommended in some old books, and some new ones, is to apply paraffin, or paraffin and milk, to a dog's coat. It might well kill the fleas, but it might kill the dog too. *Paraffin is poisonous to animals and should never be used on them.*

FLOWERS — OXYGEN INTAKE

The belief that flowers should not be left in a sickroom at night, lest they take oxygen from the patient, is a perfect example of a little learning being dangerous. It stems from the time when it was discovered that flowers breathed carbon dioxide in the day and oxygen at night. What people failed to consider was the amount of oxygen a flower uses. A bunch of flowers would in fact use a minute fraction of the oxygen a person would use in the same period. So it would take an awful lot of flowers in an almost sealed room to do any harm.

JELLY SETTING

It is sometimes suggested that if a jelly mould is stood in water containing a handful each of salt and washing soda the jelly will set much faster. Far from it. It makes the jelly set more slowly.

LEAKING PETROL TANK

There are those who say, if a petrol tank springs a leak the answer is to put in a piece of chewing gum and wait for it to be sucked towards the hole and block it. It might, but equally it might be sucked towards the outlet to the engine and block that. Use gum on the *outside* of the tank not the inside. It may not stay on, but at least it won't gum up the works.

OIL PAINTINGS

A large number of books, both old and new, recommend cleaning oil paintings by rubbing them with a slice of raw potato and wiping them with a silk cloth. Whoever started this chain of bogus know-how may have a lot of paintings to answer for. Oil paintings usually have hairline cracks through which the moisture of the potato can penetrate. Once this moisture is behind the paint the chances are it will eventually lift it. Today's improvement could be tomorrow's disaster.

POISONOUS MUSHROOMS

Many people believe that if you put a silver spoon in the pan in which you are cooking wild mushrooms it will turn black if any poisonous ones are present. Unfortunately, this is not true. Some poisonous fungi do blacken silver, but some of the most poisonous do not. The only safe method is to know your mushrooms.

RANCID BUTTER

There is a story that if you beat up rancid butter with sweet milk you get sweet butter again. You don't. Unfortunately you get soggy rancid butter and wasted milk.

VEGETABLES

Some cooking books, and articles on helpful hints, say it is a good idea to add soda to green vegetables to keep them a bright green and stop them smelling. It should never be used, because it destroys the vitamin C in the vegetables — which is after all, half the point of eating them in the first place.

WHISKY

A lot of people, it seems, believe the darker a whisky the stronger it is. This pleasant fable has no basis in fact. The colour only tells you how much caramel has been used to colour it.

INDEX

Abrasive papers 49
Acetone, dry cleaning hazard 153
Aches: deep 179; earache 186; headache
188, 190; rheumatism 192; toothache 196
Acrylic carpets, static on 7
Acrylic jewellery, cleaning 29
Acrylic velvet 153
Adhesives 9; resistance to 41; softening 37;
stains 155–156; storage 37
Afrormosia, oiling 12; gluing 41
Almonds, skinning 95
Aluminium 13
Amber, cleaning 28
Ammonia, dry cleaning hazard 153
Anti-freeze, in car 216; on steps 16; in
washing 142
Antique furniture 34–35
Ants, deterring 201
Apples, cheese with 67; cooking 67;
enhancing flavour of 87; fruit salad 87;
nightly 229; storing 118
Apricots, cooking 102; peeling 86
Aquarium cleaning 201–202
Arranging flowers 55–63
Arthritis, reducing 179
Artichokes, Jerusalem, perparing 92
Artichokes, leaf, preparing 67–68
Asparagus, cooking 68
Aspic, see Broth
Aubergines, preparing 68
Avocado pears, preventing browning 68

Babies, gripe 187; jet lag 189, teething 196;
see also Childbirth
Bad breath, cures for 162
Bakelite, cleaning 3
Baking bread 72–74
Baking cakes and biscuits 68–71
Baldness 169
Ballpoint, ink on fabric, 153–54; ink on
plastic 137; pens blocked 215

Bamboo, cleaning 6
Bananas, enhancing 87; fruit salad with 87
Basins, blocked drains 8; chrome polishing
7–8; limescale on 4; painting traps under
44; rust marks on 15; verdigris removal
from pipes 17
Baths, cleaning 3–4; stains on 4; see also
Basins
Bats in attic 202
Batteries, fading, loose 215; see also Car
Beans, broad, cooking 74; dried, cooking
81; dried, in salad 103; dried, storing 115
Béarnaise sauce, saving curdled 71
Bed bugs, killing 202
Beef, keeping 120
BEE STINGS, treatment for 180
Beeswax polish, making 4–5; marks on 5
Beetroot, cooking, peeling 71; stains 154
Belts, flapping 131; leather 136; plastic
137; polishing 131; see also Leather
bindings
Biros, blocked 215; see also Ballpoint
Biscuit beetles, hazards of 115
Biscuits, storing flapjacks 118; see also
Baking cakes and biscuits
Bites, insect 180
Blackberries, enhancing 87; storing
124–125
Bleach, hazards 153
Bleaching, hair 163; linen 149–50
BLEEDING, cuts and grazes 184; nose
190–191
Blinds, cleaning 5
Blood, stains 154
Bloody Mary, making 72
Blouses, ironing 147–8
Boards, cleaning chopping and pastry 5; see
also Floorboards
Boiling fowl tenderising 72
Books, care and storage 22–23
Boots, waterproofing 131

233

Index

Index